As a Matter of Heart

As a Matter of Heart

A nuclear engineering
professor's life-changing journey
from safety to self

~ A Memoir ~

William E. Kastenberg

Seena River Press

Seena River Press
Ashland, Oregon
asamatterofheart.com

Cover design by Frank Fienbork
Project management and interior design by Ruth Schwartz

Publisher's Cataloging-in-Publication data

Names: Kastenberg, William E., author.
Title: As a matter of heart : a nuclear engineering professor's life-changing journey from safety to self / William E. Kastenberg.
Description: Ashland, OR: Seena River Press, 2022.
Identifiers: LCCN: 2022901811 | ISBN: 979-8-9856935-2-2 (hardcover) | 979-8-9856935-0-8 (paperback) | 979-8-9856935-1-5 (ebook)
Subjects: LCSH Kastenberg, William E. | Marriage. | Man-woman relationships. | College teachers--United States--Biography. | Self-actualization (Psychology). | Spiritual biography. | BISAC BIOGRAPHY & AUTOBIOGRAPHY / Personal Memoirs | FAMILY & RELATIONSHIPS / Marriage & Long-Term Relationships
Classification: LCC HQ1059.5.U5 .K37 2022 | DDC 305.244/1092--dc23

For Gloria, my soul mate –
without her love,
this memoir would never have been written

The heart has its reasons,
which Reason knows nothing of.

– Blaise Pascal

Contents

Acknowledgements

A S A PROFESSOR at a major research university, I quickly mastered the art of writing research papers, grant proposals, and letters of recommendation. Either alone or with my colleagues, postdocs, and graduate students, I'd respond to reviewers' comments, making changes where there was agreement or giving reasons why there was disagreement. When I retired and the idea of writing a memoir became a reality, I naïvely believed that the transition from technical writing would be easy. Ha!

After several frustrating attempts at writing something personal that didn't read like a research paper or proposal, my wife, Gloria, gifted me a memoir-writing workshop in Italy, in the town of Assisi with Robert Hughes, offered by Art Workshop International. While I worked with Bob, Gloria painted landscapes and cityscapes with Gregg Kreutz, a well-known artist, art teacher and author.

I owe debts of gratitude to Bob for launching me as a memoirist and to Lynn Gernert and Charles Kreeloff for being great hosts and for organizing workshops where our creative juices could begin to flow. Thanks to them, we returned for second workshops a year later.

I am forever grateful to Shoshana Alexander, who invited me into her beginning memoir-writing group when I returned from the first Assisi workshop. Meeting twice a month for five years, Shoshana became my coach, mentor, cheerleader, friend, and—finally—my structural editor. Our original group of Barbara Shor, Judy Hillyard, Bill Ritch, and Carolyn Shaffer became intimates as we read scenes and chapters to each other, always critiquing with love and compassion, and encouraging one another to expose our deepest vulnerabilities, our triumphs, and our failures.

I was very fortunate to attend Katie Hafner's memoir-writing workshop in Big Sur and Linda Joy Myers' and Brooke Warner's *Magic of Memoir* workshop in Oakland, where I learned the art of creating scenes, developing my characters, and writing dialogue. I can only hope I've done justice to their teaching and that the lessons I learned are reflected in this memoir.

My profound thanks to Joel Lesko, who read an early version of the full manuscript, but mostly for supporting me with his encouragement and love throughout my process. And to Alan Novidor, my cousin, who read several versions of the manuscript, engaging me in many discussions about what I wanted to say and how I wanted to say it. Again, I thank Barbara Shor and Judy Hilyard for reading and critiquing the near-final manuscript after listening to me for hours and hours as I read individual scenes and chapters in group. Bill Ritch went through the near-final manuscript with a fine-tooth comb, always provoking me to be clearer, to go deeper, and to provide more specificity.

Sincere thanks to Dotti Albertini, Anna Fienbork, Frank Fienbork. Marilyn Friedman, Thomas Huffman, Alia Lesko, Sarah Marshank, Heidi Merker, David Norris, Eben Ostergaard, Trine Ostergaard, Birgitta Rhein, and Susan Stark, either for reading the near-final manuscript or for reading specific chapters and making comments and suggestions that, no doubt, significantly improved the writing and—most important—the story.

A very special thanks to Kathryn Thomas who, as my line editor, read the complete manuscript, line by line, scene by scene, chapter by chapter, sometimes three or four times, until I got it just right. In the line-editing process, Kathryn wasn't just addressing my spelling and grammar, but also pointing out where I'd use a word incorrectly or too many times in a paragraph or scene, where I'd include too many colloquial expressions, or where something I wrote just didn't make sense. Her magical touch afforded me an accurate, complete, and polished manuscript.

My sincere thanks to Frank Fienbork for designing a fantastic cover, as well as for his patience and devotion to the project as I changed the title and subtitle several times during his creative process. And certainly, to Ruth Schwartz—my book midwife—who made my dream become a reality. Her sage advice from cover to cover, designing the interior pages, and producing an actual book—my very first—makes my heart sing.

I also owe a debt of gratitude to Tim Westfeldt. He helped me process the events I describe in the last several chapters of this memoir, and ultimately arrive at the resolution delineated in the penultimate chapter.

Writing a memoir is both an internal and external process—at least it was for me. My journey to find the person behind the persona began with my beloved, Gloria, when she gave me John Welwood's book, *Journey of the Heart*, to read. She not only lived through most of the story as we travelled together along the same path, she experienced it again as we read chapter and verse to each other as I'd write, edit, and rewrite. Gloria stood for the story being factually accurate and complete, as well as accurately capturing her thoughts and feelings and—oftentimes—if I couldn't recall mine—she invariably did.

It was in the final editing and rewriting that we completed the process that began with our marriage vows. Through this journey with her, I learned more about who I am, who she is, and who we are as a married couple than from all the therapy and workshops combined we had encountered along the way! It is to her that I dedicate this memoir.

Author's Notes

THIS IS A STORY about my emotional and spiritual journey of personal discovery. It is a story of romance, partnership, and love. It is not about cults. Nor is it about physical, mental, emotional, or spiritual attainment. During my journey, I was exposed to spiritual teachers—gurus, tantric masters, consciousness change coaches and even academic mentors—some who were emotionally abusive and some who were well-intentioned and good-hearted, but often with debilitating impact. Some engaged in narcissistic coercive control directed at me or towards others that I witnessed. Some I learned about as I was writing this story and investigating the topic as part of my own healing process. I cannot in good conscience condone nor promote their methods, models, and programs, or diagnose the perpetrators or their victims. It was in the writing of this memoir that I learned about the psychology of narcissistic coercive control; how I experienced it and how it affected me. The subject is an extremely important psychological dynamic that is relevant to our time and goes far beyond what this memoir can offer. Perhaps it is a subject of further exploration for me.

On a practical note, I have occasionally adjusted timing and consolidated events for brevity and clarity. I have also changed some locations and many names—and occasionally gender—to protect privacy and anonymity. Some characters and places are a blend of more than one. Rather than writing long narratives, in many instances I made extensive use of dialogue for character development and to move the story forward. Most of the dialogue is as I recall it. Some of the conversations were as I imagined they would possibly be, but mostly, these conversations did occur. In a similar fashion, I have used italics to express my own thoughts and feelings to reflect my inner process. It is my story as I remember it, verified to the extent possible by several people who were part of it, and altered sometimes for emotional effect and dramatic arc.

ABOUT THE TITLE: While I had several working titles over the ten years I spent writing this memoir, none of them seemed to describe the main theme of the story when the journey was complete. Several titles I came up with that included the words "matter" and "heart" were already used. When, in a state of exasperation I explained this to my son Andy, he said, "Dad, when we were growing up, one of your favorite expressions was, 'As a matter of fact.' Why don't you change the word 'fact' to 'heart' and use 'As a Matter of Heart' for the title? Isn't that change what the book is about?" My immediate response was an emphatic "Yes!"

ABOUT THE COVER: I owe a debt of gratitude to Frank Fienbork who, after reading the manuscript, designed the cover which, together with the subtitle, illustrates my journey. The equations that appear in the background represent my academic career. I wrote these same equations on many blackboards during a career spanning more than forty years. Frank's colorful handwritten title emerging from the mathematics represents my fun-loving, inquisitive, whimsical "inner child" who was set free along my journey.

Introduction

SEVERAL YEARS BEFORE RETIREMENT, I was walking across campus with an esteemed colleague, doing my best to convince her to support a workshop that my wife and I were organizing called *Ethics and the Impact of Technology on Society*. We wanted to bring together a cross-cultural, multi-disciplinary group of educators, practitioners, and professionals ranging in knowledge from eastern and western philosophy and religion to physical science, social science, and engineering. As we walked, she said to me, "Do you know what your colleagues say about you? 'Bill used to be a good scientist, but he's gone soft.'" At the time, her comment landed like a dagger in my back. But as the years went by, I began to take it more and more as a compliment. Today I say, "Boy, if only they could see me now."

But how did I get to now? How does a man who was gifted with a exquisitely logical mind, who could cut a graduate student to shreds with rapier-like questions on an oral exam or tell a junior colleague that his research didn't qualify him for tenure without blinking an eyelash, end up facilitating sessions with, for example, a man whose mother beat the shit out of him as a child or a woman who was brutally and sexually abused by her father, feeling their pain and — at the same time — feeling rage at the parents who perpetrated these abominable acts? How does a man, whose marriage fails miserably and swears he would never get married again, meet the love of his life — his soul mate — and barely manage to avoid falling into the same behavioral traps as before? And how can a man who, as a boy, raged at God for taking his mother now have a felt sense of divine presence in all manner of everyday life?

These questions frame the story of my life, and that's what this memoir is about. Webster's dictionary defines ecology as the scientific study of "the relationships of living organisms to each other and their surroundings." This memoir examines how my relationships — with my parents, my mates, my children, my professional work, and God — have changed. Each chapter examines the evolution of my values, assumptions, and beliefs, my successes and failures, and my journey to find my authentic self — steps to an ecology of heart. And as the caterpillar transmutes to the butterfly, there is no return ticket.

At my age, I can say that I have lived my life within a structure; whether a familial, professional, philosophical, or spiritual paradigm, structure has provided me a level of safety within which I could grow or shrink, thrive or starve, and achieve or fail. And now my challenge is to step out in front of these structures—to be backlit by them, as it were, to become transparent—and to just be.

I wrote this memoir to reflect on where I have been and where I am now, as well as to serve as a compass heading for the future. And if any of this resonates with you, the reader, I invite you to take some steps along with me, *As a Matter of Heart.*

Chapter 1

The Singularity

A simple Child,
That lightly draws its breath,
And feels its life in every limb,
What should it know of death?
—William Wordsworth, "We Are Seven"

I KNEW MY MOTHER WOULD DIE. I just didn't think it would happen so soon.

As far back as I can remember, my mother had been going to regular doctor appointments. Once a month—on Saturdays—she would take me with her to Dr. Gordon's office. We would sit together in the waiting room, thumbing through old magazines, sharing an interesting picture or a funny cartoon, until the nurse came to fetch her. She never spoke to me about why she saw the doctor, and I never asked. Since children weren't permitted in the examining room with their parents, I'd wait for her alone, flipping through issues of *National Geographic*. Assuaging any sense of fear, I would fantasize about travels to faraway exotic places—Bali, India, China, the Amazon. Before long, my mother would return and, without saying a word, she'd take my hand and we would leave the doctor's office.

Except for harsh winter or suffocating summer days when we'd head home for comfort, we'd walk the two long blocks from Park to Fifth Avenue for a visit to the Metropolitan Museum of Art. As the years passed and I neared adolescence, handholding gave way to walking arm in arm. Little did I realize at the time that she had increasingly been leaning on me for stability and support as we climbed up the many steps to the Museum's main entrance.

After spending an hour or two viewing a special exhibit or the Impressionist paintings — our favorites — we would take the subway to my maternal grandparents' apartment, where my father and our extended family would be gathered for dinner. Entering the dining room with her, I felt whole, bathed in love, special.

As the months passed and my mother grew weaker, she would wait on a bench in the Museum's great entry hall while I explored the galleries alone. I'd stop by the Greek and Roman marble statues or explore the Egyptian exhibit. Leaving behind the remnants of an ancient world, I'd hurry off to the American and European wings, anticipating the array of bright colors — blues and reds, greens and yellows.

One Saturday when I was twelve, she must have decided to go with me to the Impressionist exhibit. I remember her sitting beside me on the bench facing one of my favorite Renoir paintings, *Madame Georges Charpentier and Her Children.* This vivid portrait of an elegant Parisian woman fascinated me—a soft smile on her face, relaxing on a sofa with her identically attired son and daughter next to her, the family dog sleeping at their feet. I was an only child and envied the idea of having a sibling, as all my friends had. But it was the feeling Renoir had captured that most attracted me—a portrayal of love, security, stability, and peace.

My mother and I had been regarding the painting in silence for some time. We were alone, almost as if the other visitors could feel our need for privacy and the painting's hold on us. At some point, she turned from the Renoir and looked directly at me.

"It's harder to lose a wife, Billy, than to lose a mother," she said.

Her voice was barely audible. She paused for a second. Unmoving and in shock, I stared straight ahead at the woman on the sofa, at the happy children, at the sleeping dog—the picture of tranquility shattered.

"I'm going to die soon, Billy," she said. "I don't have long to live. Please take care of your father."

She was forty-four years old.

FIVE YEARS EARLIER, my mother had been diagnosed with breast cancer, followed by surgery. Her decline had been almost imperceptible, though I'm sure I sensed somehow her gradual withdrawal from me, from us, from life itself. The woman sitting next to me in front of the Renoir was not the seemingly ever-smiling robust woman I'd known as a younger child. She was gaunt—her thinning gray hair framing the ashen pallor of her face.

One September day in 1952, soon after starting the eighth grade, I arrived home to find my cousin Renée waiting for me in front of the apartment building where my family lived. I froze. *Why is Renée here? Something must be wrong.* Ten years my senior, Renée was like an older sister to me—she had taken care of me on those rare occasions my parents went to a movie or a Broadway show. And, at the age of eight, I had slept cuddled in her arms when my mother was hospitalized after her surgery.

A cold shudder ran down my spine as Renée took my books from me without speaking a word and beckoned me to follow her up the three flights of stairs to our apartment. The front door was slightly ajar. My father opened it as we arrived.

"Mother won't be with us anymore," is all he said.

It would be the last time for many, many years that I would hear him speak about her. She was gone, leaving an incomprehensible void in my life—and in his. I couldn't speak with him about her and certainly not about how lonely and empty we both felt. Throughout my mother's illness, my father had remained stoic. From the moment of her death through the funeral and periods of mourning, I didn't see him show any emotion at all. As usual, he attended to all the necessary arrangements, getting every detail taken care of, but I never saw him cry or express any feelings in response to losing her.

At the cemetery, my closest relatives flocked to assist my grandmothers, who were wailing in Yiddish. My grandfathers, rocking back and forth, prayed in Hebrew. My father, standing next to me, was cold and distant—he might as well have been a thousand miles away. I was alone, facing that gaping hole in the ground.

The sound of the dirt and rocks falling on the coffin after it was lowered into the grave would echo well into my adult life. Buried with that rubble would be my capacity to be open and vulnerable, limiting my ability to form intimate and loving relationships. When the lid of my mother's coffin closed, my heart closed with it.

I RETURNED TO SCHOOL a week after my mother's funeral. That morning, walking down the hall to class, I ran into the homeroom teacher I'd spent the previous school year with. Knowing my mother had been suffering from cancer, she stopped briefly and asked me in a very cheery voice, "How is your mother doing?" Just as I hadn't been prepared for my mother's death, neither was I prepared for any such question. How does a thirteen-year-old boy explain that his mother was no longer doing anything? How does he say, for the very first time, "My mother is dead"?

I opened my mouth to answer her, and nothing came out. Tears welled up in my eyes. Terror set in. My universe turned black. I stood there in the hallway, a stone statue unable to move, while the teacher, probably confused, hurried past me and on to her class. That feeling of turning to stone would become a plague throughout my adult life, arising whenever I was confronted with a situation that touched my vulnerability.

For the rest of that school year, I lived in a shadow world, trapped in a blur of inchoate grief, garbled thoughts, unresolved and unarticulated questions. *How is it possible that a parent's death is any less painful than a spouse's death, as my mother tried to tell me? Wasn't my father supposed to take care of me? Didn't she have it backwards? Why did this happen to her? Or even to me?*

WITHIN MY SHADOW WORLD arose a tremendous unspoken sense of guilt and shame, the feeling that my birth had somehow caused my mother's death. My grandmother, her mother, had often told me stories about how I was a big baby at birth—eight pounds, nine ounces. As I was born with a black eye, the nurses had called me Jack Dempsey, after the World Heavyweight Boxing Champion. I'm sure this story was delivered with some humor, but there must have been an underlying message that accompanied it: my birth had hurt my mother. In fact, I had been told over and over again that my grandmother took care of me during the first six months of my life because my mother was bedridden.

Another story my grandmother told me several times was about how I'd kicked a glass baby bottle out of her hand while she was feeding me. She cut a tendon when she picked up the broken pieces, leaving her thumb immobilized for life. My grandmother would show it to me each time she recited the story as proof it was true. By five or six years of age, I had a clear impression that the impact I'd had on my mother and those who loved her was harmful.

Even as an adult, I would be haunted by this burden. Thirty or so years later, I was a tenured Professor of Engineering at UCLA and my father had joined me for our monthly lunch in Westwood Village near the campus. He and I were reminiscing about the move to California we'd both made when I was nineteen, and how it had finally fulfilled his previously thwarted dream to leave the East Coast. Before I was born, he told me, he had been offered an executive position at a women's clothing factory in downtown Los Angeles. With an air of regret, he added that he had to turn the job down because my mother didn't want to leave her family in New York City. California had seemed like the end of the world to her, he said.

This was the first time since her death that he had ever mentioned my mother and, to my surprise, his words carried a note of resentment. I kept quiet and just took it all in. Then he said something that knocked the breath out of me.

"Her sisters blamed you for her death," he said, delivering the statement as if it were the order for his meal.

I was speechless. *So I was the cause of my mother's death.* The dark underpinnings of my psyche had been revealed as the truth.

I sometimes refer to my mother's death and the events surrounding it as The Singularity. In astrophysics, a singularity is a region in space where gravity is so great, light cannot escape it—a black hole. The guilt and shame I carried unconsciously, believing I was the cause of my mother's death, had placed me at the edge of an emotional black hole centered deep in my heart. *If I let myself be pulled into these dark emotions, I will never come out. I will be annihilated.*

Unable to face this darkness, I had turned my gaze outward towards the precision and beauty of the natural world revealed in science. My outer success as a professor teaching at prestigious research universities had managed to hold at bay that darkness of guilt and shame, that sense of being damaged.

It would take me many years to work through the crippling emotional and spiritual wounding caused by that belief. The guilt I felt, and its underlying shame, would infuse many of my choices in life. Yet it drove me forward on my quest for discovery, release, and—ultimately—self-acceptance.

AMID THE IMAGES OF the paintings on the walls of the Metropolitan Museum of Art—and all the art museums around the world I have visited, for that matter—I'd see my mother, her gaunt features and her purse clutched on her lap, waiting for me to return from my explorations. While that image of her was indelibly etched into the recesses of my heart, the paintings filled my head with beauty. The stories my favorite paintings told of motherly love, family, and friends had covered over the pain of seeing her recede from life.

I do know that, through the profound explorations that artists have made about our relation to the world around us, I had stayed connected to her—not simply through that memory of her resisting the world, anticipating the end as she waited for her boy. Except for that brief exchange before the Renoir, I could never know her thoughts or fears, but the unspoken resignation of her imminent demise must have left preserved within me always that little boy, still hoping to find her there waiting for him—healthy and strong—after I had thrilled my soul with art.

Chapter 2

Abandoned

Blessed, praised, glorified, exalted, extolled, mighty,
upraised, and lauded be the Name of the Holy One.
—The Mourner's Kaddish

S A BOY GROWING up in a Jewish family, I knew by the age of seven or eight what was expected of me in terms of my religious education. Beginning at age nine, I would attend Hebrew School several afternoons a week, culminating in my Bar Mitzvah, welcoming me into manhood on or around my thirteenth birthday. What I didn't know was that three months later, my mother would die and, now that I was a man, it was incumbent upon me to attend prayer services every day at the synagogue for eleven months. At the end of each service, I would be required to stand up and read aloud the Mourner's *Kaddish* in Hebrew. Of course I knew exactly what the translation was—a prayer of thanksgiving and praise to God that is said in moments of darkest personal grief.

How stupid, I'd think as I recited the Hebrew by rote. *Why praise a God who would take away my mother? Give thanks for what?*

Both of my grandfathers, as well as our Rabbi, had made it abundantly clear that it was my duty to follow centuries of Jewish tradition—a tradition that would feel to me, as the months went on, increasingly hollow and cruel. In hindsight, I see that during those eleven months of mourning, I was facing an existential crisis of biblical proportions, and I was facing it alone.

Every day of my thirteenth year was spent in the synagogue attending afternoon and evening services, saying the Mourner's *Kaddish*. My maternal grandfather took it upon himself to absolve me of attending the morning service, as would be expected, because I had to go to school. He attended on my behalf and recited the *Kaddish* in honor of my mother. She was his youngest child and his first to die, and I could feel his deep anguish. But he never spoke about it —at least not to me. I never spoke to him or anyone else about my own anguish. I remember thinking, *If my grandfather can surrender to a higher authority, why can't I? And even if I could, why surrender?*

"We are in God's hands," my grandfather often said to me. "It is God's will." And I was supposed to accept that. I couldn't. That God, it seemed, had taken my mother away.

BUT I HAD GROWN up in a religious context. That was the water I swam in.

My maternal grandmother had a mystical connection with God that filled me with wonder. As an adolescent, I would be swept up in her aura as I watched her recite her morning prayers or light the Friday night candles—one for my grandfather, one for her, and one for each of her children. She'd move her hands above the flames, drawing the light from the candles toward her face and then cover her eyes as she completed her prayer.

On the first night of Passover, almost from the time I was an infant, I would sit next to my paternal grandfather, and he would teach me how to conduct a *Seder*. By the time I was nine or ten, he was losing his eyesight. I was beginning to read and speak Hebrew, so we conducted the *Seder* together. I read aloud from the *Haggadah* as he performed the various Passover rituals.

At that age, I would jump at the chance to attend Saturday morning services with one or the other of my grandfathers when the opportunity presented itself. My maternal grandfather always sat in the same place in his synagogue, under a particular fleur-de-lis, about a third of the way back from the *Bimah*, the platform where the Rabbi and Cantor stood leading the service.

"Grandpa, why do you always sit in the same place?" I once asked him.

With a big smile, he pointed to the ceiling and answered, "So He will know where to find me." After a short pause and with a twinkle in his eye, he added, "And you can always find me here too!"

While my grandmothers instilled in me the spiritual aspects of Judaism, my grandfathers supported the duties and rituals. During the year preceding my Bar Mitzvah, I had practiced chanting my *Torah* and *Haftorah* portion for each of them—and I still remember the gentle way they both corrected me and complemented me as I made fewer and fewer mistakes. Before my Bar Mitzvah, I had contemplated the possibility of becoming a Rabbi. My mother's death three months after I "became a man," and the eleven months of mourning following, changed all that.

THE WEEKDAY SERVICES I attended at the synagogue were held in a small chapel adjacent to the main chapel, which was used for Saturday morning and High Holiday services. The afternoon *Mincha*, lasting about fifteen minutes, was scheduled to take place before sundown. Then, when darkness set in, *Maariv*, the half-hour evening service, could begin. My mother's death and funeral had occurred during the Autumn Equinox, and dusk was setting in earlier and earlier. In New York, the temperature was steadily falling. Within a few months, I was running from school to synagogue in the freezing weather, sometimes through snow and ice. But I did it. I had to. I had no choice in the matter. It was my duty as a man.

I'd arrive at the door of the synagogue—transitioning from the secular realm to the spiritual realm—with hardly a chance to catch my breath. My father worked late hours and my grandfathers lived across town, so most days I was the only family member in attendance. And always, I was the only young person joining the group of elderly men there to form a *Minyan,* the minimum number required for prayer to take place. Most, like my grandparents, had come to the United States as religious refugees from Eastern Europe. I can still smell the stale odor of their suits and ties, which probably hadn't been cleaned in years. Perhaps as retired workers and laborers, these were the only dress clothes they owned. It would be their children and grandchildren who would become professionals like me.

Crying was not allowed in this gathering of elderly men. Several times, especially in the first weeks after the funeral, a tear would escape and roll down my face. Despite my clandestine attempt to wipe it away, the *Shamash*—the assistant who conducted the daily services in the absence of the Rabbi—would direct a disapproving scowl at me or give me a sharp tap on the hands with his *yad.* His actions were intended to remind me that I was now a man—there would be no crying in this place of worship. Only the tearless wailing of the Cantor chanting the *Shema* was acceptable. The daily call to Israel to remember its God floated over the murmuring men as they rocked back and forth in prayer. I quickly learned to squelch any emotion for fear of reprimand. And I rocked back and forth with them.

During the break between the afternoon and the evening prayers, the Minyan gathered around the long rectangular table in the chapel, next to the Ark containing the Torah. I sat alone on a hard wooden bench behind them. These men were a fellowship or study group focused on the Mishna: a particular text of commentaries based on the original Oral Jewish Law. The Shamash would read a line or two in Hebrew, offer his interpretation, and then various members of the group would respond with their own comments. Because they all spoke in Yiddish, I had little idea what they were discussing. I didn't ask, nor did they seem inclined to inform me.

Sitting there day after day, I certainly didn't think of praying, so I became a doodler. Palm trees were my specialty. Date palms, coconut palms—I mastered the art of all manner of palm trees—a carryover from the days I'd read about exotic places while waiting for my mother during her doctor appointments. When the Shamash was assured—according to the clock—that sunset had arrived, the evening service began.

As I was most often the sole mourner, I was the one to stand up and read aloud the *Kaddish*. My palms would begin to sweat. My heart would race. My body was hot, regardless of the temperature in the room. In my utter disorientation, I felt confused, self-conscious, embarrassed. All eyes were focused on me. I felt ashamed—a thirteen-year-old boy with no mother standing alone in the midst of a dozen or so elderly men listening intently to every word I uttered and every sentence I recited. The men would nod in silent approval when I appropriately pronounced each Hebrew syllable and correct me aloud if I mispronounced or skipped one. I felt like they were hanging on my every word, waiting to hear a wrong intonation or a mispronunciation. And when I did make a mistake, the world went into slow motion; the men becoming huge frightening figures with El Greco-like faces pointing out my mistakes and confirming what I had already surmised: something was terribly wrong with me.

Within a short time, I had committed the *Kaddish* to memory, but the congregation's reaction remained the same: nodding and correcting, correcting and nodding. *Why didn't they leave me alone?* At the time, I thought they were being critical of me, but now I believe they were teaching me to be a man, which meant being devoid of emotional needs. Their intent was to help me, encouraging me to be perfect in the eyes of God. In fact, that is what I remember hearing them say. Some of the old men might have felt pity for me having lost a mother. But that too was painful. For the men making up the *Minyan*, I was a successful Bar Mitzvah *Bucher*—I had passed the real test. For the most part, I think what they felt was satisfaction—indeed, pride—seeing me perform my duty to my mother and, in their eyes, to God.

Nearing the end of that year, I was no longer making mistakes. My tears had dried up, and I was on my way to indifference toward emotion. Still, the anxiety I felt in the synagogue each and every day of that year would follow me for years.

DURING THE PERIOD OF mourning, I spent time with my father each Sunday, his only day off. Wherever we went, whether to visit friends or relatives, or to a sports event or a movie, the first thing he did was to ask, "Where is the closest *Schul*, so that Billy can say *Kaddish*?"

Why did he have to make such a big deal of it? Why did he have to announce it to the whole world? I wanted to hide. Why couldn't I be like every other thirteen-year-old instead of having to stand up among a group of strangers, letting them know too that my mother had died?

To his credit, however, my father always accompanied me to the synagogue on these Sundays, although I don't ever recall him standing up and praying at all. After all these years, I discovered that, according to Jewish Law, while children of a deceased parent are required to say the *Kaddish* for those full eleven months, spouses are only required to say it for thirty days. I don't recall that this delineation was ever explained to me. So for many, many years, I harbored resentment towards my father, when it turned out that he too was only following tradition. But most of all, I resented his constant criticism.

If the old men in the synagogue were critical of my reciting the *Kaddish*, my father was supercritical of *me*. He criticized my grades in school. If I earned a B: "Why didn't you get an A?" If I earned an A: "How many other kids got an A?" In my father's mind, it didn't mean anything if too many kids got an A—the teacher was handing them out too easily. Sometimes it was: "Why can't you stand up straight?" Or if I left the lights on in a room: "What—am I supporting the electric company?" Just about anything and everything I did during that year of mourning, my father had some critical remark to make. I was a teenager darting from place to place to avoid constant attacks. And my father was in a state of grief too—expressed as anger—a response I now know is common after losing a beloved.

His criticism about my grades continued throughout high school. Academic success would mean satisfying my father's wish for me to "make my mark in the world," an injunction he gave me when I graduated from the Bronx High School of Science. A victim of the Great Depression, he never completed college. My success would be his success. I would go on to college and then graduate school, succeeding where he hadn't—or couldn't.

WITH TIME, I BEGAN to realize that I was now different from all the young people I knew as friends and relatives: I was motherless. I was a freak in some circus sideshow. My father worked long hours, leaving me to spend my teenage years alone or as an occasional guest in my relatives' homes. Even with my family, I felt like a stranger. An outsider. An orphan. And much like any other orphan, I learned very quickly to be thankful for any support I received, whether it was emotional, physical, or material—and to always settle for less. I learned to behave myself.

Being different was especially hard in relation to my friends. While I was in the synagogue that year, my best friends, Barry and Stuart, were home with their mothers, doing homework or playing games. The three of us had met in Kindergarten, played all manner of ball games together through grade school, celebrated our Bar Mitzvahs within three weeks of each other—we were inseparable until the Singularity. Now I was AWOL with them. It never dawned on them to come to services with me. It never dawned on me to ask them to come to my embarrassing daily ritual. Nor did it occur to their parents to say, "Go to services with Billy today. Keep him company. It'll do you good to keep up your Hebrew and say your prayers." At the end of the year of mourning, we resumed our friendship as if nothing had happened. And we never talked about my mother.

I am alone, abandoned by my mother, my father, my friends, and my family – and by God. If only I had someone – anyone – to share this with.

IF MY HEART CLOSED with the closing of my mother's coffin, it had been nailed shut every day I attended the synagogue during those eleven months of mourning. As that year unfolded, the self-consciousness I was experiencing turned to anger, the anger to rage. Through it all, I suppressed these feelings just as my father and grandfathers had, and as was expected. At the deepest level, though, I was pissed. *God be damned!* When that year of mourning ended, I walked out of the synagogue, vowing never to trust in God again. I would be an independent intellectual, trusting the solid truths of the material world. Scholarship became my *shibboleth*; teaching became my sword.

The study of science and mathematics was perfect, precise, and predictable. Order seemed to abound. My emotions, which threatened to overtake and consume me, were easily set aside by the curiosity I felt putting attention on my studies. I would sit alone at the kitchen table, sandwiched between the small refrigerator and the gas stove, and the world opened to me, like the workings of a majestic grandfather clock with everything perfectly fitting together and making sense.

I chose a career in nuclear science and engineering—at first because of the promise that radiation could detect and cure the cancer my mother had died from, and later as a pursuit that could fully occupy my attention, allowing me to excel, using acute mental capabilities, but asking nothing of me emotionally. I superimposed the image of loving families and friends in Renoir's paintings onto whatever strife may have been happening in my life. This defense kept me steady and balanced—and lost in my work. But my success in the outer world would prove to keep me imprisoned in a one-dimensional life, trapped in a positive emotional front geared to surviving the bleakness and loneliness of my loss. A week before my mother died, she had sent me a note from the hospital. "Be a good boy, do your homework, and listen to your aunt Fay." So I pored over my studies in our one-bedroom apartment in the Bronx, blocking out the pain of my mother's decline and death. I found solace in books and safety in science.

It would take more than fifty years before I would finally access the suppressed rage and sorrow I felt and express it. By that time, I was about to retire after a successful career as a Distinguished Professor of Engineering, and my closed heart was threatening to undermine my personal life. Seeking advice, I sat in front of a psychic who knew very little about my academic achievements and nothing about my childhood. In the middle of the reading, she looked directly at me and, with a surprised look on her face, exclaimed, "I have the distinct feeling there are two of you sitting on the sofa in front of me."

There were indeed two of me. I had constructed a persona—The Professor—who stood between the outside world and me. The Professor had a single purpose: to protect me emotionally by ensuring my success in the world. I had taken refuge in my head to avoid the pain of loss buried in my heart.

Chapter 3

The Dichotomy

It is not enough to have a good mind.
The main thing is to use it well.
—René Descartes

"IN THIS COURSE, we're going to have some fun with a deadly serious subject—nuclear reactor safety." I looked around at the group of twenty or so graduate students enrolled in my class on the first day of the fall quarter in 1989 at UCLA. As usual, I was nervous meeting the students at the beginning of a new class. *What's this anxiety? I've given the same opening comments so many times before.*

"Instead of homework each week, there'll be a term project," I said. "You'll work in groups of four or five students and prepare a Safety Analysis Report for a new generation of nuclear power plants that have been designed, but not yet licensed and built. The project is the deadly serious part."

I paused, wiped my brow, and noticed how much I was sweating.

"And in lieu of a final exam," I continued, "I'll convene a panel of engineers from industry, government, and academia who'll serve as an advisory board, and you will have to convince them your reactor is safe and deserves a construction permit, and then a license to operate. That's the fun part."

I paused again. Noticing the alarm on the students' faces, as well as my own nervousness, I tried a bit of humor. "At least it's fun for me."

I began to chuckle. The students seemed to have grasped how difficult this assignment would be for them. To break the tension, they began laughing along with me. I started to relax as my anxiety subsided.

I hadn't yet made the connection between my nervousness before the first lecture each semester and my experience during that period of mourning following my mother's death. The anxiety I'd felt in the synagogue had carried into the classroom, where I once again stood before a group waiting to hear me speak. With all eyes upon me, I was back in that small chapel, anxiously trying to ignore how I felt under the scrutiny of those old men.

Well, if I was going to be scrutinized by dozens—and eventually hundreds—of students, I was going to make my lectures interesting.

THE INNOVATIVE IDEA OF having students present their term projects to a mock advisory board came to me in 1980, just after I'd spent a sabbatical as a Senior Fellow with the committee that advises the Nuclear Regulatory

Commission on a broad range of safety and licensing issues. In addition to my own research project, I'd observed firsthand how such advisory boards operate. So when I returned to UCLA, I developed and taught the first ever academic nuclear reactor safety course in the country that included a model for a mock review board.

"There are three safety systems that are required in case of a 'plant fault,'" I would begin my introductory lecture. "First, a highly reliable system to detect the fault and rapidly shut down the chain reaction—the Plant Protection System."

With no laptop computers or tablets in those days to distract them, the class would be diligently taking handwritten notes. Knowing the subject matter so well, I could relax and slip into the remainder of the lecture. Over the years, this aspect of teaching became so familiar that, whenever I was asked to make some remarks at casual social events, I would joke that I could only speak in fifty-minute blocks.

"Second, redundant and diverse systems," I would continue, "to insure heat removal from the long-lived radioactive fission products—the Decay Heat Removal System."

Imparting my knowledge and experience to these young students was a far cry from reciting a prayer before the elderly men at the synagogue. Lecturing was a choice I had made—praying was in obedience to someone else's command. And having the students' complete attention was very satisfying. They too were listening to every word I uttered and every sentence I recited.

"And third, a system to ensure that the decay heat is transferred to the ocean, a river, or a cooling tower—the Ultimate Heat Sink."

By this time, I'd be cruising—the nervousness gone and the sweating over. I was in my element and the class was with me despite the complex nature of the material. Intellectually-gifted graduate students could meet me in the far reaches of my mind. The elation I would feel describing these three systems would carry me through the remainder of the lecture and throughout the ten-week course.

A bonus: the far reaches of my mind offered a safe hiding place from any messy emotions that might arise.

At UCLA, I felt part of something bigger than myself: a community of scholars—a family. I belonged. I was accepted and well recognized as an innovative teacher and a creative researcher. Mid-career, in the 1980s, I served first as an Associate Dean and was then appointed as a Department Chair in the School of Engineering and Applied Science. My academic and professional life was unfolding with ease and opportunity—just what I needed to avoid the other untidy parts of my life.

ONE DAY IN 1966, shortly after I had arrived at UCLA and taken up my post as a young Assistant Professor, I stopped by the office of a senior faculty member.

"What are you working on?" he asked.

"I've been expanding my analytical work on time-dependent nonlinear stability," I responded, "to include spatially dependent feedback mechanisms that might be applicable for advanced nuclear reactor systems."

I described the sophisticated mathematical techniques and the complex physical phenomena I was dealing with. He listened intently to what I had to say and seemed to take it all in. There were several seconds of silence after I finished speaking. He closed his eyes, looked to the ceiling as he opened them, smoothed his goatee, bowed his head, and looked directly at me over his glasses.

"That's interesting," he said, shrugging his shoulders. "Anybody could do that." He took off his glasses, fiddled with them for a few seconds, and continued. "If you want to work on some really challenging nuclear reactor problems with important societal impact … boy, have I got some for you."

I was stunned by his comment. I thought I had impressed him with my knowledge of mathematics and physics. *Was my colleague — an internationally renowned expert on reactor safety — discounting my research?* I felt like a thirteen-year-old again, and my father was reprimanding me for something I had done that didn't meet his expectations. Much as I would have done with my father, I meekly asked him what he had in mind.

He proceeded to outline some challenging nuclear reactor safety and risk issues that I might explore. When he finished, I thanked him for his advice and retreated to my office, determined to prove my worth to him.

Was I trying to take care of my senior colleague, as my mother had instructed me to take care of my father, by immersing myself in his areas of research? Would specializing in nuclear power plant safety make me feel safe? Subconsciously, I was already wading into emotional issues that would ultimately determine the trajectory of my personal life.

My colleague was right: I had been working on analytical problems that really had no immediate application to the practice of nuclear engineering. With the rising availability of mainframe computers, my analytical research would eventually come to a dead end anyway. So I took him up on his suggestion that I work on nuclear reactor safety and risk. He became my mentor. I worked diligently to prove myself in his eyes and, for the next forty years, focused my career on nuclear reactor safety and risk. Little did I know that safety and risk would also characterize my personal unfolding.

Based on my research and teaching, I was soon sought out by various government agencies for my professional opinion and advice. My reputation among my peers continued to grow with each academic and professional accomplishment in the nuclear reactor safety field. I could rely on my mind to resolve difficult technical issues. Science and mathematics provided the context within which I could excel. With reason and logic, I didn't have to feel the pain and grief of my mother's death—or any other pain, for that matter. I was in place, doing well what I had set out to do.

MY PERSONAL LIFE—that was something different. I'd often arrive home feeling as nervous and with the same sweaty palms I had on the first day of a class. When my wife would meet me at the door with something like, "Would you do something with those boys?" I felt confounded and in shock. I'd always wanted a sibling to share my innermost thoughts and feelings after my mother's death, so, for the life of me, I couldn't comprehend why our two sons would fight with each other. Never having had that experience, nor seeing how a parent might deal with it, I'd attempt to resolve whatever issue they were embroiled in by applying the reason and logic that made me so successful as a professor. That didn't work.

If the issue wasn't about the children, it might be about finances. Referencing my professional persona, my wife might say, "Well, if you're so smart, how come you don't make more money?" Or, striking at the core of my choices, "Joslyn's husband speaks at conventions in the Bahamas. How come you speak at conventions in Pittsburgh?"

Maybe her questions arose from frustration with a husband who found his fulfillment solely in his head. But they felt like daggers plunged deep into my heart. Feeling defensive, I'd respond with reason and logic.

"Joslyn's husband is the General Counsel for a large corporation," I would argue. "I chose a life of service in academia, and you agreed to it—and you're the one who wanted to move back to Los Angeles because our families are here."

I'd always felt that working at a public rather than a private university was my way of "giving back" for the undergraduate degree I had earned at UCLA and the graduate degree I had earned at UC Berkeley. Perhaps that's why working in industry didn't resonate with me. Besides, I was a natural teacher and researcher. Pouring my mind into academics was a refuge and a delight.

With time, I would also come to understand that tenure at UCLA—my alma mater—felt safe, providing a sense of belonging and the family I didn't have as a child. Essentially, I stayed in the University of California system my entire professional life. A university career gave meaning to my life and provided self-worth to a motherless child.

MY WIFE AND I had met at UCLA in 1962 while we were both undergraduate students. She was nineteen, and I was twenty-three. Our yearlong courtship formed the template for our marriage. She was living in one dormitory and I in another. This would aptly serve as a metaphor regarding our future life together. While we spent time together—studying, attending campus cultural, social, and sports events, eating our meals in the cafeteria, and visiting her family—we were removed from the reality of creating a life together. We were encapsulated in the ivory tower of academia.

During our first three years of our marriage, I was a PhD student at UC Berkeley. She was a senior at nearby Mills College the first year and a teacher at Berkeley High School the second year. Our first child was born the third year while I wrote my dissertation, and she became an at-home mother. Upon earning my PhD, I took the position at UCLA. I do not recall us ever having free time to ourselves, to explore our marriage or relationship, or to articulate our value system as husband and wife or as parents. Within seven years, we had three children—two sons followed by a daughter—nicely fitting my mental picture of what I thought a professor's family should be. In my idealized traditional family, it was her job to take care of the children and the household and mine to earn a living. It never occurred to me to deviate from that picture—or to discuss it.

For two decades, my wife and I rumbled and tumbled from one event to the next—season tickets for the UCLA basketball and football games, the Blue or Gold concert series, and the dance and music concerts at the Music Center. We entertained our friends, as they did us. As I moved up the academic ladder at UCLA, we attended fundraisers and hosted faculty and students. And we both focused on the children—birthday parties and sports events, graduations, Bar and Bat Mitzvahs, school concerts and school plays. Pre-school, public school, Hebrew school, Indian Guides, zoos, museums, children's theatre.

When the children were old enough and my wife lost interest in UCLA sports, they accompanied me to the games. One year I counted fifty weekends devoted to children's activities.

It's not that I didn't enjoy doing these things with my family. The idea of being a good father served me well, though what that would mean in terms of emotion was simply not on my radar. I have a vivid memory of staying overnight at the hospital with one of my sons when he was a toddler. There he was, in a crib covered by an oxygen tent, lying on an ice pack to break his fever—and there I was, sitting in a chair next to him, deriving a solution to a set of differential equations. I distinctly remember that, right there on that very night, I developed a matrix transformation to decouple the two group diffusion equations for neutron transport. The Professor at work—Billy's strategy to avoid feeling the terror of his mother's illness—had become medication for my own fear and anxiety. My child's was secondary. I recall dozing off and awakening to his cry as he was standing up in the crib, trying to attract my attention. Until recently, I think my children had been trying to do that their whole lives.

While my strategy allowed me to pour love and attention on my children, my closed heart could not afford them a place to land in me emotionally. Since I couldn't process my own emotions, I couldn't process theirs with them. The same dynamic that insulated me from my children's mother insulated us from each other.

My oldest son once said—upon becoming a father himself—that I was one hundred percent physically present, fifty percent mentally present, and probably ten percent or less emotionally present when I was with them.

THE DEFLATION I FELT personally was inversely proportional to the elation I felt professionally. As a measure of my success, I had received a call in early 1980 from the White House, asking whether I would be the technical consultant to President Carter's Commission to investigate the incident at the Three Mile Island nuclear power plant. This had been a "severe accident"—the reactor core had melted, and radioactivity had been released into the surrounding environment, including local communities. This was the first such accident in the United States and the President wanted a report on the causes and an assessment of how to prevent something like this in the future. Stepping out beyond the academic world and into the real world was very exciting. This was an opportunity to serve the world community in an area where I felt confident about the subject matter and of the expertise I had to offer.

I interviewed with Bruce Babbitt, the Governor of Arizona, who chaired the President's Commission. We hit it off right away, and I travelled with him to meetings and onsite visits. Having a security clearance allowed me access to places I didn't know existed. It was a rare opportunity to contribute to the nation's safety and welfare and to learn how power plants operated in actuality rather than in theory. As a bonus, I could bring this learning back to the classroom. Clearly, this part of my life was working.

Over the next year, I provided to the Commission the technical basis for "lessons learned" from the accident and recommendations for improving the operation of the nation's nuclear power plants. My reputation and success continued to open more doors in Washington DC for me to serve on review committees for various government agencies. I was flying high.

During those years as a professor at UCLA, the schism between my work and my family grew from a mere crack to a huge canyon. More and more, I became an outsider in my own family. Once again, I felt different from the people I was supposed to feel close to. Just as focusing on my homework after my mother's death had given me solace, focusing on my teaching and research at the University had provided sanctuary. My success shielded me from my painful home life and my equally chaotic but unexplored inner life. *How could I be so accepted and admired, so successful and so comfortable in one part of my life, and so out of place in another?*

When the children left home—my oldest son was living with his girlfriend as he completed his college education, my younger son was attending graduate school in the Midwest, and my daughter was an undergraduate in Northern California—I no longer had an excuse to ignore my failing marriage. By 1989, my wife and I had enrolled in a program called *Marriage Encounter* and also tried couples' counseling. These attempts at resuscitating our marriage drove us farther apart.

In *Marriage Encounter*, we were challenged to write letters to each other regarding the three pillars of our married life together — children, finances, and sex. It was said that, if one of the pillars is broken, or even two, the relationship can be repaired and survive. When it's all three, the relationship collapses. The letters we read to each other, as instructed, seemed to be filled with attacks and blame, highlighting how little respect and understanding existed between us. I recall finding myself either on the defensive or the offensive, unable to hear the pain she was feeling or blaming me for. All three pillars of our marriage were broken.

During one of the exercises with our marriage counselor, I was directed to sit in a chair with my eyes closed. My wife, eyes closed as well, stood in front of me, took my hands in hers, and pulled me out of the chair, much as an elderly couple with physical frailties might do. I saw in a flash that someday I would be an old man being helped out of his chair. However, the woman helping me up would not be my wife. It would be another woman.

Chapter 4

Another World

The unexamined life is not worth living.
—Socrates

IWAS WANDERING AROUND the Malibu Country Mart, a Spanish-style plaza, catching my breath before returning to the maelstrom of my personal life. Dreading going home after another day at the University, I had chosen a detour to admire the palm trees, the red bougainvillea climbing the whitewashed walls of the plaza, and the succulent Mediterranean plants bordering the children's playground. The events of my hectic workday slowly faded away as I took in the salty ocean breeze. As I stepped into a courtyard, the gentle clatter of wind chimes hanging in the open doorway of the Malibu Shaman bookstore attracted my attention. I could see well-stocked bookshelves lining the walls and, without further thought, I entered.

I've always loved bookstores and libraries. The act of picking up a book, reading its dust cover, and perusing a few pages is more than just a passing fancy for me. It awakens a promise of knowledge and adventure. The act recalls the weekly chore my mother had given me of removing each book from its resting place in her bookcase and carefully dusting it off, long before I could read any of them. Opening a book reminds me of when I became enamored with the content of those books and could read them.

The Malibu Shaman was not the kind of bookstore I'd ever been in before. I felt surprisingly at ease with the burning incense, amethyst crystals, soft music, and statues of the Buddha. Memories of my grandmother and her ethereal energy flooded my mind—the objects and artifacts seemed to mirror her way of being in the world, giving me a sense of comfort.

A young woman walked toward me. Her long blond hair, parted in the middle, framed her face. A red dot was centered on her forehead. Her short saffron-colored blouse revealed a tan midriff; a long maroon and saffron colored skirt hung from her hips. She was clearly of European descent, so her manner of dress seemed a little incongruous to me. *Young women certainly don't show up in my engineering classes dressed this way.* She greeted me with a welcoming smile and a soft voice.

"Can I help you find something?"

"No, just browsing," I replied. "I hadn't noticed this bookstore at the Mart before."

In fact, it seemed the bookstore had just appeared out of nowhere, like Brigadoon. She smiled at me again.

"Oh! So you've been to the Mart before?"

"Yes, my wife and I live up the road, in Cold Canyon, just off Malibu Canyon. We sometimes eat at the restaurants here."

Over her shoulder, a large cloth painting on the far wall caught my attention. It depicted the Buddha sitting cross-legged, surrounded by a number of what looked like little Buddhas.

"That's called a *thangka*," the woman said, noticing the shift in my attention. "They're religious paintings from Tibet."

I moved closer to study it. Having taken two art history courses as an undergraduate and having visited many art museums around the world, my knowledge of art was more than superficial. But I'd never seen anything quite like the *thangka* before—it was absolutely stunning. The craftsmanship, detail, and vivid use of color somehow struck a chord within me. The sitting Buddha seemed to emanate a sense of stillness, harmony, and inner peace. He seemed to call to me: "Be quiet. Go inside. Find yourself."

I would return to the Malibu Shaman many times—the young woman in the sari became an informative and pleasant guide to the bookstore's treasures. With each visit, the otherworldly atmosphere of the place became more familiar to me. I began to anticipate the calmness it provided within the frenetic pace of my professional work and my turbulent personal life. On campus, I would roll from one activity to the next—teaching class, meeting with graduate students, attending committee meetings or a distinguished guest's seminar. Oftentimes,

I was acting on autopilot, momentum carrying me through the day.

Before long, just as some people would stop at a bar for a quick one after work, I began to use the bookstore as a place to decompress before returning home.

ON ONE OCCASION AT the Malibu Shaman, a woman seated at a table was giving a tarot card reading. Of course, at the time, I had no idea what a tarot card reading was. But something about her voice sounded familiar, so I waited nearby. When her client left, she looked over at me from where she was sitting.

"I'd recognize your big blue eyes anywhere," she said.

It turned out that, almost thirty years earlier as UCLA undergraduates, we had lived in the same dorm, had eaten many of our meals together, and had even dated for a while. After she explained to me what a tarot card reading was, we agreed to meet the following week at the bookstore to catch up with each other's lives—and for me to get a tarot card reading.

"The cards indicate that a great transition in your life will take place in the very near future," she told me as I sat, intrigued by the strange images on the cards laid out before me.

I was skeptical but listened intently. As I turned to leave after her reading, I brushed against a book that was sitting on the edge of her table and it fell to the floor. When I bent over to pick it up, she said, "Ah, Maggie Scarf's new book—*Intimate Partners*. Perhaps that book was meant for you." She smiled and, with a twinkle in her eyes, she continued, "It was so nice seeing you again." Without fully registering what had just transpired, I bought the book and slowly made my way home.

Comparing my marriage with the case studies described in Scarf's book confirmed the bleakness I was feeling. Amid a failing marriage, I was offered a view of what might be possible in a healthy relationship. This was certainly not like anything I was experiencing.

I decided to talk about the book and the feelings I was having with a colleague of mine, a clinical psychology professor at UCLA, who was writing a book on relationships. We were both serving on an Academic Senate committee and would often meet on campus for coffee before a meeting. As we got to know each other, she told me about the difficulty she was having in her own marriage, seemingly giving me permission to talk about mine.

"You need some emotional support to help you through this difficult time," she said to me during coffee one day. "You should see my friend Curt. He's a psychiatrist and an adjunct professor in the Medical School. His office is on Westwood Boulevard—you can walk there from here."

That was exactly what I needed.

By THE TIME I WALKED into Curt's office for my first appointment, I had realized I could no longer try to salvage my twenty-six-year marriage. This first foray with Curt into my inner life set in motion the excruciating task of unraveling the threads that had so entangled me.

"What prompted you to act after all this time?" Curt had asked.

"Well … one clear, moonless, star-studded night several months ago, my wife and I were sitting in our outdoor hot tub." I began. "Although she was sitting next to me and I heard her words, I felt completely alone."

Curt nodded, indicating to me that he understood how I felt. For the first time in my adult life, I had the support of a kind and thoughtful man with whom I could be completely honest about my feelings.

"On what might have been a very romantic evening," I went on, "I realized that our marriage had actually died."

Opposites can attract. However, when matter and anti-matter collide, they annihilate each other. I finally had the resolve to admit that, with one more blow, I'd disappear emotionally—forever. Rather than suffer mutual destruction, I initiated a legal separation from my wife. Eventually, we divorced.

AS PREDICTED BY THE TAROT cards, my life did indeed go through a great transition. It was 1991, a year after that reading. I was living alone in a rented cottage on a cliff overlooking the ocean at Point Dume, just west of Malibu, off the Pacific Coast Highway. I was a bachelor again.

I often refer to myself during that marriage as living an "unexamined life." Rarely, if ever, had my wife and I discussed our values and the goals for our relationship. Nor did we discuss our feelings—we merely acted on them. We seemed to be locked in an ever-present battle for control of one another. When I left that marriage, I knew I wanted something different, although I hadn't yet found words to describe what was in my heart.

One day, while browsing the shelves at the Malibu Shaman, I came across Robert Nozick's book, *The Examined Life*. The evocation of Socrates' quote in that title would have a critical impact on my life's journey.

Known for his work on metaphysics, epistemology, and the philosophy of mind, Nozick was a world-renowned philosopher at Harvard. As an academic I could admire, he was a bridge for me to the world of the esoteric and spirituality that I was strangely drawn to. The book explored his experience and personal understanding of birth and death, love and sexuality, children and parents, values and meaning. It seemed like a personal invitation to the same exploration.

Thanks to Nozick's insights, I began to sense that I did not want to live my life on the surface, bouncing from one event to the next or responding to one external stimulus after another. I wanted to be present for my life. Nozick gave me the words to describe what I had been sensing: that I wanted to find out who I would be if I were not just the roles I played—professor, husband, father. Yet I had no idea what it would take to find this out, or what it would mean to expand my focus beyond what happened around me to take into account what was going on within me.

AFTER I HAD BEEN seeing him for a while, Curt invited me to attend a workshop he was leading—something he called Holotropic Breath Work—an exploration into the subconscious. He explained that, during the process, participants worked together in pairs, alternating as "the sitter," who was a supportive observer, and "the breather," who was deepening into a journey guided by the breath.

"The breather lies on a mat or futon that's covered with soft cushions and begins to hyperventilate, inducing altered states of consciousness."

"Sounds like a hallucinogenic experience without the use of drugs."

By this time, I had done enough reading while thumbing through the books at the Malibu Shaman to make the association between altered states of consciousness and hallucinogenic substances.

"That's right," he continued, "it was developed for exactly that."

"I'm willing to try anything 'reasonable' once," I said. "So I'm game."

"As a sitter, you can become acutely aware of the breather's deep emotions, often in the form of sadness, rage, or joy. And as a breather, well ..."

"I can see the possibility of releasing some rage myself," I said, "so I can attend the divorce proceedings in a reasoned and logical manner."

"At a minimum," Curt chuckled and nodded.

"Her lawyer's requests are making me angrier by the day."

That statement turned his chuckle into downright laughter. Little did I know that Curt was in the midst of his own divorce proceedings and understood exactly what I was experiencing in that arena—and the potential of Holotropic Breath Work to guide me to a new understanding and capacity for release.

DURING MY FIRST EXPERIENCE as a breather, I found myself sobbing for a prolonged period, then moving on to rage and, finally, to laughter. The breathing and the emotional transitions were accompanied by music, helping me access past experiences and deep feelings. I recall a violin sonata that provoked the deepest tears I had ever experienced—perhaps the tears not shed at my mother's funeral—although I did not make the connection until much later.

Lying quietly on the futon following my first session of deep breathing, I realized there was more to me than my body or mind. Although I found I couldn't articulate the transcendental nature of that experience to the group at the workshop's concluding round, I did recall that it felt primordial in nature. I remember hearing the sound of molten lava flowing over land into the sea and the sounds of drumming in a jungle. And I could viscerally feel the difficult sensations of my own birth. I remember comparing it to the last bit of toothpaste being squeezed from its tube.

Following the workshop, Curt suggested I attend a Gestalt therapy workshop at Esalen Institute, a retreat center in Big Sur on the Northern California Coast.

"What is Gestalt therapy?"

"Trust me," he said. "Just go. It'll do you good."

Not knowing anything about what I was in for, I took his advice, registered for the workshop, and, several weeks later, drove up to Big Sur by myself. While waiting for my room, I watched three women on the front lawn dancing bare-breasted to the rhythms of a man playing bongos. The dancers' freedom stood in sharp contrast to the captivity of the life I had created for myself. I began to sense that I'd become imprisoned by my professional success and the emotional constraints imposed by my role as The Professor. In fact, despite its rewards, that prison had held me in bondage, unable to sense my own pain, let alone react with compassion to the pain of others.

As I watched the dancers, a memory arose from several years before. I was a new professor and my secretary had arranged to be away for a week on her honeymoon. But that Monday morning, she unexpectedly showed up for work and started sobbing.

"Why are you here?" I asked, surprised.

"My fiancé jilted me on the morning of our wedding," she said. Then, choking back another sob, she added, "And my mother has had a stroke."

I was deeply sorry for her. I could feel her anguish. But something held me back from expressing any of that. I couldn't even hug her. I just couldn't do it. I was her supervisor, and students were milling about. What would my colleagues say if they caught me consoling a secretary by embracing her? Here was a young woman in emotional distress and what was going on in my mind was the concern that I might set a bad example or, worse yet, be accused of sexual harassment by offering a reassuring hug to a bereft soul.

As a young faculty member, I'd already been burned once in this prison when a colleague of mine, a man of Middle Eastern origin, clasped my arm in his as we walked together sharing some good news about a funded research proposal. The next day, both my Department Chairman and the Department Administrator separately admonished me.

"You shouldn't walk with Navid that way," they both said. "It'll give some people the wrong impression."

Such was the nature of academia in the 1970s and 80s. But not here. I was free, sitting on the lawn at Esalen, basking in the Big Sur sunshine, watching those women dance. Something was changing for me, and I was about to find out what.

During the Gestalt workshop, I heard personal stories of childhood physical and sexual abuse, trauma of all sorts, and subsequent psychological damage. These were the kinds of things we never spoke about at the University or at home. As I listened to stories of rape and incest, I began to cry. The pain of these individuals affected me deeply as I thought of my colleagues, my staff, and the students who attended my classes. I had always considered them—and treated them—as rational human beings, but they were also emotional human beings. *What does that mean for me behind the façade of The Professor?*

The Holotropic Breath work and the Gestalt workshop at Esalen helped free up something that had been locked away in my heart. To my surprise, I was a much more sensitive and feeling man than I had realized. My personal journey of self-exploration had definitely begun.

Chapter 5

Soul Mates

The deeper a soul-connection goes … the more it brings our karmic patterns and personal neuroses to the surface. So before two people make a commitment to each other, they need to find out whether they can handle this challenge.
—John Welwood, JOURNEY OF THE HEART

"HI, HOW'S IT GOING for you?" she asked.

It was Sunday lunch break at a weekend holotropic breath workshop that Curt was leading in Santa Monica, and I was happily ensconced in a chair on the deck reading the *Los Angeles Times* sports section. The annual UCLA-USC football game had been played the previous day—the first such game I'd missed in years—and I was intent on at least taking in the summary.

I looked up at her. "Fine," I responded, not quite relishing the interruption.

She looked somewhat familiar. I'd seen her at the first breath workshop I'd attended with Curt. I turned back to the *Times,* but she was still standing there. Not knowing what else to do, I introduced myself.

"My name is Bill. I didn't catch your name yesterday."

"Gloria," she replied. "My mother named me after the movie star Gloria Swanson—or maybe Gloria de Havilland. She never said which one."

"Well, it's Olivia de Havilland," I said with an air of authority.

Gloria cracked up laughing. At my preciseness and seriousness, I figured.

"Well, that's my mother for you," she said. "You can't pin her down on anything."

More than twenty-seven years had passed since I'd last pursued a woman and now here was an attractive one standing in front of me, telling me about herself. I felt awkward and shy, eager to take refuge in the *Times* and UCLA football. I mumbled a few sentences.

She smiled and said, rather seductively, "See you inside."

As I folded up the newspaper, I remembered that the previous day, when participants spoke about their intentions for the workshop, Gloria had said she was dealing with a relationship breakup. I'd been legally separated for only five months and was relieved to be alone. I didn't really want to start thinking about dating now—or did I?

During a session that afternoon, I was in my role as a sitter when I heard what seemed to be oddly familiar cries from across the room—like a baby in distress. Realizing it was a woman crying, I thought: *Whoever she is, I'd like to meet her.* Her cries brought tears to my eyes and chills to my body, and I didn't know why. There was something about her ability to go deep into herself and express this distress that touched me.

This is no doubt a woman who's not afraid to know herself—someone very different from most of the women I know.

During the concluding round, when everyone spoke, it became clear that the crying-baby voice had come from Gloria, in touch with her childhood pain.

Everyone hugged goodbye at the end of the weekend, as was the custom. But as Gloria and I held each other, something happened. I'd never felt a full body hug like that before. More chills ran up and down my spine. Of course, I would never hug a colleague at the University. And hugging my estranged wife—especially in front of our children—had become perfunctory. This was something completely new to me. My body was aroused. I couldn't get her out of my mind that night.

The next evening, I was having dinner at the home of my colleague who had introduced me to Curt. We were having a working meeting to review her section of an Academic Senate committee annual report. After we finished our business, the conversation turned personal.

"Dating anyone?" she asked. "Have you met anyone yet?"

"They always want to know," her husband mumbled from the kitchen.

"No and no," I replied, and then launched into telling her about my positive experience at the workshop. I mentioned that I was attracted to a woman named Gloria.

"Glad to hear it, but we have to hurry now," she said, clearing the table. "Two women are coming to do some energy work. By the way, they're both single. You should get to know them. And one's name is Gloria."

Precisely at that moment, the front door opened and the very Gloria I'd met at the workshop walked in. I stared at her. It was like magic!

"We were just talking about you," I blurted out, stunned by the coincidence and a bit tongue tied.

Gloria, seeming nonplussed, introduced her friend, and we briefly acknowledged that we'd met at Curt's workshop the day before. Then the two women proceeded down the hallway and out of sight.

While following sacred signs certainly was not a path I'd been traveling, I seemed ready to take this chance meeting as one. Maybe it was the time I'd been spending at the Malibu Shaman bookstore. Meeting this woman on two successive days in the greater Los Angeles area with its population of five million or so felt like more than just coincidence to me.

The next day, I called Curt and left a message asking for Gloria's contact information. Unbeknownst to me, shortly after I left the workshop, Gloria had asked Curt about me as well.

She later told me that Curt had readily responded, "Oh, he's a very nice man."

Gloria's psychologist friend Serena, listening in on the conversation, had elbowed Curt in the ribs.

"You can't give her any information about him," Serena said. "He's your patient."

And he didn't.

But Curt's response on my answering machine made up for it. The message he left will reverberate in my heart for all eternity.

"I am not allowed to give you the contact information for Gloria Hauser, an attorney living and working in Santa Monica."

No problem!

If my explorations and workshops with Curt had caused an inflection point in the trajectory of my life, helping me see patterns and trends in my past, my relationship with Gloria would change the trajectory of my future altogether.

GLORIA AND I HAD our first date at a bustling Italian restaurant in Santa Monica. At first, she talked about being a lawyer, and then I talked about being an engineering professor. But soon we dove into our personal lives—her recent breakup with a long-term boyfriend, my recent legal separation from my wife and, of course, my three children. It felt natural and easy to speak with her about these things. She was receptive, open, and interested in me in ways I hadn't experienced in a very long time. Her eyes were kind and deep. I felt I could fall into them. Time seemed to stand still.

Suddenly, after realizing that we had been deeply involved in conversation for quite a while, I became aware that our dinner hadn't arrived yet. I called the waitress over.

"What's taking so long with our dinner?"

"Well, you haven't ordered yet," she responded.

During the evening, I learned that Gloria would be going to a meditation retreat in Ojai the following weekend and then passing through Malibu on her way home to Santa Monica.

"How about if, on the way back, you stop by my cottage in Point Dume," I asked, rather shyly. "It's on the coast, a little north of Malibu. I'll have dinner for you."

"I'd love to."

I can still see Gloria's image, backlit by the setting sun, standing at the top of the long driveway to my cottage, wearing a wide-brimmed straw hat, a pink tank top, and colorful Bali pants. Even now, I feel my heart pounding as I write this. I had a deep sense then, as I do now, that we had already known each other for a long, long time, and that we were connected in some profound way. At that moment, I think I began to believe we'd met in some previous lifetime, in the way I'd read about at the Malibu Shaman. Thoughts like that were completely new for me. Yet, in relation to Gloria, they seemed natural—as if I'd always framed my world with metaphysical concepts.

I invited her into the cottage. It was small. The only furniture I had was a queen-sized bed and an armoire for my suits, slacks, and ties. A few colored pillows that several friends had bequeathed me adorned the living room floor. I'd left everything else behind and was starting over from scratch.

I began setting the takeout dinner containers on the living room floor while Gloria went into the kitchen to get plates and silverware. Peals of laughter erupted when she found every kitchen drawer and cabinet filled with my neatly folded underwear, T-shirts, sweaters, socks, and other items of clothing.

I joined her with a little laugh.

"Why buy a dresser for my clothes? And I don't cook, so I don't need the kitchen cabinets or drawers for dishes or pots and pans," I said. "The pantry makes a great bookcase, and I can even store my papers there."

"Okay," she said with a chuckle.

Gloria managed to find the paper plates and plastic utensils I'd tucked away in a corner cabinet. I brought out the real drinking glasses that my stepmother had given me, and I had managed to keep from breaking.

On that second date, we ended up in the bedroom in what felt to me like passionate lovemaking. At the age of fifty-one, I was experiencing the second woman I'd ever had sex with. I was in heaven. Lying together felt natural and right to me. I was anticipating cuddling there together for the rest of that night.

Suddenly, Gloria jumped up and quickly got dressed. "I have to go home now and feed my cats." She was gone before I could put my clothes on.

I was befuddled. I thought only men left to go home after a sexual encounter. At least, that was my impression from watching movies like *When Harry Met Sally*.

The next day, on my way home from UCLA, I decided to stop by her apartment on the chance she might be home. We briefly hugged at the door.

"I just wanted to see if you were okay," I said. "You left so quickly, I didn't have a chance to say goodbye."

"I'm sorry I left so abruptly. Of course, I did need to attend to the cats because I'd been gone all weekend and I had to be in court early this morning."

There was an awkward moment of silence as I took in what she said.

"But there's more, Bill. I got scared," she admitted, hesitation in her voice.

"Scared?" I couldn't believe my ears.

"Yes, I know this may sound strange. But since my first marriage ended, I've felt most comfortable with men who aren't available. Something feels different about you, it scares me."

"You are so honest," I said. "I'm deeply touched."

We ordered in dinner and talked for a while longer. To my surprise, she was frightened that this relationship could be the real deal, so she had run away. *How open and forthcoming she is,* I thought to myself.

Several days later, I phoned to say I would stop by her apartment on my way home after a late committee meeting. Expecting me, she'd left the door unlocked, and I let myself in. As I could hear that she was on the phone in her bedroom, I sat down in the living room to wait. It soon became clear that she was having a difficult conversation with her mother. Listening to the sound of her voice, I realized it was an agonizing call. So I walked into the bedroom, sat on the bed next to her, and held her hand.

When the call ended, she said she was embarrassed to have me overhear and learn what a difficult relationship she had with her mother.

"You'll get a first-hand sense of how damaged I must be, and you'll never stick around," she said, sobbing.

I looked into her hazel eyes and my heart burst with love.

"I'm not going anywhere," I said. "I'm staying here with you."

This was a singular moment for each of us. My defenses seemed to melt away. I felt I could be fully present and empathetic for, and with, a woman in a way I had never experienced before. I sensed that she was equally open and would be empathetic with me. Later she would tell me the same—that, with me, she felt she could be vulnerable with a man she could count on in a way she'd never experienced before.

"When you sat there next to me during that difficult phone call with my mother, I could feel my own goodness reflected back at me through your eyes," she told me. I had felt my own goodness through her eyes as well.

We made love again—slowly, tenderly—and then I held her close. She relaxed into my body until she fell asleep. I covered her with a blanket and left to go home. I was falling in love. After that night, we began to see each other almost every day.

GLORIA ARRANGED A DINNER date with Serena and her partner, A.J. When they arrived at Gloria's apartment, we clambered into the back seat of their car. Without a pause, Serena turned and said, "So what's going on with you two? I can feel it."

During the drive, Gloria proceeded to tell them everything—the encounter in Malibu, the phone call with her mother—and how scared and how tender she had felt. She recounted all of this openly and honestly.

This way of relating was refreshing to me. The talk at dinner with Serena and A.J. focused on our new relationship and then on their own personal lives—not on politics, sports, or some recent movie or show, which was the kind of social conversation I was used to. The way we talked that evening made me think about a scene in the movie *Ordinary People*. In the film, a married couple, played by Donald Sutherland and Mary Tyler Moore, are at a dinner party. One of their friends asks about their son, who'd tried to commit suicide. Sutherland forthrightly answers that the son is in therapy now and doing well. In the next scene, as they drive home, Moore's character scolds her husband for talking about family matters that she considers private.

That commentary in the film exactly reflected the social standards of secrecy that had operated in my former marriage. The screenwriter could have been eavesdropping on a comment from my estranged wife. In fact, our closest friends had been shocked when we legally separated, as were my colleagues at UCLA. We had been yet another upper-middle-class suburban couple whose inner turmoil festered beneath an idealized image presented to the world.

In contrast, Gloria and her good friends, including Curt and his new girlfriend—I'd left therapy by then— were completely candid with each other about everything. It was refreshing to begin being real with other couples and with each other.

I WAS ABOUT TO leave on a trip to Washington DC for a meeting with the Nuclear Regulatory Commission staff who were funding one of my research projects at UCLA. As we were saying goodbye, Gloria handed me a copy of a book she had been reading: *Journey of the Heart* by John Welwood.

"He describes the kind of relationship I would like to have with you," she said. "Are you up for it?"

Gloria opened the inside cover and read a passage to me: "As men and women find that they can no longer rely on old roles and formulas to get along, intimate relationship calls for a new kind of honesty and awareness, a willingness to let go of old patterns and cultivate new powers and sensitivities. *Journey of the Heart* shows how we can meet this challenge by learning to use whatever difficulties we are facing in relationships as opportunities to expand our sense of who we are and deepen our capacity to connect with others."

I was listening intently.

"I feel moved to work out these patterns inside a relationship—the best place for them to be healed, since that's where they will come up," she added.

I readily accepted the book from her, turned it over, and read the synopsis on the back cover. *"Journey of the Heart* offers a new approach to intimate relationships—as a path, an unfolding process of personal and spiritual discovery whose challenges awaken our deepest strengths and resources."* I looked up at her, smiled, and, with a big gulp, put it in my briefcase.

My understanding of married life and what I thought were intimate relationships had been shaped by old television sitcoms—*The Adventures of Ozzie and Harriet, Father Knows Best,* and *Happy Days*—in which family issues would always be resolved in thirty minutes, including commercial breaks. My own marriage and family life, of course, had been nothing like that. Father didn't know best and there weren't many happy days. *Could marriage be more for me than being a good provider, raising children, entertaining other couples, and going to the theater or sports events together? Could I be open and honest and live an examined life in relationship with Gloria?*

I could feel Gloria's excitement about the idea that whatever difficulty came up in an intimate relationship could serve as a foundation for spiritual growth. She had been a meditator for many years and Welwood—a therapist and a meditation teacher—was revealing how relationship could be a vehicle for self-discovery.

On the return flight from Washington, I read Welwood's book and was intrigued by his ideas. He advocated using whatever issues might come up between a couple as a means for self-discovery in the same way a meditator uses whatever comes up during meditation as something valuable to be aware of, but without identification or attachment. Welwood's words sounded good to me. Little did I know that I would need time—two decades—to really understand and act upon them.

Gloria met me for dinner the next night after I got back.

"Well, are you up for the kind of relationship Welwood describes?"

My response was flippant.

"Yeah, of course I can do this."

Chapter 6

Commitment

*Childhood is not elective. Our earliest relationships are not chosen
by us, and we do not decide how they function.*
—Stan Tatkin, WIRED FOR LOVE

About a month after our first date, Gloria and I were walking on the beach in Santa Monica, when she told me something that turned out to be more than just passing interest. Our conversation had been meandering through various aspects of our lives as we were getting to know each other, and she mentioned that, just before we met, she'd had a reading with a psychic. By this time, I was pretty open to accepting alternate realities alongside the more predictable workings of science and mathematics. So the idea of a psychic reading was starting to feel more normal to me. I was actually curious.

"The psychic told me I would have a relationship with a man who has big blue eyes," she began, kind of off-handedly. "She said his mother's name was Rose, he was a professor at a major university, and we'd move north together. She saw the man and me standing under the Golden Gate Bridge. Isn't that interesting?"

"Wow," I said. "I have blue eyes and I'm a professor at UCLA. That's a major university. But my mother's name wasn't Rose."

Gloria laughed. "Well, chalk that one off."

"But my grandmother's name was Rose. She *was* like a mother to me," I added. "At least, she played a very big role in my life when I was growing up."

Gloria stopped walking and stared at me. I went on, explaining that my grandmother Rose took care of me during the first six months of my life because my mother was bedridden following the difficult delivery she'd had with me.

"My grandma Rose was also a pillar of strength for me later, during my mother's struggle with breast cancer, and then after my mother died."

Gloria was still just staring at me. A little puzzled, I rambled on.

"When I was sixteen and got hit in the eye with a baseball, I was blindfolded and confined to my bed for a month. It was my grandma Rose who took care of me again."

Gloria was silent.

"But I don't know about the moving north part," I said.

I launched into telling her how happy I was at UCLA when, suddenly, she took off running down the beach.

Gloria was a dedicated runner. By the time I caught up to her, all I could do was to just stand there taking in gulps of air, bewildered and concerned.

"I ran away," she finally said, "because I got scared again. What you said in response to the reading gave me hope that the relationship I've wanted for so long might become a reality. After being single for so long, I guess I'm afraid it's too good to be true."

With the sun reflecting off the waves rushing to the shore, Gloria began telling me about her birth and infancy. Her account was similar to what I'd told her about mine. Her mother was depressed and withdrawn after her birth. After having a daughter—Gloria's older sister—her mother had dearly wanted a son. Unfortunately, she had a stillborn baby boy. A year later, Gloria was born.

"Because of my mother's depression, I spent my infancy in the hands of a nanny. I never quite bonded with my mother, or my mother with me," she said. "I remember feeling lonely as a child. My mother was distant and removed. She was pretty controlling. I never felt heard by her."

She too had felt like a motherless teenager.

"My father was the neighborhood pharmacist," she continued after a short pause. "He spent most of his time behind the counter in his drugstore. If I wanted to talk to him, I'd do it between customers or filling prescriptions. All of that added to my loneliness."

I nodded as I took all this in. I could relate.

OUR RELATIONSHIP PROGRESSED QUICKLY, from spending the night together a couple of times a week to being with each other every night. The workweek was spent at Gloria's apartment in Santa Monica and the weekends at my cottage in Point Dume. Despite our different histories, we had an amazing number of things in common. We were both born and raised in East Coast cities, we were children of Jewish immigrants from Eastern Europe, and we enjoyed a similar lifestyle regarding food and exercise. We both liked to read books and keep up with the news. We shared a similar value system regarding education and politics, as well as a sense of familiarity in each other's presence. And then, of course, there was that magical "something" that would reveal itself over time — a "something" that matches people up perfectly to work out their "stuff."

Gloria and I often talked about our childhood and how our parents influenced us emotionally. I recall one conversation where we discovered the similarity between my father's behavior towards me and Gloria's mother's behavior towards her.

"Thank you for giving me a baby boy," my father had written on a congratulations card he gave my mother at the time of my birth. I found the card affixed to a page in a family photo album, along with a picture of her holding me at my grandmother's home. I could see how frail she was, even then.

Was I imagining that, even in that note, it was more about him than my mother or me?

I also found a letter my father wrote to my mother, postmarked August 5, 1943. I was four years old. My mother and I, along with some of my aunts and cousins, were in the Catskill Mountains vacationing and avoiding the dreaded polio virus. In the letter, my father described his comings and goings in a chatty manner and, towards the end, he wrote, "Does Billy ask for me?" He didn't ask about Billy.

"He always wanted something from me rather than for me," I realized aloud. "He seemed to want something from me in order to feel good about himself."

Gloria had been listening intently.

"Isn't a parent supposed to be there for their child and not the other way around?" I asked rhetorically. "Could he have been a narcissist?"

I began to wonder how many of the mentors I'd chosen were narcissists.

"My mother had narcissistic tendencies," Gloria said, without hesitation. "Her reaction to me always seemed to be about her. She saw me as an extension of herself. Not to mention that she was always critical of me."

Now I was listening intently.

Gloria continued, sighing. "I absolutely felt I had to manage her reactions. And 'handle' her. 'Dave, she's killing me' or 'Dave, she's embarrassing me' were standard things she said to my father when she was upset with me. Or even when I was upset or had a problem."

She started to weep.

"I can't remember my mother ever being truly empathetic with me. In fact, I'm not sure she ever saw me. I grew to feel it was my job to dance around her emotions and take care of her feelings, rather than the other way around. She sounds like your father."

She paused, gathering her thoughts. Then she sat down and put her head in her hands. I sat down next to her.

"Except, maybe because she was an immigrant, I grew to believe it was my job to teach her how to be a mother," she continued. "Isn't that crazy?"

I felt her pain in that moment and held her hand—just as I did that day, sitting on her bed after the phone call with her mother.

"Am I trying to teach you how to be with me in the same way I did with her?"

It was a rhetorical question at the time. Yet it offered a clue about how our unprocessed emotions were part of an issue that would soon give rise to conflicted dynamics between the two of us. It was a question that would eventually require an answer.

JOGGING ALONG THE VENICE boardwalk every morning during the week—along with what felt like half of Santa Monica—was one of our regular activities. One beautiful morning, I glanced over at Gloria as we made our way south, past Rose Street. Her long, dark hair, drawn into a ponytail, swung back and forth with each stride. I was mesmerized.

"I heard from Noel, the man I was dating before I met you," Gloria said. "How would you feel if I saw him?"

I was surprised. Not that Noel had called her, but that she was asking me how I felt about it. I took her question in and thought for several moments.

"It doesn't feel right to me," I said.

There was no professorial mental assessment of the situation, as I might have done before—just a gut feeling. I was speaking the truth of what was in my heart and not my head.

Gloria responded with a big smile and, right then and there, in our sweaty running clothes, we fell into a full body embrace so encompassing that it enveloped us in our own world. The crowded boardwalk with its skateboarders and joggers passing by in both directions seemed to disappear. The world was just the two of us and our love and our joy. Right then and there, we became a committed couple.

The lonely professor had embraced something that would carry him in love far beyond anything the motherless child had ever imagined. And in return, it would demand everything he had in body, mind, and spirit.

Chapter 7

Sacred Union

I take you to be sacred to me as my wife/husband according to the teachings of Moses and Israel.
—Traditional Jewish Wedding Vow

SIX MONTHS AFTER OUR MOMENT on the Venice boardwalk, I would propose marriage to Gloria in an unpremeditated moment of love. My heart was propelling me into a new life.

Having recently completed a funded research project focused on managing severe accidents at nuclear power plants, I had been invited to address an international audience of academics and professionals in Tokyo about my results. Intending to have a short vacation after the conference, I had invited Gloria to travel with me.

"If you could go anywhere in the world after the conference, where would it be?" I had asked her as we planned our trip.

Her one-word answer: "Bali."

Little did either of us anticipate how our "little romantic holiday" would turn out.

Friends would later jokingly remind me that, after my first marriage fell apart, I had adamantly and often pronounced, "Never again." Gloria was fine with that proclamation. Remaining an unmarried woman was an acceptable, even popular, choice in those days of independence influenced by the Women's Movement. Besides, her early and painful marriage had also left her skeptical of the institution. We had declared ourselves to be life partners on the boardwalk in Venice and moved in together as a committed couple. Still, marriage had never been mentioned.

Before we left on the trip, some friends had mentioned that the spiritual depth of the Balinese people created a resonating field that was life-altering for visitors—if they opened themselves to it. I wasn't sure what they meant. But Bali began working on us almost immediately. I could feel the magic our friends had described, and I recognized there was something different about this place.

By a stroke of luck, we were given the presidential suite at the beautiful Amandari Hotel. That was all they had available when we arrived. Our room was an elegant marble-floored pavilion perched on a hill at one end of the property overlooking the countryside. On the far side of the living room from where we entered, two sliding doors opened onto a private Olympic-size swimming pool. Another set of sliding doors on the adjacent wall opened to a view of emerald-green rolling hills covered with rice paddies leading to a river below. Bare-breasted women were harvesting rice while men with oxen-driven plows made new furrows behind them, zigzagging their way down to the river. And on the third side of the living room, a door opened to a private atrium enclosing an outdoor bathroom with a sunken tub. Upstairs, the master bedroom suite had a panoramic view of the surroundings.

Shortly after we settled in, I was sitting in the living room when a Balinese steward magically appeared — seemingly floating in — bearing a bowl of tropical fruit, a bottle of champagne, and two champagne flutes. After he left, I opened the champagne and poured two glasses. But where was Gloria?

Searching the "palace," I looked into the atrium and there she was, waiting for me in the sunken bath. The sight took my breath away. Champagne glasses in hand, I moved towards her. Fortunately, reason and logic could not compete with my feelings. As I approached, I felt as if my chest cracked open and love was pouring from my heart. She looked at me and it seemed as if her love was pouring back. For a moment, I was Gloria, and she was me. And we hadn't even started drinking the champagne. Nothing like this had ever happened to me before — my heart resonating with another human being's heart in this way. I knelt beside the bath, handed her a glass, and looked into her eyes.

"Will you marry me?"

Tears welled up in her eyes. "Yes, I will."

That evening, when we entered the Amandari dining room, the maître d' met us and showed us to our table. Two place cards faced us: "Mrs. Kastenberg" and "Mr. Kastenberg."

How did they know?

I HAD JUST TURNED FIFTY-TWO and was now engaged to be married. Our pavilion provided a backdrop for us to experience each other now as a fully committed couple. Curt had given us a gift of sacred medicine to take with us—and encouragement to partake of his prescription if we found the perfect set and setting, as he had instructed us before leaving on our trip. The pavilion was indeed perfect and now, as a newly engaged couple, we travelled together into a transcendent process that would set a tone for our future life together. We "knew" each other rather than "thought about" each other in ways I couldn't explain but were more real than anything I'd ever experienced. In one moment, Gloria was my young lover—beautiful, voluptuous, sexy. In the next moment, dancing on the razor's edge of life's mystery, she was a crone, the woman of my distant future—the woman with whom I would grow old.

Later, when we spoke about our process, she told me that she'd seen me morphing from a young Adonis to a decrepit old man and then back to my current age and state. I felt the resounding joy of knowing deep in my bones that I'd met what I would only call my soul mate. Thank God for the tutorials at the Malibu Shaman and, of course, Curt. If my heart had burst open the night before at the vision of seeing Gloria in the sunken bathtub, my mind blew open as I perceived the world with all my senses at the same time. Time-lapse photography, I'd call it later—only it was the integration of sight, smell, taste, sound, and touch. I'd met myself in a whole new way: a way of being that encompassed the past, present, and future all at once. Inner and outer no longer felt separate to me.

Bali created a seismic shift inside me. Its sensuousness invited mine. We were surrounded by music and floral scents carried by the trade winds, exotic birds and flowers, endless rice paddies and canals—and monkeys. Ah yes, the monkeys. They were hilarious. Each morning on our jog down a dirt road from the Amandari, one particular monkey would greet us. It would sit on a brick wall and, as we approached, would cover its eyes until we passed, looking like the see-no-evil member of the triumvirate. The laughter we shared on seeing that monkey every day was washing away the years I'd spent being so serious and tense.

As PREPARATION FOR OUR MARRIAGE, Gloria suggested we do a "cord-cutting" ceremony.

"What?" I drew out the word as if it contained three or more a's. Bali had certainly opened me to new things. Back on the mainland, however, I still had to apply my critical thinking in life. Gloria hastened to explain.

"This woman I know, Lynn, is a powerful shaman steeped in Native American tradition," Gloria said. "She has a sweat lodge on her property where I've done ceremony with her. It's a way to pray and offer what you no longer need to the fire—the heat opens you up and the circle creates a sacred container."

While I had been legally released from my ex-wife, there were other ties. The final divorce decree was signed by the court a few weeks after our return from Bali, and all financial and property issues were settled. However, she was awarded substantial alimony payments—to which I had fully agreed—that would last until I retired, died, or she remarried. That prospect alone caused me anxiety. We had shared our lives for twenty-six years, so I figured we must be inexorably connected in some kind of bond. And she would always be the mother of my three children.

Curt had both warned and advised me that I could lose the connection to my children if I didn't communicate to them how my life was changing and that, even though they were adults, it would be difficult for them to see their "parental safety net" disappear. Added to this, I had the fear that they would feel responsible for taking care of their mother now that I was no longer with her. Although my sons appeared to take all this in stride, my daughter seemed to have difficulty embracing Gloria or my newfound happiness.

My daughter had been my companion at sports and entertainment events during the last years of my marriage to her mother. As most fathers of my generation, I treated her differently from my sons, especially when she was a teenager—she had me "wrapped around her little finger." When I met and was falling in love with Gloria, my daughter was spending an academic year abroad studying in Europe. She arrived home about the same time Gloria and I returned from Bali. And even though I had visited her previously and told her of my new relationship, my intended marriage plans seemed to be a shock to her.

While Gloria could feel the impact of these entanglements, there was something else concerning her. She attributed the difference to the psychic bonds that held in place unaddressed resentments and underlying familial patterns. The *Ordinary People* syndrome, as I came to call the dynamic my ex-wife and I suffered of not being open and forthcoming about our thoughts and feelings, had imprinted on my children. Gloria couldn't help noticing that I seemed to be one person when I was with them and my extended family, and another person when I was with her and our growing circle of friends who were open and honest.

"You have years of 'muck' between you and your ex that was never resolved—never spoken about or worked out within you. I can sense it," Gloria said as she described her cord-cutting vision with Lynn. "This isn't going to magically take all of it away. But we can recognize it and begin to resolve it."

Would that ceremony help me feel less "stuck" in the closed familial system she described? Or would it help me more fully transition into the open system that I was beginning to relish? I was willing to entertain the possibility. Although I was skeptical about the sweat lodge, I would try anything to get relief.

A cord-cutting ritual in a sweat lodge might be just the thing.

Gloria and I met Lynn at her home several times to develop and prepare the ritual. On the appointed night, along with Serena and AJ as witnesses, we entered a small dome-shaped tent made of wooden poles still clad in their outer bark, covered by various animal hides. Inside, at the center, was a pit filled with red-hot rocks that had been heating all day in a fire. We sat in a circle around the pit wrapped in towels—Gloria, Lynn, our witnesses, and me—and hot steam filled the enclosure as Lynn poured dippers of water over the glowing rocks. I don't recall what any of us said in the darkness and intense heat, but I remember Lynn being in some altered state of consciousness, praying and chanting for us. I actually felt her taking us with her on the journey. I envisioned myself free of the chains that bound me—the prison that had grown up around me—that my previous marriage supported. I could see myself ready for the marriage Gloria and I wanted to create together.

Afterward, I felt surprisingly light, as though an emotional weight had been lifted from me. In Bali and in the sweat lodge, I was beginning to realize a new understanding of consciousness. At the Malibu Shaman bookstore and at Esalen, when I heard or saw the phrase "altered or expanded states of consciousness," I had assumed it was about an altered or expanded state of mental capacity, a way of interpreting the world around me using reason and logic. Now I was beginning to understand that consciousness also had something to do with emotional and spiritual states — new ways of sensing and feeling — that, in the years ahead, would have a profound impact on my way of "being" in the world.

AT SUNSET ON MAY 3, 1992, Gloria and I were married in Malibu, California, on the deck of a beach club overlooking the Pacific Ocean. An auspicious day and time for the wedding had been chosen with the help of an astrologer, who had done some readings for us individually and as a couple. Having the same birth sign — Cancer — we were good crabs, loving to hole up together for long periods of time, alone in our shell. So our marriage ceremony with more than a hundred family, friends, and colleagues in attendance was our huge coming-out party.

All three of my children attended the wedding. While we had some challenges along the way, I especially felt my two sons' support. My daughter — that was another matter, which would surface later.

Rabbi Stan Levy had worked with us in the months preceding the wedding, giving me a different understanding of Judaism from the one I experienced in my childhood. He helped us create a ritual not unlike those we participated in before our wedding. He invited us to write our own individual vows and blessings—we could say anything we wanted, just as long as he heard the words that make up the traditional Jewish wedding vow: *Harey at M' kudeshet Li B'tabaat Zu K'dat Moshe V' Israel*—I take you to be sacred to me as my wife/husband according to the teachings of Moses and Israel.

Of course, this was not a problem for us. We felt we were already sacred to each other.

Surrounded by the beauty of the Malibu cliffs at sundown and the sounds of the Pacific Ocean as the waves rolled in, we exchanged our vows in that sacred understanding, speaking aloud for the first time what each of us was promising for our relationship, Gloria first, then me:

> *May we remain ideals in each other's eyes, concentrating on all that is good in each other so that we come to embody those ideals.*
>
> *May we not dwell on each other's faults but, rather, through compassion and acceptance, recognize the Divine in each of us.*

While we did not yet know how we would struggle to embody these words over time, we felt their power and appreciated the power of our souls' journey that had brought us to this moment.

> *May we share our mind's ever-changing tides, discovering the truth in each moment as a beacon for growth.*
>
> *May our love and commitment guide us and light our way.*

We felt with gratitude the blessings of the myriad souls of our ancestors who'd made this journey before us and contributed to our very nature.

> *Let us be ever mindful of God working through us that will, in time, reveal our true nature.*

> *May we remain conscious in times of pain so our relationship can serve as a means of healing.*

We declared our marriage to be a vehicle for personal growth and an offering of service.

> *May our special love and acceptance of each other serve as a model for our relationship with community.*

> *May our understanding of love deepen through our years together, and may that love be an offering of service to life and the greater good.*

Our vows launched us on a path of no return. We'd spoken aloud in the presence of witnesses about who we were and who we could become through our relationship. Finally, we recited the final part of our vows as one voice.

> *May we work this lifetime together, ever mindful of the love that goes beyond form.*

We had committed to the individual work of personal growth we knew we each had to do, while affirming the goodness and guilelessness we deeply felt in each other.

One of our favorite wedding pictures shows Gloria and me leaving the *chuppah* — the marriage canopy — after the traditional breaking of a glass and the first marriage kiss. In the photo, Rabbi Levy and our wedding party are in the background, and we are in the foreground, running hand in hand into our new life together. I was in a profoundly heightened state of consciousness. A dear friend quipped that the picture should be captioned "Professor and Mrs. Einstein stepping out into the unknown far reaches of the Universe."

While not quite the far reaches, certainly it is The Professor running innocently toward what none of his mathematical analyses and formulas could have predicted or explained.

Chapter 8

After the Ecstasy,
The Agony

The most frequent entryway to the sacred is our own suffering.
Countless spiritual journeys have begun in an encounter with the
difficulties of life.
—Jack Kornfield, AFTER THE ECSTASY, THE LAUNDRY

"COULD YOU MAKE DINNER tomorrow?" Gloria asked me one evening, several weeks after our honeymoon. "I'll be working late."

"I don't cook," I announced.

"Oh?" The look on her face was quizzical. I guess I had succeeded thus far in concealing my feelings about being in the kitchen. Up to that point in our relationship, I'd always managed to find something very important I needed to take care of—reading a student's thesis, paying bills, repairing an appliance—while Gloria was in the kitchen preparing dinner. Or often, we went out to eat.

When I invited her for that first takeout dinner in my cottage at Point Dume, I'd told her that I didn't cook, which I figured was also pretty apparent, given the contents of my kitchen drawers. I suppose it hadn't registered with her that I seriously meant this. Or maybe she just forgot.

But that evening, something was arising that would reveal a deep and more extensive undertow in our new-lywed relationship.

"How about I leave you a simple recipe?" she offered.

"I wouldn't know where to begin ..."

She quickly cut me off. "Recipes are self-explanatory. I can find something with pictures."

"That's okay ..." I said matter-of-factly, despite feeling vulnerable. I receded behind the thick layer of fog that often descended when my vulnerability was confronted. The fog brought back memories of my thirteen-year-old self—Billy—facing his teacher in the hallway, unable to speak when she asked about his mother.

The day after Gloria's request that I cook, I probably ended up just getting some takeout on my way home from UCLA with the excuse that I'd had a busy day too, which I'm sure was the case. Over time, the dense fog separating the vulnerable, confused boy inside from the puzzling onslaughts of the outside world had become a thick defensive wall, providing protection from anything painful or embarrassing. It was a rampart The Professor found useful in supporting an identity that assured him a sense of value. The wall also guarded the incongruity between my inner feelings and my outward actions. My facial expressions, my body language, and the words I spoke were elements of a well-practiced attempt to sustain my exterior identity and to protect the vulnerable, unsure boy inside.

Now, despite enjoying my new life with the woman of my dreams, my attachment to this identity as The Professor would end up wreaking havoc in our relationship. In the complex world of emotions and feelings, how could The Professor manage to do everything correctly? Billy's right to exist was guarded by having his external identity confirmed as a man who knew what he was doing. However, The Professor was now being thrown into an arena of emotions and feelings he had no idea how to navigate, as well as being challenged where he wasn't an expert—cooking. This overlay of ubiquitous expertise would take years to dismantle. Meanwhile, much to my chagrin, the cooking conversation continued to come up, always fraught with my defensive excuses.

"My mother hardly ever cooked because she was very sick, so I didn't learn anything about the kitchen."

"My father didn't cook, so I didn't have a mentor."

"My ex-wife always made dinner for me and the kids, so I didn't have to cook."

Perhaps what I didn't say aloud—to either of us—was not only that The Professor was an important man and cooking was a little beneath him, but also that having food prepared for him still felt like the currency of love for the grieving boy inside. Early memories of my mother cooking for me held profound meaning. It had been my special time with her as I sat at the kitchen table studying, watching, and feeling her near me while she prepared my dinner. Even though I would be engrossed in my studies, she was nearby, and her simple meals were endowed with her love and care.

After her death, at the homes of my grandmothers or aunts, food continued as the expression of love, adoration, and nurturance that I craved.

"*Esn, mayn kind.*" Eat, my child—my grandmothers' invariable welcome when I arrived at their homes. "*Bubbe* made this just for you, *mayn aynikl.*" Their attempts to heal their grandson's hidden but absolutely broken heart with brisket or roasted duck would establish an inviolable link between food and love. Many years later, in the company of colleagues at a restaurant in Durango, Colorado, I would order the specialty of the house— roasted duck. My colleagues watched with astonishment while tears streamed down my face as I tasted the first bite, and those buried memories of nourishing food began to emerge from the sealed-off chambers of my heart.

Mingled with the savory aromas of roasted duck and brisket emanating from my grandmothers' kitchens was the memory of the entire family crowning me The Golden Boy. For most of my childhood, as the only male grandchild, I carried the family name and the hope of a better life than my working-class immigrant family had. My destiny held much bigger things than cooking. "This is America," my grandparents would always remind me.

"If you study hard, you can become anything you want to be."

My hidden sense of male entitlement emanating from my golden-boy identity effectively served to cover over the insecure orphan—Billy, hidden within my sealed-off heart—and to elevate my exterior importance. No doubt these were the origins of what I would later call The Professor.

The Professor's voice was insistent: *You are above the task of women's work in the kitchen. You have differential equations to solve and nuclear power plants to keep safe. You shouldn't waste your time chopping tomatoes.*

Even now, in the kitchen with Gloria, he would still whisper these things to me, keeping me isolated from my feelings, distant and far removed, behind that wall of fog covering over the dichotomy between specialness and shame. If I found myself helping Gloria in the kitchen, my heart would pound, and my hands would sweat. The loud-and-clear message, *You'll fail if you try this,* conveniently translated into *Why should The Golden Boy help in the kitchen when he has better things to do?*—a question that was not addressed until many years later. In the increasingly uncomfortable emotional realm of marriage, this required hiding behind a wall of silence. If I had to admit I didn't understand or couldn't do something, who would I be then?

GLORIA BROUGHT HER OWN childhood challenges into the marriage mix. Faced with my idiosyncrasies—silence, sudden change of subject, taking refuge in words that didn't match my facial expressions or body language— she was suddenly catapulted back into interacting with an irrational mother. She would try to explain things to me simply and clearly and would use her tools as a lawyer to present very convincing arguments for how we might work better together. Despite her attempts to be compassionate and helpful, I, like her mother, would grow more and more distant in response.

One evening, after another of our "discussions" about helping in the kitchen, Gloria tried the gentle approach.

"Sweetie, isn't this a perfect opportunity to use Welwood's idea of exploring the pattern that stands in the way of your learning something new as part of our spiritual growth?"

It was a valid question, considering what we had so recently pronounced in our wedding vows: John Welwood's formula of using whatever issues arise in relationship as grist for the mill in spiritual growth. Now, however, I heard her question as an accusation rather than as a reminder of our promise. When Gloria took those wedding vows, she included our process, or what she considered context, as the clue to our spiritual issues. I, on the other hand, although habituated to content, never considered that spiritual issues might have anything to do with something so mundane as cooking— or whatever other daily issues would arise. *How could the internal conflict I'm feeling possibly be a window into our growth individually and as a couple?*

When Gloria's default position as The Lawyer, making logical courtroom arguments, met my default position as The Professor, who had to know everything, we were left feeling disconnected—alone and abandoned, just like during our childhood. We were locked in a dynamic that would take years to unravel. Increasingly for me, Gloria's insightful observations about my behavior and her incisive questions felt like she was a prosecutor. In my confusion and silence, I felt like a defendant.

For more than twenty years, Gloria and I would remain pawns of a dichotomy that held me in bondage—my feeling of being abandoned, damaged, and unworthy competing with my golden-boy persona—alongside my fear of having this dichotomy exposed by anything that smelled of imperfection. This conflict of identity in me left Gloria sad and lonely at times, unable to feel my heart and be close to me—something we both dearly wanted. And it absolutely mirrored the confusing messages that had been imprinted on her psyche during childhood.

When our hearts were open, Gloria and I were perfectly matched, and we were able to feel the goodness and guilelessness in each other. However, we fought the realization that we were also perfectly matched when our family-of-origin conditioning and wounding masked the possibility of connecting authentically with open hearts. This disparity would ultimately lead us to deepen our relationship and spiritual growth. Meanwhile, we were thrown into the fire more than once, especially when The

Professor, over his head in an unfamiliar field, had no idea how to be an expert.

ONE DAY, A FEW MONTHS after our wedding, one of my sons called me with an exciting, yet expected announcement.

"My fiancée and I are getting married. Would you and Mom walk me down the aisle?"

He was referring, of course, to his mother, who was now my ex-wife. *Oh shit! How am I going to handle this situation?*

"Sure thing," I replied.

Although the hostility and tension between his mother and me were still alive and well, for the love of my son and his bride-to-be, and for the sake of family appearances, I felt perfectly willing to do this. Gloria was delighted upon hearing the news; however, she was apprehensive about meeting my extended family as my new wife—especially my ex-wife's side of the family. And, of course, there was my daughter.

Leading up to our own wedding, my daughter had a difficult time accepting Gloria. In fact, we were sufficiently alarmed at her resistance that we sought couples' counseling. As Curt had become a personal friend, we sought the help of another psychiatrist he recommended, Jack. I'll never forget his helpful advice.

"If you want to get off to the right start with your new marriage, make sure that you and Gloria are connected. Be on the same page and present a united front," Jack had told us with respect to my daughter — and to all my children and family, for that matter. "Let them know you are a unit."

Since my family had operated more like the characters in *Ordinary People* — by skirting emotional and personal issues rather than being open and honest about them, the conversation with my daughter had not been an easy one for me. Still, with Gloria's support, we managed to have a gentle, frank conversation with her about our wedding and our concerns. I let her know that, if she would be uncomfortable, it wasn't necessary for her to come. She did choose to attend and to support us. But the very thing Gloria feared — my being pulled back into the *Ordinary People* dynamic of being closed off and noncommunicative — was beginning to manifest.

One day, not long after my son told me about his proposed wedding, he took me aside.

"I don't want Gloria to be in the receiving line." He paused, studying my face for a few seconds. "It would be too much for my mother to take in."

Although I cannot recall what I said to him, I recall feeling shocked, hurt, and in a quandary. I heard Jack's advice in my head: show up as a united front. *What should I do?*

I sensed myself slipping into the old dynamic from my previous marriage — an experience completely different from the dynamic with Gloria in the years I'd been falling in love with her and then marrying her. Now here I was, standing in two different worlds that had the potential to tear us apart, and a rift between us was being created.

With Gloria by my side, I had managed to hold frank and honest conversations with my daughter, but this situation was very different. Rather than dealing with one adult child, I now was entangled in a whole family constellation: my son, his fiancée, my ex-wife, my father, and the generations of traditional souls who were onlookers—all called in when we stood under the *Chuppah* at our own marriage. This was complexity beyond the pale.

I felt the freedom I had known as a single man dissolving, displaced by the familiar pull of the electromagnetic field created in the marriage I had left behind.

"WHAT WILL YOU DO?" Gloria asked. I heard her question as a demand. At least, to my ears in that moment, it sounded like a demand.

"I don't know."

How could I stand in the receiving line welcoming guests without my new wife by my side? On the other hand, how could I abandon my son and his bride and drift off to the sidelines to be with Gloria? This was a no-win situation—no matter what I'd choose, I'd lose.

I wanted to celebrate my son and new daughter-in-law, and I wanted to honor and acknowledge my beloved partner. Inside, I was Gloria's. Outside, I had a role in my son's newly expanding family. I had a dilemma: how could I resolve the habituation of being, while in my children's company, the person who had been married to their mother and had created a closed system dynamic, with the person I was now creating in my new marriage, which I liked to think was based on openness and honesty?

This was not my wedding; I didn't get to set the ground rules. This was my son's wedding, and I wanted to give him the same respect he had given me when I married Gloria. Also lurking somewhere in my subconscious was the old need to earn approval from my father. These motivations combined to throw me into what might be described as a catatonic state whenever I tried to broach this subject with Gloria.

On the other side of the equation, Gloria was struggling to be big enough and spacious enough to let go of the concern and hurt she felt about being left out. More importantly, I was becoming unrecognizable to her in the way I was showing up.

Although our experience with Jack still resonated in the psyche of my beloved, I didn't think to ask for his advice. Even worse was that, in a twisted effort to protect Gloria, I failed to speak with her about my predicament for fear I'd hurt her. If she brought up the subject, I couldn't hear her. Whatever she said sounded to me like my ex-wife making demands.

The hold of the magnetic field was so strong that I didn't even know how I felt. By default, I tried weighing the risks and benefits of each choice in my "brilliant mind." But as my dilemma defied reason and logic, this strategy got me nowhere in navigating these tricky waters.

Although Gloria must have advocated that we seek advice from Jack, it never occurred to me that there might have been a solution—that I could have simply talked with her or asked Jack to help us work it out. Only years later would I learn that speaking together about the fact that we were both triggered by the situation could have actually connected us rather than driven us apart. Instead, in this moment, faced with the issue of the receiving line, we simply didn't know how to have empathy for each other's difficulty or sympathy for each other's dilemma. I reacted to her as if she were my father or worse, my ex-wife, and she reacted to me as if I were her mother. We both wanted connection but couldn't find it.

TRUE TO MY WORD, I walked down the aisle on one side of my son and his mother walked on the other. Escorted by her brother, the bride looked magnificent in her ivory-colored 1920s wedding gown, tiara, and veil. Gloria sat with the bride's mother in the front row, next to an empty seat reserved for me. I delivered my son to his bride and took my place next to Gloria, emotionally frozen, still unsure what to do.

When the ceremony was over and the receiving line was starting to form, I made my choice. My father, nearly ninety years old, was already in the line. The family electromagnetic field was strong.

I looked at Gloria, mumbled something like, "I'll be right back," and slowly walked away, as if on automatic pilot, leaving her there alone. I joined the line, standing without my new wife, ignoring Jack's advice about protecting our fledgling marriage at all costs.

I was one person with my family and another in my new marriage.

When Gloria would later bring it up at couples' sessions or workshops, I resented her for what I viewed as rubbing it in. The idea that this schism—my unconscious attempt to shore up the dichotomy of my competing selves—could have constituted grist for the mill just escaped me. The schism this circumstance created and the way we attempted to handle it would take almost thirty years to resolve and, in fact, even as I am writing this, we're still working it out. It was a hard lesson for me to learn.

Years later, Gloria and I were driving on a freeway listening to an audiobook—*Hold Me Tight* by Dr. Sue Johnson—and there we were. Dr. Johnson was talking about a relationship dynamic we later referred to as "attack and defend." She was describing us, whether we were confronted by issues related to cooking or weddings or whatever else came up between us. I had to pull off the freeway and listen to it again—and again. I finally could hear a description of the dynamic that we got into when our childhood imprinting—and now, my prior relationship history—collided. In this dynamic, one party is perceived as aggressive, critical, or demanding, and the other party is perceived as defensive, distant, or withdrawn. The key word here is *perceived*, as we would find out. It was this attack-and-defend dynamic that had been continually showing up in our marriage, and we had been helpless in the throes of it.

Despite it all, our love for each other remained unquestioned, and we sought understanding wherever we could find it. We delved into the childhood development literature to learn about the role of the brain's limbic system in a growing child's emotional experience. A mother attuned to her infant's emotional states creates a limbic resonance that ultimately leads to what psychologists call "secure attachment." It produces emotionally secure children, we read. Lack of it causes emotional insecurity and avoidance or ambivalence in personal relationships. Clearly, we both had work to do in that arena.

Although Gloria and I had been struck by the similarity of feeling abandoned in infancy, we hadn't yet understood how the breaking of that mother-infant bond had affected us as adults and in our relationship with each other. It wasn't that we couldn't relate to each other emotionally — we'd known depths of that relatedness, starting when we first met. Rather, it was that, under emotional distress, our default position would become an attack-and-defend dynamic, founded in the fear of an abandoned infant. I became the defendant, hiding my shame and unworthiness behind the face of The

Professor, while she was hidden behind the safety and security of The Lawyer.

Ultimately, we would learn how to provide each other with that secure attachment described by Dr. Johnson arising from her seminal research working with couples. It would take years of commitment in which we provided for each other the emotional safety that we hadn't received as children, as well as years of unraveling the patterns I had established in my previous marriage and the ones Gloria had as a single woman.

Chapter 9

Beginner's Mind

*The fate of all explanation is to close one door
only to have another fly wide open.*
—Vincent Fort

"YOU ARE PERSISTENT," I said, laughing. "I just wanted to see if anything has changed for you since we last talked."

I had received a call from the Chairman of the Nuclear Engineering Department at the University of California at Berkeley, shortly after our honeymoon.

"How'd you like to transfer from UCLA to Berkeley?" he had asked at that time. "I'm getting ready to retire in a year or so, and I'd like you to be my successor."

The Chair was now asking me once again whether I would consider such a transfer. I had declined his offer the first time since Gloria and I had just started our new life together as a married couple. She was working for a law firm as a litigator, and I was ensconced at UCLA. Now, eighteen months later, she was finishing up her work with the firm and we were planning a six-month sabbatical leave—for intellectual enrichment, the

University calls it. Gloria intended to start a private mediation practice when we returned.

My previous sabbaticals usually sparked something new for me in the way of teaching or research, so this was an interesting prospect, and I was open to it. In that way, the invitation was perfectly timed. Our personal lives seemed to be calling us north, just as Gloria's psychic reading had predicted.

"Well, yes … my wife and I come up to the Bay Area quite often to visit her family and my cousins," I said. "And after the Governor reappointed me to the Independent Safety Committee at the Diablo Canyon Nuclear Power Plant, I've started coming to PG&E headquarters in San Francisco a few times a year."

"Those are two good reasons to transfer to Berkeley," he enthusiastically replied. "You won't have to travel so much."

"Gloria and I are leaving on an extended trip to India during the first part of my upcoming sabbatical," I told him. "I'll mull the idea over while we're traveling."

"Why don't you come to Berkeley for the second half of your sabbatical and see how you like it? I'll provide you with an office."

"Sounds good. I think Gloria would agree. She has activities in the Bay Area as well."

As I hung up the phone, I secretly marveled at what seemed to be one of those inexplicable coincidences.

What I hadn't told the chairman was that Gloria and I had another reason for visiting the Bay Area. On one of my trips to PG&E headquarters, I'd taken a walk through the San Francisco Arboretum with my cousin, a long-time Berkeley resident. As we walked, he told me about his teacher and colleague, Dr. Jackie Margoles, a clinical psychologist, and the communication model she had developed for resolving conflicts among individuals and groups. He had found the model useful in communicating with his partner, soon to be his wife, and thought it might be something that would prove useful for Gloria and me in unraveling the resistance and resentment that was building up between us.

My cousin was a member of Dr. Margoles' training team and served on the board of her non-profit organization, the Center for Holistic Systems. He also thought her communication model, based on open living systems, might be employed at a professional level in my research program at UCLA on risk and systems analysis for managing toxic waste. Moreover, he and his partner had been at our wedding and recognized in our commitment, a way of being in relationship that seemed to resonate with the communication model.

Gloria was interested in enhancing her skill as a mediator and I believed I might be able to help Dr. Margoles find a more public venue to get her work out into the world through my contacts in academia and industry, possibly catapulting Gloria's mediation practice into reality as well. The idea of collaborating with my cousin together with Dr. Margoles heightened my interest.

So he set up a meeting for Gloria and me on our next trip to the Bay Area.

In the conversation with the chair, I was reluctant to even suggest any flaws in my personal life motivating me to make such a move, or that working with Dr. Margoles also meant that I would be engaged in deep psychological excavation.

THE AROMA OF FRESHLY brewed coffee mingled with the scent of jasmine in the early morning air. My cousin had arranged for us to meet with Dr. Margoles in the lush garden of a restaurant in Berkeley's Gourmet Ghetto that offered the best pancakes in town—and maybe the world. The meeting felt convivial, suggesting the possibility that, ultimately, my relationship with Jackie would open me to a new way of thinking—poking holes not just in The Professor's façade, but also in the academic paradigm that was the basis of my world view.

Despite her short silver-gray hair, Jackie, as we came to call her, appeared youthful. She was friendly, polite, and good-natured, putting me at ease as we engaged in a broad range of technical topics I understood well. After breakfast, we entered into an esoteric conversation about general system theory—the differences between open and closed systems, as well as between linear and nonlinear systems. That Jackie could meet me on these topics impressed me.

"I'm fascinated by the correlation between your model and open living systems," I told her. "I've researched nonlinear physical systems, which are basically closed, for my dissertation and have read James Gleick's book, *Chaos: Making a New Science.*"

The nonlinear nature of open systems theory was fast becoming the basis for the future of engineering. I wanted to hear more, even though my own work focused on engineered systems—nuclear power plants, aerospace vehicles, environmental clean-up systems—all having fixed-boundary conditions, which meant that they were closed systems obeying the deterministic laws of classical physics—a linear process.

A lively discussion ensued about how this linear approach shaped the way western society has perceived and interpreted the world for the past three hundred years, and how the possibility exists that we are approaching a new epoch, as nonlinearity might herald a change in our way of thinking. I was excited by the conversation that fit the depth and breadth of the intellectual stimulation I was experiencing at the University as we made the bridges between science and its humanistic implications—bridges I'd need for my research to be successful.

"I've tried to teach a model that is congruent with the fact that all human beings, be they individuals or in groups, are open living systems not limited by a reductionistic and deterministic view of the world," Jackie explained. "If you assume the world to be holistic and events random, rather than determined by an equation, the possibility to navigate the existing complexity we encounter in communicating can be mastered and can be more accurate and complete."

I listened carefully, challenged by Jackie's delivery, which was commensurate with the complexity of her ideas. Although I felt embarrassed to admit that I was having a difficult time communicating with Gloria, I decided to step into the unknown and asked Jackie to say more.

"As humans, we are continually exchanging information with the people around us in the form of messages or signals. We speak, and there is body language and other signals that we are unconsciously reading," she explained. "Just as any living system exchanges food, air, or water with its environment, we exchange these signals and interpret them."

"I see that," I said.

"I've developed a grid or map that helps people interpret the signals necessary to keep communication congruent with its non-linear nature, while eliminating a direct causal relationship that leads to blame and other nonproductive behaviors, but rather, seeing the signals as mutually influencing each other," she said without taking a breath.

"Doesn't Buddhism talk about events mutually co-arising?" Gloria asked.

"Yes, and some people correlate aspects of my work with Buddhism," Jackie responded. "I'm describing the nature of things as is described in Buddhism."

I could see how Gloria's interest was sparked by the correlation with Buddhism, and that she seemed familiar with the language—no doubt from the spiritual work she'd done before meeting me. My mind began to wander. Jackie had been describing her work in scientific terms I could understand, and now the conversation was shifting. No doubt sensing my momentary inattention when the subject of Buddhism came up, she asked me about my work at UCLA with environmental cleanup systems.

"My colleagues at UCLA and I have a grant from the State of California to develop technology for managing toxic waste," I began. "But there are heated and often emotional conflicts among the various stakeholders when we try to implement a solution at an actual clean-up site. I'm running up against this kind of conflict at the nuclear power plant too."

"Perhaps we can collaborate around an environmental issue like that," Jackie said. "We could try demonstrating the model. But I'd have to train you in its use."

I asked what that training might entail. Jackie offered to spend several weekends with us, describing her process and the map she had developed. We would meet for half or full days and basically work with whatever conflicts arose in the group. In that way, she would demonstrate how she uses the map, all the while helping translate our habituated closed system language into the more open system approach. And while she trained us, I would look for ways to incorporate her work at UCLA.

"I'm intrigued," I told her.

"We'll be coming up to the Bay Area on a regular basis," Gloria chimed in. "I have family here—my parents are still alive—and Bill comes up quite often to visit PG&E."

Little did I know that Jackie had learned from my cousin about the personal conflict also motivating us to consider training with her. Towards the end of our meeting, she mentioned her success in using this work to help couples resolve their relationship issues.

"The model can be difficult to learn," Jackie said as we were leaving the restaurant. "People have difficulty unlearning old patterns and changing their ideas about communicating. At the same time, they must simultaneously learn a new way of speaking, along with a new way of viewing and making sense of the world. Essentially, I help people make a shift in mindset—from linear thinking to nonlinear thinking."

Gloria enthusiastically agreed. "This means that doing your work helps you understand yourself, correct? You can't unlearn your viewpoint if you don't know what it is."

"Yes, exactly," Jackie responded.

"I'm looking forward to giving it a try," I said.

"It's a difficult shift," Jackie cautioned. "You have to become a novice—with 'beginner's mind,' as Buddhist teachers like to say."

OUR UPCOMING TRIP TO India started me on the journey of understanding beginner's mind—apropos to visiting the birthplace of Buddhism. It was also a big step in fulfilling my childhood fantasies of going to exotic places—those *National Geographic* dreams I'd had while waiting in the doctor's office for my mother to finish her appointments. Professionally, I had a reason for visiting as well: learning about India's burgeoning nuclear power program, as well as the successes and failures of its Green Agricultural Revolution. These subjects were among my ongoing research projects at UCLA. But there was one other reason for going to India: Gloria.

Gloria had suggested that we could bridge the growing gulf between us by finding a shared spiritual connection. Early in our relationship, she had told me about her experience as a disciple of Swami Muktananda, an Indian spiritual teacher who had established meditation centers in the United States. The profundity of the Swami's effect on Gloria was not lost to me.

While Gloria had told me a lot about herself, I hadn't asked about Muktananda's teachings or what they meant to her. As I had little experience with eastern religion and philosophy, I didn't even know what to ask. Until now, my inquiries had stayed pretty much on the surface. I understood that her time with him had a profound impact, but my mind equated it with earning an advanced degree, rather than something that expanded her mindset and opened her being. I tended to stick with conversing about things I already knew, and I considered myself naïve to spiritual matters. My curiosity lay in the physical—not the metaphysical—world, despite some evidence to the contrary. While I'd been curiously drawn to the Malibu Shaman and had already had several powerful and life-changing experiences—not to mention my downright magical and mystical grandmother—I didn't think I had a connection to the metaphysical world. But I was wrong.

"Muktananda helped me develop my capacity to be open—to have a vision of how to hold my most difficult experiences in a space of love, and even beyond that," Gloria had explained. "But I wasn't in a relationship during those years. These days, I'm finding it nearly impossible to stay connected to that center of love and acceptance when I'm triggered. India may reboot that inner fire for me and maybe have a shared experience with you. And it will be an adventure."

"I sure hope so," I said.

"I don't know that we'll meet anyone who will have such a powerful impact on you as Muktananda had on me," she said, "but India has got to be an opening experience."

I was reminded of Curt's advice during my last session with him: "All you need to do is to open up. Just follow Gloria to any workshop she suggests."

So India it would be.

IN FACT, I ALREADY had more of a foot in the door of the spiritual world than I realized. Although I'd left Judaism behind after that fateful year of mourning following my mother's death, the tradition still exerted a pull on me.

My ex-wife and I had seen to it that our children had a Jewish education, were Bar and Bat Mitzvah'd, and even had been confirmed. Our intention had been to expose them to their Jewish heritage and, of course, to please the four grandparents.

I had already been exploring a renewed connection with non-traditional forms of spirituality before I met Gloria. When we became a committed couple and started planning our marriage, we attended Stan Levy's *Shabbat* services to get to know him. Stan, trained as a lawyer, was not a traditional Rabbi, which suited us, and his services reflected a new-age sort of Judaism. Moreover, he conducted *Shabbat* services at his home, rather than at a synagogue, which was also more palatable for me. Services with Stan were as much social events as they were spiritual or religious events. The high holiday services were filled with song, dance, and laughter—a far cry from the somber services I had experienced as a child. Stan's teachings felt true, real, and relevant to me.

My grandfather had taken me to a Sephardic temple once, and the recursive melodic chanting between the congregants and the Cantor felt infectious and compelling. These Sephardic Jews, having emanated from Spain and its environs, were draped in colorful prayer shawls, whereas we Ashkenazi Jews, emanating from Eastern Europe, were always draped in our black and white shawls. Being with Stan conjured up that memory of the joyful *Shabbat* services in the Sephardic temple and awakened a different understanding of what it meant to be religious.

The awareness gained from Welwood's book, the breathwork, the sweat lodge, and our experience with Stan Levy combined to ignite a new understanding of spirituality in me. But beyond those forays into expanding my spiritual understanding, there was something else: a desire was emerging in me to understand several experiences in my life I hadn't been able to explain rationally; paranormal events that felt bizarre or sometimes frightening to me.

In my early thirties, I had several experiences in which I had the physical and visual sensation of being blasted through hyperspace at warp-speed—as I would later see depicted in science fiction movies such as *Star Wars*—before blacking out. In the first blackout experience, I was walking through my front door and, fortunately, had enough presence of mind to grab the doorframe to prevent falling. The experience felt like an emotional eternity but probably lasted a few microseconds. I had a half-dozen or so similar events over a ten-year period, and then they stopped. I never thought of them as a health issue—I was young and strong—but I hesitated to tell anyone. I simply told myself I was working too hard or had a dizzy spell. However, that fear was now changing to curiosity, and I began to wonder if those experiences might have been spiritual breakthroughs or spontaneous forays into other states of consciousness that spiritual exploration entails.

Later, in my forties, I had several "out-of-body" experiences while I was teaching. In each of these, I had the distinct sense that I was standing in the back of the classroom watching myself teach. There was no sound—just a silent movie playing out before my eyes. On the way back to my office after class, I had no memory of the material I covered in the lectures or what I had said. Yet it was clear—based on their homework and exams—that the students had received the information they needed.

One particularly profound out-of-body experience happened during an international conference in Seoul, South Korea. At the suggestion of my host, I had spent the morning visiting a Buddhist shrine set in the center of a park that encompassed a square city block. Cherry trees with pink and white blossoms surrounded the shrine. It was spring—or so I thought until I realized during the taxi ride back to the hotel that it was a cold, drizzly day in November. The realization sent a chill down my spine.

During my presentation that afternoon, I once again had the experience of watching myself from the rear of the auditorium. After the session, several colleagues I knew from around the world commended me: "Great talk, one of the best you've ever given."

"Thanks—what did I say?" I responded, only half joking.

I hesitated to tell anyone about these events for fear they would think I had lost my mind. Maybe they'd conclude I was unfit to teach and put me away in a straitjacket. I continued to categorize them as dizzy spells and kept them to myself until I met Gloria. To my amazement, she was excited for me. I'm sure my revealing these occurrences to her was part of what assured her that even The Professor was a candidate for spiritual experiences in India.

Chapter 10

Who is Asking?

When you return to your Self, this is called awakening, liberation, freedom.
—Sri H. W. L. Poonja, known as Papaji

"I LOVE THE SMELL OF dung in the morning," I joked.

It was mid-December 1993, shortly after the fall quarter at UCLA had ended. We were standing on the veranda of the Carlton Hotel in Lucknow, Northern India, where we had spent several days recuperating from jetlag. My cousin, who was also the publisher of a Buddhist journal, had recommended that we travel to Lucknow to experience *Satsang* with Papaji, a preeminent Indian sage who taught Self Enquiry. Although I didn't have a reference for Papaji's credentials, Gloria's excitement and my cousin's assurances that he was quite esteemed by his circle of western Buddhist teachers left me curious and excited too.

We hired a bicycle rickshaw driver to take us to Papaji's home, where *Satsang*, the spiritual gathering, would take place. Mr. Sweetlal pedaled cheerfully through city streets crowded with traffic of all kinds, moving in all directions, seemingly all at once—cows, camels, and even elephants seemed as welcome as the pedestrians and motorized vehicles. The streets were alive with activity—a man getting a haircut and a shave on one street corner, and a woman selling strings of bright orange marigolds on another. It felt as if all of humanity occupied these streets. The transcendental mood that I experienced in Bali came rushing back; the sights and sounds were intoxicating.

Holding on for dear life in the back seat, bumping along through potholes and puddles, we headed out of the city and into the suburbs. We saw women wearing brightly colored saris washing clothes at the edge of the river, while others sat along the side of the road, breaking up large rocks with a sledgehammer to be carried away by other women in baskets on their heads. I was later told that the smaller rocks would be used to make concrete for roads and the overpass for a busy boulevard intersection. *I wonder if they use the same process here to build the concrete containment for nuclear power plants.*

Mesmerized by the array of colors, smells, and sounds that stimulated my senses, I felt alive and filled with wonder. However, as an engineer and scientist involved in environmental cleanup issues, I was absolutely aghast at the air pollution, the garbage on the streets and floating in the rivers, and the loose cattle wandering the roads leaving random piles of manure. It took me a while to realize that the numerous clay disks sticking to the walls of every structure—each with a handprint similar to the ceramic gift kindergarteners give their grand-parents—were dried manure briquettes used for the fuel that produced the smog hovering over Lucknow. That morning, I'd read in *Times of India* about the World Health Organization's study on environmental illness and the malnutrition of India's children. Seeing first-hand the pollution and the undernourished children playing in the garbage and rubble prompted my academically trained rational mind to immediately start thinking of solutions.

Why not a program to recycle all those plastic bottles that litter the streets? Or how about corralling the loose cattle? Why aren't the water treatment processes that are cheap and readily available being used to clean the water? I realized that emission control for the single stroke motors propelling the myriad vehicles jamming the roads and highways would be a more challenging problem—but I believed it could be engineered, both technically and socially.

When we arrived for Papaji's *Satsang*, Mr. Sweetlal assured us he would wait and then take us back to the Carlton, as he did every day for the next several weeks. Being newcomers, we were ushered to the front row where we and other first-time attendees could ask questions at the end of the talk. Sitting cross-legged on a meditation cushion in front of the guru, surrounded by seekers from the far corners of the world, was utterly strange to me. I could only imagine my colleagues at UCLA thinking I'd gone off the deep end if they saw me there.

Nonetheless, at the appropriate time, I scooted over to the center of the area ready to ask my question, which went something like this: "What's the difference between the I and the Self you spoke about?"

Papaji's response puzzled me. "Who is asking the question?"

I thought he wanted to know who I was. So I began to tell him I was an engineering professor at UCLA and about my research. He burst out laughing before I could finish. His big belly laugh was contagious. His devotees, sitting around me in a big semi-circle several rows deep began laughing. I turned toward Gloria. She was laughing too.

Did she know something I didn't? Was she laughing at me? What had I missed? Was I the butt of a joke? I felt small and insecure for the first time in public as an adult. Without hearing a further response from me, Papaji turned to answer someone else's question.

Unlike my encounters with Gloria where The Professor managed to mount an adequate defense, this experience with Papaji opened an innocent, tender, and emotionally exposed aspect of myself—the vulnerable boy locked in my heart—that wasn't at all what I had come to know as "me." But I couldn't find the words to express my feelings or to acknowledge the boy.

At lunch that day, Gloria tried to explain to me what Papaji meant with his response to my question.

"He was asking you to look beyond your sense of Self," Gloria said. "Beyond your personal identity."

I don't recall that any of it made sense to me. Besides, what did it matter when there was so much of the outside world to distract and fill my senses? I did what I trained myself to do when feeling vulnerable or confused: look at the outside world rather than attend to my feelings.

DETERMINED TO REDEEM MYSELF in Papaji's eyes and, hopefully, Gloria's, I decided to stick with a subject I did know something about. Of course, I had no idea of my true motive at the time. Having been directing a research center for hazardous and toxic waste control at UCLA, I actually wondered if I might help with Lucknow's pollution problems. I thought Papaji and I could engage in an intellectual conversation where I might be on equal footing with him. He was well known here and must have had some influence. Clearly, I was trying to impress him with my awareness and knowledge of the environmental health issues in India, but mostly, I didn't know what else to ask.

"What can I do to help clean up the environment here in Lucknow?" I asked Papaji a few days later, in my professorial voice.

Papaji listened intently as I explained my concern. When I finished, he waved his hand across the expanse of the many devotees present and said, "It looks clean in here to me."

The room roared with laughter, much louder than the last time. Papaji paused to take in the laughter and then began laughing too — that big belly laugh. When the room quieted down, he wagged his finger at me.

"Just clean up your mind."

At first, I thought he was playing with me. It was difficult for me to imagine that Papaji wasn't concerned with the environmental pollution in India. I later understood that he was trying to deliver a spiritual message to me — to provide me with an insight as to our "true nature." But at the time, the message eluded me.

Papaji, of course, was referring to what he saw as the pollution in my mind: my internal world and my identification with my expertise, to begin with, and then my identification with everything else I thought of as "me." Intellectually, this made sense to me, but I still found it confusing.

"Of course you were confused," Gloria said later when we were alone. She compassionately took my hand. "But you were so courageous, jumping back into the fire."

I remained silent and expressionless. I felt my face flush with embarrassment as she attempted to explain her understanding of Papaji's philosophy.

"He was talking about non-dualism — asking you to look beyond the dualistic mind that compartmentalizes the world into good and bad, right and wrong," Gloria said. "Being free of those judgments and seeing everything as 'what it is,' he wouldn't necessarily see pollution the way we do."

Although I listened intently, I didn't understand. Unable to admit my incomprehension, I said nothing.

Gloria, triggered by my silence, upped her ante. "That is how he teaches. He is not there to answer questions about cleaning up the environment. He is there to answer questions about discovering your true nature."

"Have you ever experienced the non-dual?"

"I've had glimpses," she shyly replied. "Enough to have a sense of what he was pointing you toward."

Embarrassed, I receded into myself, compelling her to double her efforts to reach me—a strategy that never ended well for us. However, as the days passed, something shifted for both of us. She let go and, as we continued attending *Satsang*, his teachings touched me in surprising ways despite my lack of understanding.

Nearing the time we would leave Lucknow, I was moved to seek a private audience with Papaji. There in his living room, I began to realize that I wasn't who I thought I was; rather, I was playing a variety of roles dictated by life's circumstances—professor, husband, father, teacher. This was a revelation.

Much to my amazement, over the remaining days we spent with Papaji, a sense of spaciousness began to arise in me. Listening to the answers he gave to his followers' questions, I began to recognize that what I called "myself" was in no way static or representative of all of me. At first, in fleeting moments, and later in more substantial ways, I began to see The Professor as a persona or a role I played, along with all the other roles. While I couldn't feel all of them, starting with The Professor felt like an enormous breakthrough.

Uncomfortable as it had been, *Satsang* with Papaji launched me on the path of finding out how The Professor came to be, the role he played in my life, and who I'd be without him. New questions arose inside me: *Who's asking the question, if not The Professor? And then what?*

AFTER THE PENETRATING COLD of Lucknow, heading to Southern India was an attractive proposition. We flew to the city of Kochi in the state of Kerala, where we spent a few days sightseeing. Throughout Kochi there were pictures of Amma, known as the hugging guru, everywhere we ventured, from the seemingly infinite number of street vendors' stalls to the dashboards of the myriad taxis roaming the streets. As Amma had an ashram in California, we'd heard of her. We decided to head to her ashram deep in the jungle. Traveling in an open-air boat down an inland waterway that wound itself through Kerala's tropical landscape was breathtaking. Along the way, the boat stopped at a hut on the shore for a lunch that was served on a banana leaf and eaten by hand, as was the custom in many parts of India. We washed our hands before and after eating in the brackish waterway. The bathroom consisted of a ditch in a small clearing beyond a clump of banana trees. By this time, I was used to the customs and sanitary conditions we found along the way, so I didn't attempt to solve any environmental problems in my head. Perhaps I was beginning to recognize that the environment, at least in India, is what it is.

After nearly a full day cruising along the waterway, we were deposited in what seemed like the middle of nowhere.

"Are you sure this is the right place?" I asked the boatman when he stopped at a small, rickety wooden dock. He simply gestured several times toward a jungle trail, repeating "Mama."

Gloria and I picked up our luggage and trustingly trekked forward on foot. About fifteen minutes later we arrived at a large clearing surrounded by a sea of palm trees. At the clearing's center sat a magnificent, ornately decorated pink building that reached toward the sky. I was in awe. Except for the color pink, the set and setting reminded me of the Emerald City in the *Wizard of Oz.*

As was the custom at the ashram, Gloria and I would be separated into women's and men's quarters for the several days we spent there. Each day, walking together towards the main hall for *Satsang,* we would see hundreds of Amma's Indian devotees waiting to enter the building. One day, out of curiosity, I walked up several flights of stairs to the roof garden, where I could see lines and lines of Amma's devotees coming from several directions. The lines snaked through the jungle for miles along dirt paths, as far as the eye could see. The ashram was among the most sensual places I'd ever been—the smell and taste of the food, the sounds of chanting reverberating along the wall, the cold water running over my body as I showered—I felt truly alive and aware of each moment in time.

On our first day, an American devotee of Amma's had stopped us at the main entrance to the hall and ushered us through a side door to the "western section" of an auditorium, close to the stage. A day or so later, Gloria and I were invited up on the stage to sit on Amma's lap, the typical welcome for new guests. I sat comfortably on her right knee and Gloria did the same on her left, as we took in the aroma of sandalwood incense that seemed to emanate from her body. We learned later that it was unusual for a husband and wife to sit on her lap together.

Amma spoke to her gathered devotees for several minutes in *Malayalam*, her native language, and then looked at each of us with the sweetness of a succulent plum. Next, she gave us a big hug—a blessing for our union—and, for each of us, a kiss on the cheek. As she kissed me, I felt my own mother's lips touching my cheek and I began to weep with a mixture of joy and sorrow that came from a place deep inside me. The tenderness of the moment washed over both of us.

In sharp contrast to my experience with Papaji, where I had been confused and embarrassed, I felt bathed in Amma's love and acceptance, something I obviously longed to experience. The distance and misunderstanding Gloria and I had come up against in Lucknow now subsided in Amma's arms. Bathed in her clear expression of what her followers called Absolute Love, I had a glimpse of what might be possible if the steel bands that kept our hearts in bondage when we were afraid, were freed. It was as if Amma had given me the marriage blessing from my own mother that death had denied me. Her blessing left us with the certainty of our bond and love for each other, as well as a deep recognition of the power of such a "love field." Now all we had to do was figure out how to make that work in daily life.

Chapter 11

Shaktipat

... the visions I saw in the sleep of tandra-meditation were quite genuine. I would see something that was going to happen, and it would actually happen.
I would see somebody come, and then he would come.
—Swami Muktananda, PLAY OF CONSCIOUSNESS

I WAS IN A MEDITATIVE state, eyes half-closed, sitting cross-legged on the floor of Swami Muktananda's Samadhi Shrine in Ganeshpuri, India. The main feature in the building was a large white block of marble sitting atop his burial place. Next to it, a marble pedestal held a pair of silver sandals I would later learn represented the power of the guru's grace. Gloria was chanting in the meditation hall, and my intention here was to pay homage to the guru for his influence on Gloria's spiritual life.

We had arrived at Muktananda's ashram the previous day after a long and harrowing taxi ride from the airport in Mumbai. Despite the glow remaining from our stay at Amma's ashram, the ride had jolted my nervous system. But this morning, upon entering the Samadhi Shrine, the tightness in my shoulders had relaxed, my breathing had slowed, and my mind was still.

A dozen or so devotees were also sitting in silence in the dimly lit shrine. After a while, I noticed that, before leaving, they'd walk quietly towards the marble block, bow, and touch their foreheads to the silver sandals. With hands clasped in the prayer position on the heart, they would then walk slowly backwards towards the open doorway of the shrine, turn, and exit.

In deference to the Swami's devotees, I waited until everyone left. After several minutes, I stood up, approached the block, bowed, and touched my forehead to the sandals.

A bolt of lightning just struck my head – its electric charge surged through my body.

In that moment, I knew I was going to transfer to Berkeley and establish an interdisciplinary research center for nuclear and toxic waste management. In that moment, I knew how I would obtain long-term funding for the research center and who would participate in its activities. In that moment, I could clearly see how to reorganize and manage the Nuclear Engineering Department at Berkeley and resolve a host of professional and personal issues related to the transfer.

What had happened? How could I have received all that information at once?

This download happened much the same as the blackouts had occurred—instantaneously and beyond time and space, yet replete with information. Although any explanation of how this could have happened would defy logic and reason, I didn't doubt for an instant the truth and legitimacy of the information. Hands clasped to my heart, I hurriedly backed out of the shrine, turned, and went looking for Gloria. She was just coming out of the meditation hall when I met her. I motioned for her to sit down next to me on a grassy knoll overlooking the shrine.

"I just had an experience that literally and figuratively blew my mind."

It took me more than an hour to describe to her that instant of time. After we sat in silence for several moments, Gloria looked at me and smiled.

"I am so happy for you. You've clearly felt the energy of this place and of the guru. I'm so happy that you had the presence of mind to take it all in." She closed her eyes as if to recall her time with him. When she opened them, she said, "Let's talk about Berkeley and all that later. For now, I think we're sharing something we came to India for."

I listened intently.

"My own early experiences with Muktananda were like falling in love," she continued, "especially when he placed his left hand on my head, pressed his thumb between my eyes, and, with his right hand, bopped me on the forehead with his peacock feather."

She described how this was a way the Swami imparted Shaktipat—a jolt of primordial cosmic energy—to his devotees.

"The first time, it felt as if the top of my head blew off and I was nothing but white light," she said. "All of a sudden, everything the prophets and sages said seemed true to me in one gestalt. I was in bliss. I couldn't work for days. I don't think I've been the same since."

Now I was finally able to appreciate, take in, and actually physically sense what Gloria had experienced with Muktananda. Gradually, I would find myself more open to the reality of mystical experiences.

One day, near the end of our trip, we were sitting along the banks of the Ganges River in Varanasi, watching clouds of white smoke rising from the burning corpses of the newly deceased. By now, even this practice seemed normal.

"It's amazing how at ease you are with all these unusual experiences—like at the Samadhi Shrine, and now sitting here watching the bodies burn," Gloria said to me. "It's so far beyond your typical reality, and beyond what I even imagined when we planned the trip."

I'd been thinking the same thing myself.

"When I was a boy, I often sat beside my grandmother when she recited her morning prayers."

The image was vivid in my mind—of her standing by her living room window, her long silvery-grey hair, normally tied up in a bun, hanging down to her waist, glistening in the morning sun. Although she couldn't read, she held an open Jewish prayer book, never missing a word or sentence, as I later realized when I learned to recite the prayers myself in Hebrew school.

"She seemed to be in a transcendent state of consciousness as she swayed back and forth reciting her prayers," I said.

I paused for several minutes to savor the memory, and then went on.

"I'm just now realizing that, as I listened to my grandmother, I felt like I merged with her and the prayer. It felt like the safest place in the world for me. Being here in India conjured up those memories and feels similar. It feels normal and safe."

"Perhaps that is why you never felt frightened when you had those out-of-body experiences while lecturing and teaching," she said.

"Well, the experiences themselves weren't frightening, but I was afraid of what others would think or do if I told them," I said. "Now, after having had these experiences with you, I no longer feel the fear."

We both paused as another funeral pyre went up in flames.

"Approaching my mother's death, I was terrified of anything related to death," I continued. "I've avoided thinking about it and being anywhere close to it, as if I just pretended it doesn't exist. Yet here we sit, watching the reality of death. It still feels distant, but I can bring it into my awareness."

"How does that feel?" Gloria asked.

"Freeing."

India had done its work. And now what was in store?

UPON RETURNING FROM INDIA, Gloria and I spent three months in Berkeley testing the waters to determine whether or not we wanted to make the move. This also gave us a chance to digest the profound experiences we'd had in India.

I'd heard it said that a trip to India would bring up karmic baggage of the kind described by John Welwood. It didn't take long to understand what that meant. Along with the ecstasy of my new experiences and an expanded point of view, came the hard work of translating those into my daily behavior as a more conscious human being. At the same time, I seemed to be even more sensitive, easily taking Gloria's words as criticism, feeling hurt by a look from her or a misunderstanding. Apparently, an expanded awareness simply wasn't enough to dislodge stubborn patterns. Something needed to be unwound in me. The work of cleaning up my mind would make our relationship more profound and, at the same time, much more difficult.

The transmission of information I had received in an instant of time at Muktananda's Samadhi shrine irreversibly altered the trajectory of my life. Not only did the transmission point the way for our move to Berkeley, but new worlds were also being illuminated, along with possibilities for a deeper relationship with Gloria. The door to the emotional and sensitive part of me had opened at Esalen and in the holotropic breath workshops. I also had opened a crack in the door to the spiritual part of me again in India. The rational paradigm that I had lived and breathed throughout my adult life no longer applied in every circumstance. I was traveling through uncharted territory inside, while exploring a new world outside.

We loved the beauty and intellectual stimulation of the City of Berkeley, and I enjoyed going to the campus each day, meeting faculty and staff, and imagining new avenues of research with new colleagues. I discussed ideas about an innovative center for the management and disposal of toxic and nuclear waste with engineering faculty and talked with humanities and social sciences faculty as well. All of this exploration was rooted in the information transmitted to me at Muktananda's Samadhi Shrine, although I could never tell anyone I talked to about that. I assumed they would never believe it or that they would think I meant it as a joke.

One evening in Berkeley, Ken Fowler and his wife Carol invited us for dinner at a posh San Francisco restaurant. Ken was eager to hear my decision about his proposal, as well as Gloria's thoughts on the transfer. After a delightful meal and fluid discussion regarding the virtues of the Bay Area, we got to right to the point.

Ken turned to Gloria: "Do you want to move to Berkeley?" By the end of the meal, he already knew my answer.

"Yes, if you can make it happen quickly," Gloria responded—a tall order for a university that often does things at a glacial pace. Gloria didn't want to spend nine months to a year in limbo before beginning her new mediation practice. If we were moving, she wanted to get settled as soon as possible.

"Of course," Ken responded, as if it were already a done deal.

"I have some misgivings about moving to Berkeley," I confessed as we drove home. Gloria listened in silence.

"Los Angeles has been my home and UCLA my sanctuary for almost thirty years," I continued. "It'll be tough for me to leave."

"I understand," Gloria said, "and I'm so sorry. Leaving LA, your family, UCLA — that must feel challenging. Still, it's such a great opportunity for both of us." For Gloria, that meant working with Dr. Jackie Margoles.

"My children are adults," I said. "They're establishing their own lives and can take care of themselves. It's my father I'm worried about."

Since my father was close to ninety years of age and had become quite frail, I had been unconsciously following my mother's directive: "Take care of your father." As the good son, I had believed it was my duty to manage several details for him and my stepmother. I would routinely go to their home and pay their bills. When necessary, I took him to his doctor's appointments and prepared his daily insulin injections. Although I cannot remember anything we talked about, I do remember looking forward to those visits. Although his memory was fading and his body slowly deteriorating, a certain sweetness had emerged from him.

Shortly after our return from the three-month trial in Berkeley, my friend Seth had asked my father, "What do you think of Bill and what he's achieved in life?"

"I don't know about all that," he responded. "I only know he is the most important thing in my life, and I love him!"

I wept. I had been waiting all my life to hear that.

Having finally heard those words from my father, I no longer felt obliged to take care of him. Those arrangements could be made from Berkeley. I now had his permission to leave home.

By January 1, 1995, two and a half years after our marriage ceremony, I was a Professor of Nuclear Engineering at UC Berkeley and the Chair of the Department. After almost twenty-eight years at UCLA, however, I realized I had become uncomfortable with the comfort. I was back at the place where graduate school had prepared me for my professional life.

Little did I know that I was moving back to Berkeley to prepare myself for my emerging emotional and spiritual life.

Chapter 12

A Clash of Paradigms

*A law that cannot even be demonstrated to one group of scientists
may occasionally seem intuitive to others…. Before they can hope to
communicate fully, one group or the other must experience the
conversion we have been calling a paradigm shift.*
—Thomas Kuhn,
THE STRUCTURE OF SCIENTIFIC REVOLUTIONS

THE HARD CHAIR, THOUGH uncomfortable, would at least keep me alert. I was in a wood-paneled antiquarian courtroom that could have served as the set for a black-and-white Wild West movie. Two dozen rows of wooden benches faced a massive table where I and the other committee members were gathered for the quarterly meeting of the Diablo Canyon Nuclear Power Plant Independent Safety Committee—the first such meeting since we had moved to Berkeley. As Chairman, it was my role to field questions from the various stakeholder groups attending this meeting.

I watched as people started coming into the courtroom. The group sitting on one side of the room I recognized as a contingent from an environmental group, along with some others, all of whom I'd met at previous meetings and who lived near the power plant. This group had been opposed to construction of the plant and now felt vindicated in their position after the meltdown of the nuclear reactors at Three Mile Island in New Jersey and Chernobyl in Russia. They would, of course, advocate for shutting the plant down.

City and county officials walked in and took their seats on the other side of the room. I already knew they would advocate for continued operation of the plant because of its contribution to the local economy. I also recognized representatives of the utility that owned and operated the plant, who I'd met during my plant visits and inspections. They would be making presentations to the Committee, followed by public comments and questions. At issue that day was the storage of spent nuclear fuel and radioactive waste, as well as some necessary equipment upgrades to the safety systems at the power plant.

As usual, when I had to face an audience, especially a passionate one like this, I'd break out into a cold sweat—just like my first day in a classroom or standing alone in the synagogue reciting the mourner's *Kaddish*. As people took turns delivering their perspective, I listened intently, nodding my head occasionally to let them know I'd heard them. Then I dispassionately asked a few questions, offered answers to their questions, and thanked them for their input. But as emotions from each of the stakeholders escalated, my calm exterior belied my chaotic interior.

I felt shame and helplessness in the face of these accusing voices. Only much later would I recognize that these public demands were bringing up the same feelings of powerlessness, confusion and ineptitude that had come up so often in my first marriage. "Would you do something with those boys?" was now translating inside me as "Would you do something with that nuclear plant?" I was a deer in headlights.

Although confident I could help resolve the technical issues they were bringing up, the emotional issues—here and at home—were leaving me confused, defensive, isolated. *How could I manage this meeting when I can't even deal with emotion in my personal life?*

ONE EVENING NOT LONG after that meeting, Gloria and I were in our kitchen preparing dinner in our new home high in the Berkeley Hills overlooking San Francisco Bay. We had moved to Berkeley and bought a house. Gloria started a mediation practice while I was busy chairing the Nuclear Engineering Department. On weekends, we began working with Jackie Margoles, learning her model.

I was standing next to Gloria, cutting some vegetables for a salad. Making salad was one of the few things I felt competent to do in the kitchen. I was busy cutting the carrots and celery along their length when Gloria glanced over at what I was doing.

"Would you cut the vegetables cross-wise?" she asked. "They'll be in smaller pieces, easier to chew and digest."

A tightness rose in my chest.

"Stop telling me what's wrong with what I'm doing," I snapped.

She looked shocked. "Who are you talking to? Are you talking to me?"

Her question only made me angrier. I felt attacked. Inept, helpless, wrong. And then I had a monumental flash. Time raced backwards. I was a boy again, forty years before, standing in front of my critical father instead of my beautiful wife. That boy, frozen in time, was angry and hurt. Gloria was right. I was hearing my father's criticism instead of hearing her, and I had been hearing his criticism over and over in all my intimate relationships.

In that moment, something opened in me. I understood that when I felt criticized by my first wife or by Gloria, and even by my mentors or a critical audience arguing about a nuclear power plant, I reacted by becoming silent or defensive. I would resort to the same protective strategy that young boy had used in face of his father. Suddenly, I remembered something Jackie Margoles had been telling us during our trainings—that all previous events are embedded in our present experience.

"I'm so sorry," I said tearfully. "I answered you as if you were my father."

Gloria silently nodded her head in agreement.

"I'm realizing that I still haven't come to grips with how much his constant criticism and negative attitude toward me after my mother died has colored my life."

Working with Jackie, I was acquiring the ability to track how my past was influencing the present—an understanding that's probably elementary in any psychological model, but one that was huge for me.

"Thank you," Gloria said, with tears in her eyes too.

MAYBE THERE WAS HOPE—at least at home. Hope continued to be a primary motivation when working with Jackie. However, I knew I'd have to build some skill with her model to speak about it intelligently in a professional setting.

Gloria and I, along with my cousins, were exploring possibilities for using the model in an academic or business setting. My cousins had graduate degrees in Organizational Development and, with Gloria's mediation skills and my expertise on risk and systems analysis, we'd make a formidable team. I knew how to obtain funding for research projects, having done so at UCLA and now at Berkeley. We were hoping that our team, armed with our increasing know-how using the model to work out communication issues among ourselves, could bring the work into the world quickly. In the meantime, I was trying to find a test case, at least for Jackie to demonstrate the model's efficacy.

Personally, I hoped to put my new Center for Nuclear and Toxic Waste Management at Berkeley on the map. By introducing an innovative societal problem-solving method to my multidisciplinary center, which included the social sciences and humanities, I would take my career beyond the scientific and technical accomplishments I had achieved at UCLA. This could be the capstone of my career and a powerful motivating force for me and for The Professor.

I had long been captivated by C.P. Snow's book, *The Two Cultures*, which spoke about the challenge of bridging the sciences and the humanities. If we could effectively make this bridge, it would certainly put my Center at the forefront of environmental conflict resolution, and we would be on the road to resolving difficult and important societal problems. Moreover, I would be satisfying my father's wish for me to make my mark in the world — his blessing and directive upon my graduation from the Bronx High School of Science. And to top it all off, if I could solve these problems in my professional life, no doubt I would be addressing the cultural divide in my relationship with Gloria.

ON A CLEAR, CRISP SATURDAY morning during our first spring since moving to Berkeley, our little band of explorers — Jackie, my cousins, Gloria, and I — set out on a hike along a trail in Marin County's Tennessee Valley. The valley was resplendent with purple lupine, yellow buttercups, and orange California poppies. As planned, we were spending the weekend together learning the model and using it to sort out the myriad issues that would come up. I was beginning to feel at ease as we got to know each other on a more personal level. At the same time, Jackie acknowledged once again the difficulty of an accomplished professor becoming a novice embracing the beginner's mindset necessary to learn her work.

About halfway along the trail, we came upon a small meadow where we stopped to admire the flora and take in the serenity of the valley. Near the far periphery of the meadow stood a waist-high tree stump about three feet in diameter. The fallen tree, lying several feet away from the stump, had a notch hewn out lengthwise that served as a bench for hikers. Heeding the invitation, we headed over and sat down. The trees gave me a sense of calm, like old friends there to comfort me.

I'd been thinking about the difficulty I was having introducing Jackie's model to my new colleagues. In an effort to acknowledge The Professor by playfully embodying him, I walked over and stood behind the stump, pretending it was a lectern.

"I've been finding it difficult to introduce Jackie's model to the academic community. I can't seem to get across to them that what she has to offer is new and innovative," I began.

I explained that no matter how I tried, my description of the model always came through as if I were introducing something linear, no different from any other conflict resolution tool or therapeutic intervention. I was able to break the model down into its parts, as any good reductionist-determinist scientist might do, yet I knew it had to be explained from a holistic perspective. At that point, I always stumbled. If we were to have any success, I had to find a way to get the ideas across.

Playing along with me, Jackie raised her hand to speak. I called on her.

"I'd be willing to go to UCLA with Gloria and do a training if you could arrange it," Jackie said. "Maybe that would work."

"I can arrange that, and maybe you can give a lecture at Berkeley too," I responded. "There's something else I thought we might do. How about we write some research proposals to fund a project using the model to address a real-world environmental issue?"

"We could try non-profit foundations interested in conflict resolution or government agencies like the EPA," Gloria said enthusiastically.

"I'll do some searches on the web," my cousin's partner chimed in. "I'm curious to see where we might find some support."

We all nodded our heads in agreement. I stepped down from the lectern, satisfied that we had a plan for moving forward.

That evening Gloria and I sat down together on our deck overlooking the vastness of San Francisco Bay—cities, towns, and freeways at the foot of the hills surrounding this great body of water with its single opening to the Pacific Ocean.

"I love this view," I said. "It's always been my dream to have a view of the Golden Gate Bridge. It's amazing to me that we are here."

"Remember that reading I told you about when the psychic said I'd meet a professor with blue eyes, whose mother's name was Rose?" she asked.

"How could I forget?"

She laughed and continued.

"She also saw me near the Golden Gate Bridge, with a group of people resolving conflicts or something like that."

The familiar chill ran down my spine.

"I love that we are all doing this together," Gloria said. "As I learn the model, I feel so much more capable in my mediation practice. I'm thrilled to be getting this training. Thanks for doing this, Bill."

"Well, if the psychic saw it, I guess it was meant to be."

"I'm serious, dear. I really appreciate your efforts and enthusiasm."

"I struggle using the model, but I do enjoy everyone's company," I said. "Sometimes I get frustrated. I lose the thread and get impatient. At least I can contribute, making things happen at the University. I'll try to find us a real-life environmental conflict for a test case."

"I think you know more than you realize."

She smiled, coming up beside me. I put my arm around her as we looked out at the sun setting behind the Golden Gate Bridge. I felt very fortunate in that moment. I was optimistic we'd find funding for our project, and I hoped I had learned enough about the model that I wouldn't let her down. I wasn't accustomed to being conscious of my insecurity, so with some trepidation, I turned to her.

"I really want to communicate better with you," I said. "It does seem like it's easier between us since we've been working with Jackie. Don't you think?"

"I do." Gloria was smiling. "I feel very close to you right now."

EXCEPT FOR FINDING FUNDING, the plans we set in motion in Tennessee Valley were slowly being realized. I'd arranged for our team to give a training for the environmental engineering group at UCLA, to present papers at several international conferences, and to facilitate a meeting of executives at a national laboratory.

Our team would gather to work on writing papers and proposals but, more often than not, we had group training sessions. These sessions served as a way for Jackie to teach us the theory behind her facilitation. She would use her methodology to resolve any conflicts that came up in our group—and the group didn't disappoint. While Jackie would facilitate the conflict as if working in the field, she also showed us how she was doing it—how she would deconstruct our communications—all the while illuminating the elements of the model.

Being a novice was a struggle for me as I tried to keep up with the group. I felt anxious faced with this novel approach to learning. Worse yet, I was too embarrassed to admit I was struggling—not getting the model fast enough—the opposite of my experience learning new concepts at the university. I was also aware that memorizing the model's terminology reinforced my mental capacity but did not enhance my intuitive understanding. I felt very uncomfortable when Jackie emphasized that I was a beginner: I wondered how The Professor could be a novice when his sense of authority was needed to assure success for our collective project. As long as he and his expertise were needed, how could I fulfill my role of being a beginner? I felt pulled apart, trying to hold myself as a novice and an expert at the same time.

One evening, months into the training, I decided to tell Gloria about my difficulty.

"I want to share something with you," I said.

"Great," Gloria responded.

"When I'm trying to use the model in our group, I feel like a novice chess player who knows how each piece moves on the board but can't comprehend the overall changing pattern of the pieces well enough to play the game intuitively. It's so frustrating for me."

Gloria squeezed my hand.

"I understand. I'm grateful you told me about your dilemma. It's not something you would've done before. Sharing your feelings with me—that is the most important thing."

I let go of Gloria's hand as she looked at me.

"I'm so proud of you," she said, "even if you get lost trying to track it all every time you open your mouth."

We both laughed. A magical evening ensued—one that reminded each of us of our love for one another. But it wasn't always like this.

At one of our weekend gatherings, Jackie started the work by turning to Gloria.

"Is something going on for you that you want to use as practice today?"

Jackie explained that she'd noticed Gloria fidgeting in her chair. This body language—along with Gloria's tone of voice—had alerted her that something was disturbing Gloria. Following the model, she was checking out what she saw and sensed.

"Yes," Gloria responded. "A conflict between Bill and me came up this morning."

My heart sank. While I'd gotten used to speaking about our issues with friends, I felt at a disadvantage in this setting because Gloria was more fluent using Jackie's model. Besides, I thought we were doing better.

"I totally get how upsetting this might be for you, Gloria," Jackie said, "given that you came to this work with a lot of hope and promise."

"I can't tell Bill how I feel about *anything* without him jumping to a solution or disappearing behind his defensiveness," Gloria said, weeping. "He says he's working on himself but, unless the work has to do with something connected with the University, he isn't interested. He only tunes in when your theories remind him of what he already knows."

Here was my wife, clearly in distress, and although she seemed to relax when Jackie made some soothing comments, I was stuck in my head, attempting to articulate an accurate response. I got so defensive — thinking I'd done something wrong — I missed the opportunity to acknowledge that something was going on for Gloria and really connect with her. Since her distress had to do with me, I felt afraid or criticized. Instead of trying to use the model correctly, and perhaps be coached by Jackie in responding, I tried to be funny.

"I'm a theoretical guy," I interjected.

Frowning, Gloria got up out of her chair with a motion of exasperation.

"See how defensive he is — making a joke out of my heartache."

"Let me help you," Jackie said. "Is that okay with you? How about you, Bill? Are you okay with us talking about this?"

Gloria nodded yes, as did I, reluctantly. Using the language of the model, Jackie proceeded to demonstrate how to deconstruct the dynamic she had been observing during our interchange. In the process, she reframed Gloria's interpretation of my behavior and my response. As usual, I began to get lost trying to follow her long sentences and phraseology: "jumping over the fence" and "making up a story" to name a few.

In response to Jackie, Gloria began describing her disappointment in long sentences that no doubt included a description of what she noticed and how she felt when I tried to be humorous, and from her perspective, no longer engaged.

"You're right," I said, turning towards her. "I didn't hear what you said, even though I'm interested in what you have to say, and in learning the model."

I watched Gloria sit back in her chair, take a deep breath, and relax. Then I went on.

"The words began to sound like jargon once you started using Jackie's terminology. I got lost in the language and missed everything else. And then I disengaged. I can't seem to keep up with where Jackie's headed with this exercise."

"Bill, let me explain learning theory and how you are in the beginner's phase of learning something new," Jackie said, looking directly at me. "No doubt this challenges your self-image as someone who is extremely competent. But if you keep on practicing, you will eventually …"

Her voice faded into the background and became noise to me.

DESPITE MY GROWING RESERVATIONS about the jargon and the difficulty I was having learning the model, I had already arranged for Jackie to make presentations at two international conferences—one in Italy and one in Crete—where she would address experts in the field of environmental conflict resolution. I was operating on blind faith, as she had agreed not to try to train the audience. She would meet them where they were and make the work accessible. I was naïve to have believed that was possible.

Gloria and I sat in the audience at each of Jackie's presentations, trying to understand what she was saying. Her remarks seemed unintelligible to me, and to the audience as well, as confirmed by the negative comments I heard during the coffee and lunch breaks. She seemed to ignore my input; hearing other talks did not seem to change her style of presentation. I felt frustrated and embarrassed, wondering why I had arranged a second event in Crete when I saw how unreceptive the first audience had been in Italy. I blamed myself, believing I'd made a big mistake in front of my colleagues.

My feelings of shame and failure were overwhelming. When no one in our group expressed sympathy and understanding—except for Gloria—I ended up feeling blamed by our group for my lack of understanding of Jackie's work. Not that anyone was blaming me—I just took it in that way.

Professionally, Jackie and I continued to disagree, even in areas where I considered myself expert: writing research grant proposals and presenting and publishing results that arose from a free exchange of ideas, methods, and models—essential tenets of academia. From the outset of our work together, Jackie had held her work proprietary, with herself as the sole owner of a business product that required tight control over its dissemination. Her reasoning was that it was important that the model be used only by those who understood it—apparently meaning trained by her. While my priority was to use the model as a way to improve my communication skills, personally and professionally, it seemed that Jackie's priority was to get her work recognized and accepted on a larger scale. Although that was our initial agreement, increasingly, it was clear to me that we were pulling in different directions.

One evening, as Gloria and I sat on our deck relaxing, I tried to express the issues I was having with Jackie.

"I'm troubled about having introduced Jackie into the university setting," I said. "She and I have very different approaches to navigating academia."

"I think Jackie might be trying to change the academic paradigm," Gloria responded. "Her confronting the academic mindset had to be jarring to your colleagues, in much the same way it is to you. And she doesn't have their agreement to be confrontative in that way. Staying true to her vision has made it impossible for her to create any meaningful change within academia."

"She is the expert regarding her methods, of course," I went on, "but I know how academia works. If she could get my point of view rather than trying to change it, I might be able to trust her. My colleagues are inviting her in only because they trust me, and I'm afraid I'm losing that trust."

I knew Gloria well enough to see the disappointment written on her face. But I now also understood that, if I openly shared my conflict and dilemma, she could stay connected to me. I was learning. I took a breath and delivered the truth.

"I'm sorry. My relationship with Jackie has become untenable for me. Although my communications with my colleagues at Berkeley and the public at Diablo Canyon have improved immensely, thanks to Jackie, I just can't work with her anymore."

"We've learned a lot, and it's been great, but I can feel you are at an impasse and—quite frankly—I'm disappointed too. I had hoped she could've bridged the gap. But for someone who developed such a sophisticated communication model, she seems strangely unable to communicate it to others." Gloria let out a big sigh. "And while I'm grateful to the whole group, this is clearly not working. I agree that we may have gone as far as we can with her. I can see that your boundaries are compromised—you're trying to be a novice with her and, at the same time, a professional whose services the project relies on."

AFTER WHAT I CONSIDERED a fiasco in Crete, our project ended. As usual, our group had held a debriefing session where I expressed—diplomatically, in keeping with my experience as administrator—my dissatisfaction with Jackie's presentations. Jackie didn't seem to take in what I was saying. From her perspective, it seemed, any issue I had with her presentation was my problem. Although this is a common dynamic in many therapeutic models, as I would experience much later, it is also a common trait of innovative leaders with big egos.

Coincidentally to ending my working relationship with Jackie, I came across Thomas Kuhn's book, *The Structure of Scientific Revolutions*. Kuhn, a physicist turned philosopher, coined the phrase "paradigm shift" to explain a fundamental change in a scientist's way of perceiving, understanding, and explaining the material world. I found Kuhn's ideas about incommensurable paradigms—illustrated by the shift from Newton's immutable view of space and time to Einstein's relativistic view of space and time—a compelling way to explain my conflict with Jackie. I would tell others that she and I had been in two alternative realities.

Kuhn writes: "The transition between incommensurable paradigms cannot be made a step at a time, forced by logic and neutral experience. Like the Gestalt switch, the transition must occur all at once or not at all."

I had remained stuck in a linear—reductionist and deterministic—paradigm, whereas Jackie lived in a nonlinear—holistic and stochastic—paradigm. In working with Jackie, I hadn't achieved an Aha moment after which the world would feel and look different and there would be a behavioral revolution leading to personal change. Nor had Jackie made the shift to understand the mindset of academics—especially regarding understanding what I needed in this setting. Yet the seeds of that Gestalt switch were planted in me and would be harvested several years in the future. I completed this phase of my work with

Jackie by explaining to my colleagues at Berkeley that we would explore other methodologies for conflict resolution that served our purposes better than hers.

It had been almost five years since we first met Jackie at that breakfast meeting, and then our relationship was over. We remained close to my cousin, now his wife, and they continued to work with her on personal matters. At the same time, my cousin continued publishing a spiritual journal while his wife returned to her work as a personal trainer and bodyworker.

MY CHILDREN WERE MARRIED by now, and I had become a grandfather for the second time. While some of our freed-up weekends were spent traveling to Los Angeles to visit family and friends and to participate in our grandchildren's life-cycle events, Gloria and I were now ready to explore another way to bridge our divide. Although I had become a better communicator and had learned much about human nature and the mind, the work with Jackie had been dry for us. And Gloria and I were wanting to rekindle the magic we'd shared with each other.

More and more often during the final year of our work with Jackie, we had been stealing away for an evening to explore tantric practices and workshops. The kind of new-age music I'd fallen in love with at the Malibu Shaman bookstore would be playing and, as we danced and moved our bodies, the mental tension from our days working with our little group fell away. I remembered the way I'd felt in Bali and India; my heart opened and I found that I could relax and be playful in this setting. It was very different from my academic life or our weekends in group, struggling to get through to each other. While I considered the work with Jackie important, I imagined there might be another way to learn it—a way that could bypass my mental process and get to the heart of the matter. I could see the same thing happening with Gloria in these tantra gatherings, and we'd come home refreshed and inspired. We were ready to discover new ways of communicating that were physical—as well as heart-based.

Chapter 13

Sensuality

*The most important person is the one you are
with in this moment.*
—Leo Tolstoy.

THERE'S AN OLD ENGLISH adage that says, "The way to a man's heart is through his stomach." I disagree—it is definitely through another part of the male anatomy—at least it was for me. I quickly learned that detour when Gloria and I attended a series of sensuality workshops.

GLORIA AND I WERE AT our first sensuality workshop, and I was thoroughly enjoying this way of being freed from my mind.

"When you touch a woman, pay attention to how it feels for you," the teacher was telling us. "If it feels good to you, it will feel good to her. If it feels awkward to you, it'll feel awkward to her."

The light bulb went on for me. I did feel awkward kissing Gloria at times, especially when I was in my head. No wonder it felt awkward for her too. Blushing, I had to admit it—to her, and to everyone present. Feeling vulnerable in this situation was easier for me to accept than when working with Jackie. Here I was anonymous; my professional credentials weren't known or necessary. This series of sensuality workshops was certainly more compelling than a dry and mental approach to communication that left me emotionally and physically disconnected. Instead, I felt open to learning about communicating through the doorway of the body. Although Gloria and I had also been exploring ways to address our issues in a couples' workshop and, of course, with Jackie, this step towards mastery and excellence in the sensuality domain—mastery and excellence being unwavering goals for The Professor in any domain—was a lot more fun. It seemed that fun was something I was sorely lacking in my life, and this was an opportunity to experience it.

"Do you think we have to complete this phase of our relationship before we can move on to anything else?" Gloria had asked with a chuckle in her voice when we began attending these sensuality workshops. "It seems easier for you to focus on physical sensation and women's pleasure than on the discomfort of sitting on a meditation cushion."

Feeling the lightness in Gloria when we spoke about the workshops and our homework meant everything to me. I felt lighter, too. And I welcomed the relief after a prolonged period where self-exploration had become heavy and serious for me. I had, in fact, given the meditation route a decent try, but with the same results I had with Jackie's process. Early in our relationship, Gloria and I attended a ten-day meditation retreat, an activity that had been part of her life. I had no problem focusing my mind on a mantra or even quieting it. That was something I had learned to do proficiently as a student. Still, I never linked how that quiet mind activated the witness state needed to explore my inner world rather than the familiar outer world of science and math. After that retreat, I joined Gloria in meditation every morning. After several months, noticing my eagerness to get on with my day, I allowed my practice to slowly fade away. Focusing my attention on a woman's pleasure—well now, that became quite compelling.

"Enjoying this sensual work sure makes it more attractive," I answered. "My teen years were so serious. Most of my energy was focused on academic goals. And being on the tenure track at UCLA, my attention was elsewhere."

I'd been with only one woman before Gloria, so what did I know about the pleasures of sensuality? My sexual experience had basically consisted of wham-bam-thank-you-ma'am—under the covers, in the dark, after the children were asleep. Though married more than a quarter of a century, I was a novice in this arena. To compound my awkwardness, I felt self-conscious about my body.

Gloria too had jumped into a very early marriage, but when she divorced, she'd entered the freedom of the sex, drugs, and rock-and-roll generation. While I was married with two children and another one on the way, she was reveling in the mud at the famous—or infamous—Woodstock Music Festival. Later, she'd taken on the serious task of becoming a lawyer and, of course, as a devotee of Muktananda, her focus had shifted. Relationships and sensuality had ended up on her back burner.

There were times I could feel the teenager inside me clamoring for sexual exploration, while Gloria enjoyed reigniting the sensual flame of her youth. Sensuality—the Bay Area version of tantra—provided a way to approach sexuality as a spiritual exploration, even if, at this point in our process, it was also laced with fulfilling our teenage fantasies. It helped each of us open and expand in a way that included the body and it seemed to bring us closer.

Reaping the benefits of Gloria's previous sensual experience was exciting for me when we began our relationship. Lighting candles, turning on music, slowing us down to spend hours languidly hanging out, and talking and laughing together in an intimate setting changed the sensual context that I'd known. However, having Gloria as my guide in this arena became fraught with difficulty. There were times she just wanted to surrender to me.

The same patterns that had operated in the kitchen were cropping up in the bedroom. When Gloria attempted to convey what gave her pleasure, The Professor was quick to jump in, hearing her requests as criticism. While our kitchen issue may have been resolving, The Professor was even more vehemently determined to protect the boy, who still heard his father's criticism — even in his grown-up bedroom. The fact that the boy had no business being in that bedroom was beside the point.

On the other hand, I could easily hear about what a woman wanted from a complete stranger in a workshop — or even from one of Gloria's girlfriends — without the voices jumping in between my conversation partner and myself. I had no karmic patterns or mother projections to work out with them.

"That was a little too hard," Gloria would say, after I touched or kissed her a certain way.

"Well, that's the way I've always done it," I'd respond.

Or she'd say, "I can't breathe, darling — lighten up."

And I'd respond defensively: "But I need to support my body." It was as if our old kitchen conversation had crept into the bedroom.

Although Gloria said many times during the early years of our marriage that she was very attracted to and turned on by me and that my sexual energy was great — translation: my body was physiologically responsive, eager, and able — but I really didn't know which end was up in trying to create a playful sensual exploration. At times, I simply felt clumsy and stiff. And it seemed that the closer we became, the stronger this impediment to closeness became. Fortunately, Gloria did not see my sensual naiveté as a problem. Instead, she welcomed it as unique and loved the guileless quality she found in me.

"Your innocence is refreshing," she had said several times when we first met, "especially after being a single woman in Los Angeles for many years and meeting a long string of bad boys."

Once the so-called honeymoon period was over, Gloria wanted more depth, and my vulnerability took over. Our new exploration seemed to be the remedy—at least, it provided an exciting adventure for the teenage part of me. Still, as long as I fell into a defensive stance that couldn't be unraveled, Gloria and I were sure to encounter the same patterns that had emerged in the kitchen. Couple that with me embracing the project with the same testosterone-driven quest that led to my academic success, as might be predicted, the sensual path created a whole new set of interpersonal issues that I would have to confront over the next several years.

EVENTUALLY GLORIA AND I joined the ranks of the Bay Area tantra community and met a group of people exploring sensuality and sexuality, both as a spiritual path and as a means of living and loving in community— often in expanded relationship. There was a basic assumption that it wasn't necessary, or even possible, to get all our needs met by our partner. So, if there was enough "goodness" in the relationship, other people could be invited in to fulfill the needs that were lacking. Joining this lifestyle was exciting, instructive, and at times confrontative. And, on occasion, the self-doubt and insecurity I suffered made it even more challenging.

Many of the people we met in the community were grounded in the transformational technology originated by Werner Erhard in the original EST training and, later, the Landmark Forum. While Gloria had enrolled in these courses during the 1970s—which had led to her meeting Swami Muktananda—she was willing to do the new iteration of the Forum with me. She thought it would be an important complement to our ongoing sensual exploration. As I understood it at the time, such transformation had to do with freeing people from their preconceived notions of their identity and their worldview by changing or expanding their concepts of themselves and the world around them—something I sorely needed and felt a bit more able to change. I now was sensing in me what Welwood had called the "soul-cage"—a concept I didn't understand when I first read his book. I always thought the cage was outside of me: the persona. Now I clearly sensed it within me, made of the unconscious patterns that locked me into an automatic response to Gloria that, despite the sensuality trainings, often precluded spontaneity and the true communion we longed to experience with each other.

We attended the Forum with Julianne—Gloria's best friend—commuting from Berkeley to San Francisco each day and taking our meals together. During our dinner conversation one evening, I got one of the concepts they called the "racket," which could be defined as an unproductive or fixed way of being or acting that includes a complaint or assumption that something shouldn't be the way it is.

"Do you think my avoidance of cooking is a racket because I'm afraid to make a mistake?" I asked Gloria and Julianne. "And complaining that no one ever taught me how to cook, so I can't do it now?"

"Brave of you to take that one on," Julianne said. "If it is a racket for you, what's the payoff?"

"I hate to admit it, but it gets me off the hook of doing something I really don't want to do," I said, more as a question than a response.

"Do you think that's true?" Gloria asked. "Because if it is, wow."

"Maybe I'm just a patriarchal asshole."

My companions laughed as we gathered our coats.

"But a very cute one," Gloria said.

"And—very kind and lovely," added Julianne.

As I picked up the check and paid for all of us, I found myself laughing as well. Catching up with the women, who were already walking back to the venue for the evening session, I noted the significance of this moment and my dawning awareness. *I am running a racket. I really don't want to learn how to cook, and not just because failure would be embarrassing. I actually do have better, more important things to do.*

For the first time, I had a glimpse of The Professor who, in the parlance of the Forum, was running a racket to not only protect me from making a mistake, but to make sure I didn't fall into an emotional black hole. And he would eventually be called out as a patriarch.

As a result of taking the Forum courses, I began to understand how I did, in fact, create my own interior reality and external worldview. I was now curious about how and why I was finally arriving at this reality. Maybe what I had learned with Jackie prepared me to understand these Landmark courses more readily. In any case, subsequent Landmark trainings confirmed what I'd learned about how context determines what we see and don't see and reinforces ideas regarding personal accountability, responsibility, possibility, and perfection.

As I was being encouraged to step outside my comfort zone, I was simultaneously being filled with the delights and opportunities offered by exploration into couples' communication and sensuality. The seriousness of my inner exploration was now balanced by the adventure offered by the sensuality workshops. While I may have been bypassing the deeper inner work needed to get to my childhood wounding, I was resonating with this exploration in a way I hadn't imagined possible. I'm sure that my private life gave me the *joie du vivre* that made my work at the University even more robust.

AT HOME GLORIA AND I were earnestly practicing our assignments. What we were learning in the workshops seemed to be alleviating the attack-and-defend dynamic in the sensual domain. Initially, when the instructor had presented what he called the "training cycle," The

Professor had resisted, affronted by the notion that he could be trained like a dog, especially in intimacy. But practice was making perfect, or at least opening some effective doors. After a day at a sensuality workshop, we would do our homework that night.

I'd place my hand on Gloria's arm or leg and begin to stroke it gently.

"Oh, that feels really good," she would say. "Could you do it a little slower?"

I would respond by slowing down the stroke.

"That's really great. Could you apply a little more pressure?"

And I would apply a little more pressure.

Receiving positive acknowledgment followed by a correction worked for me — a suggestion delivered this way effectively bypassed the memory of my father's criticism. The downside, however, was that it sometimes took us out of the spontaneity of the moment — keeping me in that soul-cage, which could be frustrating, but was definitely illuminating it to me.

Receiving feedback and course-correcting in the interpersonal domain were starting to feel more familiar, like a feedback control system in engineering. I remember thinking it was like the thermostat in a home, correcting the ambient temperature when it gets too cool or too warm. I smiled at this belated awareness. At last, I was understanding Jackie's notion of being recursive in linking the mental and physical domains by taking in feedback. *How come I could get that analogy in bed, but not in a group?*

I was also finally learning how to learn. The sensuality workshops provided ample opportunity to practice with many different women, removing the charge I felt with Gloria, who was still a father projection for me. Sometimes in a workshop, the women would sit in an inner circle while the men would move in an outer circle, practicing the lesson for four or five minutes with the woman they faced. With each workshop, I grew more comfortable and more attentive to each woman. Surprisingly, I often felt a sensual arousal in my whole body, a sensation beyond the typical sexual arousal I had known most of my adult life. When I stroked a woman's arm or leg, I began to feel the sensation in my own arm or leg. This perception changed my relationship with sensual pleasure. I found that giving pleasure could be just as enjoyable as receiving it. Something inside me began to soften as well; I found that I could lose myself in the process.

In time, I realized I could not only read my own physical response to touching and kissing Gloria, but I could also discern her physical response to my initiative. As a scientist, I'd been trained to have a keen sense of visual observation in my work. In this sensual world, I was translating that visual ability to all my body senses: in addition to sight, I began to "observe" through touch, sound, smell, and taste.

Observing the external physical world, not to mention my body sensations, was much easier for me than attempting to understand my internal psychological world. As long as I focused on improving our physical interactions, I believed my endeavors were supporting our marriage. While I wasn't necessarily resolving the conflicts that had emerged between us, at least The Professor's façade was softening, which would later make it easier to crumble.

"I'D LIKE TO MAKE A RESERVATION for two tables with two people at each." I was calling Rivoli, one of Berkeley's finer restaurants. "And the two tables should be at the opposite ends of the dining room."

There was silence on the other end of the line. It seemed to be begging for an explanation.

"You see, my wife and I often go out to dinner with this couple, and I end up talking to the man about men's stuff, and she talks to the woman about women's stuff."

More silence at the other end.

"So we're going to do something different. I'm going to have dinner with his wife, and he is going to have dinner with mine."

Still silence.

"In this way, we can get to know each other's spouses beyond the usual small talk," I offered.

"Great idea," the voice at the other end finally responded. "Maybe we should sponsor a whole evening like that." I laughed to myself, feeling particularly risqué. I'm sure they had no idea what we were up to.

Lisa and Steve were joining Gloria and me at Rivoli for dinner. Afterwards, we would attend a formal dance party our tantra teachers had planned. Gloria and Lisa had become good friends, having led women's empowerment groups together. They coached women on how to articulate their needs and desires, how to get them met, and how to find creative ways to be happier. Part of women's empowerment also meant being satisfied sexually. "If momma ain't happy, ain't nobody happy" was a euphemism I often heard in the Bay Area tantra community.

Lisa and Steve had taken all the sensuality courses that Gloria and I were now taking, and they were delighted to be our mentors in this arena. Their goal was to create more fun and connection for us and for themselves in the process. They operated on the principle that adding more turn-on and seduction would open more possibilities for us as a couple. Gloria was curious about Lisa's lifestyle and admired the way she and Steve related to each other. She was also curious how it would feel to be with a "trained" man. We were game to give it a try.

So there we were, ready to jump in. Lisa was dressed in a floor length, black velvet, off-the-shoulder evening dress cut low enough to distract any man, with matching diamond earrings, necklace, and bracelet. Her precisely styled strawberry-blond hair brushed along her bare shoulders each time she moved or tilted her head. And there I was, dressed in formal attire: black tux, studs, bowtie, and cummerbund over a bright white formal evening shirt. As requested, we were seated in one corner of the dining room, and Gloria and Steve were in the opposite corner, dressed in a similar fashion. I felt young, giddy, and yet manly; turned-on just watching and listening to Lisa—a feeling I'd never permitted myself to have with a woman who wasn't my wife. I couldn't believe I was almost sixty.

Except for our age—Lisa was twelve years my junior—we could have been mistaken for high-school seniors on prom night—the prom I never attended—-at least that was how I felt. Attending my actual senior prom was so mixed up with the seriousness I felt during my teens that I missed that social rite of passage at the time.

As we waited for our champagne, Lisa reminded me of our first meeting the previous year. She and Steve had hosted a Halloween party at their home in Woodside, an upper-middle-class community in Silicon Valley. When Gloria and I arrived, they greeted us at the front door. Lisa had graciously led me arm-in-arm towards the great room where the party was taking place, as did Steve with Gloria. About halfway down the hallway, Lisa stopped, looked up at me, and smiled.

"You and I are going to get to know each other really, really well."

Those were Lisa's first words to me, and how prophetic they were. Indeed, this evening at Rivoli was an opportunity to spend social time with a woman outside my marriage, my family, or my profession. Lisa talked about her childhood, her parents, and her likes and dislikes. I was on a date, and I listened intently.

"You remind me of my father," she said. "He was a professor at Berkeley too."

As the evening unfolded, Lisa and I spoke and acted beyond established social mores—a little flirting here and there, some teasing, even eyes locking in for a few sensual moments. Maybe even a sexual innuendo or two. What mischief could possibly befall us amid forty or fifty people in a public setting? Little did I know at the time that, within three months, I would get to know Lisa "really, really well."

The whole evening was a test of my ability to focus on a woman without being distracted by thoughts of work or the surrounding environment, without doing mathematical calculations in my head or commenting on the social makeup of the restaurant's clientele. I also began to let myself experience sensual pleasure outside the bedroom—taking in the fragrance of an unfamiliar woman's body, feeling her hand gently touching the back of my neck while dancing, or watching the sway of her hips—all of these exciting my five senses.

Gloria often wondered why I wasn't looking at or admiring women on the street or seated across from us at a restaurant. I thought she was odd for wondering, or that she was accustomed to the bad-boy behavior she'd known before me. On this evening, I was beginning to understand what she was talking about—it was more about being open to sensual pleasures. Something was making sense to me as I realized what I'd been missing: being fully present with all my senses.

I now found myself wondering what it would be like to have an affair with Lisa. Or with some of the other women here. I'd never permitted myself to even have such thoughts during my first marriage and especially as a professor at the University. Yet at this appropriate time and place, with an appropriate woman, I wouldn't "get in trouble." Intimacy was actually encouraged.

At the formal party after our dinner at Rivoli, Gloria and Steve danced with each other. Lisa and I did the same. At times, I felt as if we were the only couple in the room. We also traded partners with other couples, many of whom were friends and fellow attendees at our sensuality courses. Putting my full attention on the women I danced with was a new experience for me. At first, I felt self-conscious. Over the course of the evening, I opened to it and became comfortable. Prior to this party, I usually shied away from dancing. My first wife had been a professional dancer, and I had felt awkward and intimidated by her. This awkwardness had carried over to Gloria, who was also a good dancer. Given the encouragement to dance with other women while I was learning to get out of my head and into my body was freeing. I started to enjoy getting lost in the music and the energy exchange with each dance partner.

Precisely at midnight, as planned by the organizers, Lisa and I joined Gloria and Steve, to stand with our spouses, as did everyone else. I thanked Steve profusely for the opportunity to entertain Lisa that evening, and Steve reciprocated. Gloria and Lisa thanked each other as well. We ended with a big hug all around.

Steve and I then began a conversation regarding the upcoming football season—Steve being a 49ers fan and I being a Raiders fan—as Lisa and Gloria took off arm-in-arm for the ladies' room. We both shared the unwritten male rule of never talking to other men about our intimate relationship with our wife and, by extension, any other woman in our lives. If anything were to be said about this evening, it would be Lisa who would inform Steve, not me. On the other hand, I assumed that the women would be talking about the men they had spent the evening with.

Gloria and I were enthusiastic on the drive home.

"Steve sure did make me laugh a lot. And I loved the dancing." Gloria said. "It was a very fun evening. He was a perfect gentleman."

"I'm delighted you enjoyed yourself, and I'm happy about how Steve treated you." I sincerely felt joy.

"Lisa was impressed with how you kept your focus on her, and your playfulness," Gloria said.

"I was surprised too, without my to-do list coming up," I said. "I figured if she wanted to know about what I did, she could look me up on the University website."

"You really are learning how to translate the laser-sharp focus on your work to relationships with women."

"And it was titillating flirting with another man's wife, knowing there'd be no repercussions," I added.

Gloria smiled, nodding her approval. When I was open to exploration, Gloria was happy—whatever domain we were in—and she was clearly having a good time herself. She had become serious in her pursuit of the law in her career, and now she was taken back to her carefree Woodstock days. Life with The Professor had gotten too serious, and if this experience could open me up, she was ready to welcome it.

As Gloria and I pulled up in front of our home, I sensed the openness I had felt all evening still alive in me. It continued for the rest of the weekend. I was absolutely thrilled.

Our relationship with Lisa and Steve didn't end with the party. We developed a deeper friendship with them over the next several years, traveling together on vacations and spending time at the community house where they lived. During those fun-filled times, we learned about community living and explored intimacy beyond just sensuality. Best of all, I never laughed as long and as hard as I did when we were together.

"WE'D LIKE YOU AND A professor from MIT to review the final safety and risk analysis report for the Cassini-Huygens mission to Saturn," an Air Force Colonel said to me during a phone call around the time of our dinner party at Rivoli. "President Clinton would like an independent review before he signs off on the mission."

The Cassini space craft electronics were powered by radioactive thermoelectric generators utilizing an isotope of plutonium to create an electric current. All heads of state must sign off on any mission carrying radioactive material into space, as required by an international treaty. An accident at launch or an unplanned reentry could release radioactivity into the environment, potentially leading to public and environmental exposure worldwide.

"I've got three months to review a lot of analysis and documentation," I said to Gloria after I accepted the task. "It's set to launch in October."

"Wow," Gloria said. "That's a lot of responsibility."

"And it's scheduled to achieve orbit around Saturn exactly on my sixty-fifth birthday."

"Seems like you're leading a double life," Gloria joked.

I chuckled at the thought.

AS DESCRIBED ON THEIR WEBSITE, "Lafayette Morehouse is an intentional community aimed at maximizing our potential, both as individuals and as a group, and to have life be as much fun as is possible." When we met the members of Morehouse who offered courses in sensuality, they'd been successfully living and teaching together for more than thirty-five years, led by their founder, Dr. Victor Baranco. The cornerstone of their philosophy and lifestyle is the notion of "perfection" with a working premise that people are "right the way they are" and everything else builds from there. The coaching and teaching were always couched in a person's perfection as a starting point. This premise made sense to me and felt familiar as I'd been hearing it from other sources—Jackie, Papaji, Amma. And even the training cycle was based on it. With that in mind, I could try to reframe feeling criticized when Gloria asked for something, to being trained to "play the game" better, much like a tennis player learning how to improve her swing by turning her wrist a bit. This idea resonated for The Professor, who had been protecting me from the trauma of criticism. Still, it was just an idea—an abstraction. Putting it into practice was perhaps beyond my grasp. *Could I even accept myself?*

The teachers we met at Morehouse applied their principles to community living as well, operating under the assumption that gratified people will "treat others with more compassion and love." They were training us to embrace these principles by working with the body—absolutely a new step for me.

According to the Morehouse faculty, Vic, as he was affectionally called, "recognized that it was imperative to handle communication, sensuality, and decision-making in order to sustain a cohesive group of two or more people." Their courses represented the findings of their lifestyle experiments and research related to communication, money, and power—and, of course, sensuality and sexuality. By enrolling in their courses, we would be introduced to a method of emotional softening I could relate to: a clear formula with a relatively predictable outcome. Vic had been associated with the notion of the "one-hour orgasm," demonstrating that the duration and intensity of a woman's orgasm was limitless. This learning opportunity seemed limitless to me, incredibly eye-opening, and, at the same time, fun. In fact, fun in the sensual domain wasn't something I had prioritized until I met Gloria. So we continued our sensual education at Morehouse, taking it to another level—sexuality.

I could hear from our Morehouse coaches the link between communication and sexuality in a language I could understand. I learned the art of "pulling withholds," a technique designed to reduce emotional charge between a couple without having to analyze it. This was helpful before any activity, they explained— sexual or otherwise. We didn't get to the deeper emotional underpinnings that gave rise to the charge. However, getting the charge out of way, without my head analyzing it, felt freeing.

"Tell me something you withheld from me," I would ask Gloria.

"I hate it when you leave the sink full of dirty dishes."

"Thank you. Tell me something you withheld from me," I'd repeat.

"I was upset when I saw you spending time with Alexis at the party last night."

"Thank you."

No matter what inner reaction I might be having in the moment, the idea was to just notice the emotional charge and, without denying it and without getting caught in it—to continue with the exercise.

"Tell me something you withheld from me," I'd go on.

"I wish you'd put the toilet seat down when you're done peeing."

"Thank you."

As instructed, the process would continue for ten or twenty minutes until any emotional charge Gloria might have had seemed to dissipate. Then it would be Gloria's turn to pull withholds from me. Sometimes I went first and sometimes she went first. Sometimes we'd finish with a big laugh. Or finish with a big cry. At the end, we'd ask each other whether there was anything we wanted or needed to discuss. When we felt we had cleared the energy and any stuck emotions, we could then move on to any intimate domain of activity, if and when the spirit moved us. It was surprisingly effective and rewarding to us both that I was willing to explore this edge of vulnerability. It became freeing to be able to say anything that came into my mind with no fear about how it would be received. I was "reprogramming" myself about communication.

After completing all the prerequisite courses at Morehouse, Gloria and I each elected to enroll in an open-ended, individually designed course called Expansion of Sexual Potential or ESP. I received instruction on everything from female anatomy and physiology to pleasing a woman sexually. And the goal wasn't just sensual or sexual—it was to maximize human potential in every area of life by embodying their notion of "perfection and training ourselves to be present with the focus on giving and receiving pleasure to our fullest capacity." Along with laboratory classes, I would be unlearning my former beliefs and behaviors and then learning anew a philosophy based on "feeling good about myself the way things are." While this was quite an assignment for The Professor, the rewards were huge for me.

No ESP would be considered complete without a visit with Vic at his home in Hawaii. Vic grew up on the streets of Oakland, played collegiate football at Berkeley, was an ex-Marine, and had a manner that could only be characterized as thuggish. However, he was incredibly bright and perceptive and had had what can only be described as an enlightenment experience, which drew many followers. For us, sitting with an enlightened person who talked like a thug was disarming in and of itself.

We flew to Hawaii to spend five days with him. Before we were considered qualified to have an "audience" with Vic, we had to complete the "hexing" course. The premise being that, if there was something deep down that you felt insecure about but denied, a hex would put it back in your face. Vic was a master at this game.

As soon as we sat down, Vic called me out. "Ah, so you're the New York, pseudo liberal, Jewish commie symp ..." I can't even remember the rest of it.

Who the hell is this guy? Oh yeah, this is a hex, but what the fuck? Nobody has ever talked to me this way.

He seemed to have my number.

The whole five days could be described as one big hex. Vic deftly attempted to expose our self-deceptions as we tried to wrestle our way out of his hold. At every turn, I was bumping up against my ego. It wasn't a pretty sight.

"The point is that you think you can wow her with your intellect," he said at one point.

"Well, we do enjoy batting around intellectual ideas," I responded. "Just today we were talking about ways to improve infrastructure ..."

He cut me off.

"The only infrastructure she's interested in is in the folds of her vulva," he said, right to the point. "You guys are invested in this bullshit and, if you don't get rid of it in this course, you don't have a chance."

"Which bullshit?" My question was sincere.

"The bullshit that you aren't a patriarch. That you don't want to control her," Vic answered. "You think she should be different. Put up with your bullshit. Or is there another belief you are afraid to admit?"

"What is that?" I asked earnestly.

"The fear that you are sexually inadequate." He didn't mince words.

I couldn't hear another word. My head was spinning and, before I knew it, I had jumped out of my seat, pulled Gloria out of hers, and dragged her toward the door.

At that point, the room almost went black. Mario—I couldn't tell whether he was Vic's bodyguard or a bouncer—had tackled me to the ground. The next thing I knew, Gloria and I were both back in our chairs and Mario was holding me down in my seat.

"Okay, man, that was a hard one to admit," Vic said. "It's your fear that's the issue."

"I am afraid I can't satisfy her." I was nearly weeping.

"Then why be so uptight about it?" Vic asked. "You've been hexed. This is what you signed up for, man. I'm telling you what you want to hear."

Now, he *definitely* had my number. Destroying egos and, of course, The Professor's façade was his forte. Every time I opened my mouth to speak, he pointed out the arrogance in my words. Every time I attempted to express my opinion, he pointed out how I was talking over Gloria. He called me a male chauvinist and showed me the ways I was ignoring Gloria and being a coward by not telling her how I felt and playing know-it-all instead.

Vic was no easier on Gloria.

"Bill never butts up against me," Gloria said at one session. "He never tells me to 'get off it' when I'm off-base."

"He didn't sign up to be your policeman," Vic retorted. "Grow up, lady!"

At one point, after she had named all her complaints, he looked at her point-blank and said, "Lady, the only problem you have is that you can't shovel it into every orifice fast enough."

We were both stunned.

One morning when we arrived for our session, Frankie, another member of the Morehouse community, was playing the song "Sweet Caroline" on the piano, the song made popular by Neil Diamond. Gloria had been complaining about her girlfriend Caroline, a single woman, being infatuated with me.

Vic wasn't having it. "Would you want to be with a man that no other women wanted?" he asked when he entered the room. "It turns you on, lady. Let's face it."

Another rebuke came when Gloria attempted a rescue, interfering when Vic began to lob one at me.

"Stop it!" Vic scolded. "The kindest thing you can do when someone is falling down from a knockout punch is to let them fall. The unkindest thing is to help them up."

After a week of very straight talk, Vic finally succeeded in showing us something that we didn't know: the two of us had both bought into male chauvinism—patriarchy. That, behind my insecurities, I just didn't *want* to cook. That I considered myself too important and had weightier matters to attend to. That cooking was her job. And, on some level, that I didn't want to hear about her needs, her wants, or that she was smarter than me. I began to see that I couldn't accept her ideas unless I thought they were mine. Or that she had learned how to plant seeds in me, so I thought her ideas were mine.

We went through all of this for five full days. As the last day approached, I asked Vic, "Can you tell me how I can stop overriding her?"

"Are you asking me how you can love her better? It's metaphysical, man—it's all about being present. That's your ESP, if you let it in."

I tried to take in everything Vic said. I began to understand that what Vic meant was that being in a relationship was a paradox. "Women call and men respond," was a favorite saying of his, using the analogy of the female-male peacock mating ritual. But at the same time, women will only call when men are open to their call. A chicken and egg situation—the Schrödinger's cat paradox—that makes relationship metaphysical. And the challenge was following the call and not being a little boy.

Gloria had many lessons as well but was surprised that she hadn't recognized her own male chauvinism, which was as deep as mine. For her, being able to finally admit her truth about expressing her needs was a challenge she had brought into our marriage.

While our heads were still spinning when we returned to the Bay Area, a new course for our relationship was being charted. And the persona I came to know as The Professor had been exposed as a patriarch.

AT THE SAME TIME, I was traveling back and forth to Washington to work on the Cassini project and other nuclear safety undertakings, I was meeting with my ESP guides at Morehouse—Fred and Mabel—an older couple who guided me through an experiential process once a week for a year. Each tutorial session began with Fred or Mabel pulling withholds from me for twenty minutes. And as with any good science course, each session ended with a laboratory component and assigned homework for putting into practice what I had learned. I would also write, in exquisite detail, every sensation I had experienced and every thought I had about the experience—everything I could remember, at least—and then debrief that experience with my guides at the next session. Next, under my guides' supervision, I would be a "giver" of sensual pleasure to a woman who was a "certified receiver," followed by a short debrief. The journaling and debrief prompted me to pay attention to my body in ways I never thought of before.

Gloria did the same program as a "receiver" of pleasure. For her, she told me, this work had a spiritual component, requiring surrender to pleasure "without reaching for it—being present for every sensation." Raised during the women's movement, Gloria had developed a yang edge that motivated her to reach or push for pleasure. This year-long training had ramifications for both of us beyond sexuality.

In some regards, the mentoring relationship I had with Fred and Mabel was like the relationships I had with my doctoral students. But here I was the student, and The Professor accepted that. The physical world was much more fun than the mental world. At the end of my ESP program, I had a graduation and even received a diploma—handed to me by the head of the Sensuality Department at Morehouse.

Exercises such as the training cycle and pulling withholds were immediate and temporary ways of reducing or eliminating emotional charge, which served us well—at least for a while. For the long run, we would need something deeper, more permanent. Meanwhile, I thought I had it made. Women were attracted to me. Gloria and I were working out a new kind of relationship in which I felt confident and comfortable with her sensually and sexually in ways I didn't even know were possible. And I was reaching the pinnacle of my professional career. Who could ask for more? I had yet to find out.

Chapter 14

Consciousness Change

*Divide each difficulty into as many parts as is feasible and necessary
to resolve it.*
— René Descartes

IT WAS NEARLY Y2K and the turn of the century —
almost the end of one millennium and the beginning
of another. It was early December 1999 when Gloria
and I took a hike in Tilden Regional Park above the
Berkeley campus. And my life would change once again.

FOR MORE THAN FIVE YEARS now, I had been Chair of
Berkeley's Nuclear Engineering Department and Director
of the Research Center for Nuclear and Toxic Waste
Management. At work, I was flying high. I had recently
been awarded a Distinguished Chair in recognition of my
scholarly research accomplishments and had been asked
by Governor Gray Davis' office to chair a scientific panel
reviewing California's low-level radioactive waste issue. I
was nourished, feeling proud and very satisfied in my
professional life.

At home, my relationship with Gloria had reached a quiescent time with periodic bumps along the way. I guess you could say we were integrating all that we'd been learning from Jackie, Landmark, and Morehouse, as well as the various sensuality workshops we had attended. Still, there was something I'd describe as a faint rub or friction between us that felt like a wagon with one wheel slightly off its axle. When we hit a bump in the relationship road, we too easily drove the wagon into the ditch.

Unfortunately, I sometimes felt criticized when Gloria told me what she wanted, even with her new softer approach. Despite the clarity I had after visiting Vic in Hawaii and all the withholds we'd been doing, I felt stymied at times, trying to tell Gloria how I felt. For example, when she interrupted me, rather than simply telling her to wait a minute and saying, "I'm not finished speaking," I hesitated, keeping my comments to myself and boiling inside. She noticed—as if she could see the steam emanating from my body—and we'd be off and running.

While I'd become proficient at putting my attention on her physically with the sensuality techniques I'd been mastering, I never dared to ask her how she felt or what she needed. I was afraid her answer would confirm my fear of inadequacy—a fear that Vic had brought to light.

Still, I felt close to Gloria when we had intellectual conversations about the professional work we were doing, and even closer when we were in workshops together, whether they were about relationship, sensuality, or holotropic breathwork. Being in those spaces cleared my mind of an academic life filled with myriad details that, over time, bogged me down. Our weekend activities as a couple seemed to release me from whatever constrictions kept me from speaking my truth. Invariably, during those weekend workshops, I'd feel connected to myself and, as a result, connected to Gloria. Resuming my university activities and responsibilities each week, I'd contract.

My difficulty in making the transition between my professional life and my personal life highlighted a frustrating dichotomy. Noticing that my preoccupation with my professional work created a mental space that made it difficult for me to be present with Gloria, I wondered how I could hold both ways of being that were required in my life. Or—better still—whether there might be another way of being that didn't require making this shift.

While my ongoing relationship with Lisa offered some uplifting personal pleasure, I longed for a way to connect with Gloria without feeling so defended. I felt trapped in this familiar dichotomy. Some nights, during quiet moments lying in bed listening to Gloria breathing in her sleep, I longed for the joy and lightness of our early days together—even with all the relationship input I was receiving.

Despite the pleasure I received from my professional success and sensual diversions, the chasm between my personal and professional life was exhausting me emotionally, and I simply did not know how to cross the more subtle but still growing divide. Still, although Gloria and I had emotional disconnects, we shared a strong intellectual bond—despite Vic's hex to the contrary—that left us feeling satisfied and sometimes in tune with one another. I could reach her by exciting her intellect as well as her body.

Toward the end of the time we were engaged with Jackie's work, we discovered Ken Wilber's *Integral Approach* for understanding the evolution of human knowledge and consciousness. His work intrigued me. It seemed that he touched on ideas Jackie had been offering, but I had more access to them through his extensive writings. Gloria and I enjoyed reading parts of his book, *A Brief History of Everything,* to each other, and when we dropped into deep conversations about his work, I felt nurtured, seen and heard by her—albeit intellectually. Much of Wilber's four-quadrant approach regarding "subjective and objective development in both individuals and collectives" resonated with me. My own use of four-quadrant Cartesian coordinate systems enabled my use of logic diagrams and truth tables—fundamental to my understanding game theory and the success or failure of engineered systems—that were still alive in me. Here I could make a conceptual extrapolation that slowly but surely allowed other connections to enhance my grasp of life's complexities. Our conversations became a satisfying entry into a better understanding of myself.

Given the closeness I felt with Gloria when we shared an intellectual focus, it was no surprise that, when we started talking about my next sabbatical leave coming up in seven months, I became animated as I tossed around ideas with her. Thinking it might be an opportunity for us to continue our intellectual conversations — remembering Vic's admonition about listening to her ideas — we started talking about whether there might be a project we could do together during that year. The Accrediting Board for all engineering programs in the country had recently announced a new requirement for an educational component in ethics and social responsibility, and that had my wheels turning.

I wondered if Gloria and I could do something together in this context, and in a subject we both found interesting. Certainly, ethics had been related to her work as a lawyer and mediator, as well as to her deep interest in spiritual growth. And my research center had already been exploring social responsibility.

So one weekend in early December 1999, during a hike in the hills above campus, I recall proposing the idea of creating a course in engineering ethics. Gloria remembers this idea as hers, yet such ideas weren't real for me unless I created them in my own thoughts and words. Through the years, this discrepancy led to many conversations about why many men need to make an idea their own in order for it to be real — a topic we had spoken about with Vic, which he categorized as emanating from the patriarchy.

"I don't think I can go with you and give up my mediation practice if you're planning to do a sabbatical project that requires travel," Gloria had said, "unless it's something I can do with you that would be meaningful."

"I've been trying to figure out how I could bring that new ethics requirement into our curriculum at Berkeley," I offered.

Gloria was immediately interested, so I talked a little more about the requirement as we made our way up a steep narrow path and stopped at the crest of the hill. The spaciousness of the San Francisco Bay Area was spread out before us—the Golden Gate Bridge to our left and Mount Diablo to our right. It was a broad and promising view.

"What if engineering ethics is the project we could do together?" Gloria asked.

"What's your idea?"

Maybe, thanks to Vic, I am learning to listen more often to what Gloria is suggesting.

"We'd use the subject of ethics to see how each of us views the world differently," she continued, "so we could understand each other's mindset better."

This just might work.

I took a deep breath.

Gloria pointed out that I had become an expert in nuclear reactor safety and risk, the "hot" technology of my early academic days.

"What if you cap off your career by articulating a new mindset and ethic for engineers? A mindset that's congruent with the nonlinear science behind the emerging technologies you've been reading about."

Gloria was referring to two special issues of *Science Magazine* I'd recently read—one titled "Complex Systems" and one titled "Supramolecular Chemistry and Self-Assembly." Both addressed the changing landscape of scientific discovery and technological development.

"Imagine, Bill, what if we could figure out a way to encourage engineers to move from a linear mindset to a nonlinear one?" Gloria continued. "And maybe even to develop intuition—though we wouldn't call it that. Or maybe we would. That could give students a better sense of the ethical and social dimensions of the new technologies. The very things we're working on personally can combine with the research and teaching. That would be amazing!"

"I'm beginning to get it. You're equating ethics with a shift in mindset—the way an engineer thinks about problems and solutions—and suggesting we find a way to teach them how to make that shift," I responded. "If I understand you correctly, you're saying the study of ethics is a personal process, not just an abstract study of theories."

Sensing that we were in a groove with each other, I felt elated. Euphoric. We were on to something. I recalled Vic saying at our audience, "Women call, and men respond."

She's got a good idea and I can make it happen.

It felt good to be taking in her ideas, even in my field of engineering education, rather than automatically resisting them. Previously, I had pushed back if I felt she was trying to change me. But this was a mutual exploration we could do together that could possibly change both of us. The idea of linking personal growth with my professional work was astounding to me. We had tried doing so with Jackie, but now this was something we ourselves were generating. This time, we were on the same page with one another.

I began thinking out loud, contemplating how our students would eventually be involved in projects that would go well beyond the material venue of traditional engineering that tended to focus on machines and structures. By this time, Dolly the sheep had been cloned, nanotechnology was in its infancy, and the Internet was taking hold in everyone's lives.

"Right now, engineering education and training are still focused on balancing the risks, costs, and benefits of any engineering project—the economy of technology rather than the ecology of technology," I said. "Engineers will have to start considering how new projects affect the ecology of life itself."

Gloria nodded. Clearly, this was of interest to her. I went on, encouraged.

"We're still operating with the mentality, 'If it can be done, let's do it.' We need more concern for unintended consequences and a means to intuit them," I said. "I think you're talking about influencing a change to the prevailing mindset."

"What I'm suggesting is that, if we were successful, engineers could really feel their impact on society and develop compassion," Gloria said. "Imagine if, when you were studying nuclear engineering, you were also able to envision the nuclear waste problem that would ensue. You'd need a much broader vision."

"Yes. The radioactive waste disposal issue was considered at the time, and a site was chosen in Kansas," I said, "but the public's negative reaction wasn't considered, even though it was similar to what we encountered at Diablo Canyon."

"Well, you understand the technical aspect of engineering advances. Add to that a change in mindset in the people creating those advances that come from a broader, more compassionate, more intuitive vision," Gloria replied. "We'd be immersing ourselves in the change that we want to teach."

"Nurturing our own compassion would be great."

"Wasn't the lack of compassion a bind in the development of nuclear weapons?" Gloria asked.

"You're right," I said. "Maybe the shift in ethics is, 'Should it be done at all?' That's the question Oppenheimer should have asked when he led the development of the atomic bomb."

Gloria's response was succinct and clear. "I believe a change in human consciousness is necessary for resolving these kinds of ethical issues."

I wasn't surprised at her clarity. This line of conversation seemed promising. If we were to spend the year together while I was focused on work, it would have to be a project that she could relate to and that would bring us closer as we explored it together. The whole project would be geared toward releasing us from our soul-cage prison and helping others start exploring and considering theirs.

"Okay, let's do it. I'm game," I said, not fully comprehending the difficulty of the task.

In charting our journey to enter academia together, I would later discover that, while I was focused on changing the consciousness of engineers, Gloria would remain primarily focused on a more personal project—our own evolution. I was interested in the partnership, but she wanted to bridge the gap caused by the difficulties we had in connecting. Being reductionistic by nature, I tended to compartmentalize—meaning that, if we connected intellectually, I assumed we were connecting in all domains. Accordingly, when I heard her speaking about her goal— bridging the gap between us—I invariably became frustrated and defensive. It sounded to me like she was telling me what to do.

Oddly, Gloria realized that I was best able to hear her when we talked about engineers. I suppose that satisfied her enough to agree to undertake this research with me. Of course, while we joked about her goal to change the consciousness of one engineer—namely me—I suppose this response represented her real aim when our friends asked why we were doing this project together. In truth, the exploration of consciousness change would become my intention as well, although I struggled with it at the time. It was easy for me to see it for engineers in general, or in a consciousness changing workshop. However, whenever she asked me to look, I couldn't see this in myself.

Planning my sabbatical was an amazing experience for me. Despite my struggles with Gloria, I now had, in her, an intellectual and research partner, and that was exciting. I also had a girlfriend, Lisa, and the Bay Area tantric-sensuality community that I found fun and supportive.

GLORIA AND I WERE ATTENDING a holiday gathering at Lisa's and Steve's home in Woodside several weeks after our hike in the Berkeley Hills. At one point, I saw Gloria in the dining room speaking with a man named Paul who I didn't recognize. He seemed to have some notoriety as a small group of people had gathered around them, seemingly hanging on his every word. After watching for several minutes from afar, I walked over so I could hear the conversation too.

As I approached, Gloria began explaining to Paul the context underlying the courses we had taken at Morehouse — by this time we'd both graduated and had our diplomas in sensuality. Listening in, I'd gathered that Paul was interested in why so many of the people he met at the gathering had taken these courses. After answering his question, Gloria turned to me to ask whether I had anything to add.

"No," I said, admiring how succinctly she articulated the Morehouse philosophy. "I think you summed it up very well."

After introductions, I learned that Paul was a philosopher and psychologist, working as a private consultant with multinational companies seeking to integrate a culturally diverse work force. For twenty-five years before that, he'd been a trainer with an international firm offering personal development programs and seminars regarding consciousness change. Most of our friends at the party had taken the courses offered by his company. Although Gloria hadn't met Paul personally at that time, she had taken most of the intensive seminars offered by the firm and, through that association, she had come to know Swami Muktananda. Paul also represented the organization during the Swami's funeral, so they seemed to share a common language.

Françoise, Paul's life partner, walked over to where we were standing and joined the conversation. She listened intently, making some comments now and then about perception and thought. As I recall, I was immediately taken by her graciousness and old-world European charm and depth. I had pleasant memories of the year I had lived in Europe during a sabbatical twenty-five years earlier, and the many deep friendships I'd made.

"You must stay with us when you come to France next summer," Françoise said towards the end of the evening.

I'd mentioned to her that Gloria and I would be initiating my sabbatical the following June, with a trip to Europe as part of our engineering ethics research. In fact, we'd be about an hour's drive from their home, as I would be delivering a series of lectures at the French nuclear research center in Cadarache.

"I'm drawn to them," Gloria commented later that evening. "I'd like to get to know them better."

"Really?" I replied. I suddenly felt as though chalk had scratched my blackboard, and I didn't know why. I was conveniently disregarding the fact that I had wanted to get to know Lisa better a year or two before.

OVER THE NEXT FIVE MONTHS, we delved into the literature on how value systems in different cultures affect individual and group choices, reminiscent of the early talks I had with Jackie. We talked about how western civilization—and scientists and engineers in particular—made meaning of the world based on reason and logic, leading to the reductionistic, deterministic, and objectivistic mindset that we call "linear thinking." Descartes had reduced the world to pieces, and Newton had ascribed specific functions to these pieces that lead to specific outcomes. This mindset resulted in us perceiving ourselves as cogs in a Newtonian-Cartesian machine.

As an example, my own education, training, and practice of engineering were based on these Newtonian-Cartesian ideas. I understood the limits of their applicability, but I hadn't developed the ability to hold the "and" between linearity and nonlinearity in my personal life that I was now being called to understand.

"How would you explain the difference between linear and nonlinear systems to an engineering ethics class?" Gloria had asked me one evening at home while we were getting dinner ready.

It was working—our shared interest was distracting us from that painful dynamic that had separated us. Eager to talk about this topic, I didn't even mind being told what to do in the kitchen, at least for the moment.

"I'd give them an example," I began, as we sat down. "Take a car, for instance. You're driving along a highway in a vehicle whose parts are made all over the world, yet when assembled, they work together in perfect harmony—reductionism at its best. Step on the gas pedal and the car lurches forward, step on the brake and the car slows down, all predictable from Newton's second law of motion."

"That's my experience every time I drive, objectively speaking." Gloria smiled.

"Now consider this," I went on. "You come to a patch of ice, and what happens? The frictional force between tire and road diminishes to basically zero. There is nothing for the engine to work against, so the car's inertia carries it forward according to Newton's first law of motion."

"I've been there," Gloria said. "Good example."

"However, the car's response is no longer deterministic, it's emergent—the behavior of the car emerging from the interaction of all the system elements, especially the driver."

"So that means," Gloria added, "that every car hitting the ice patch will behave differently depending on the driver's subjective prior experience and consequent actions."

"That's right. The outcome is emergent—some cars will skid, some will spin, some will fishtail, and some might come to an abrupt halt when they hit an immovable object—that's nonlinearity in action."

"Okay, good," Gloria said. "Then we'll need to find an ethical approach that is emergent and that has within it the possibility of different outcomes and subjectivity. I can see how that might also apply to us, Bill, and how we relate to each other. That means that if you and I can really hear each other and take in what the other says, something new can emerge."

"I just realized something too," I mused. "Jackie was right when she said, 'when enough differences that make a difference, and only those differences that make a difference, are articulated,' conversations can become wholistic. I feel like dancing with joy."

I took her into my arms and whirled her around the floor.

"I do want to know how you experience nonlinearity relating to us," she responded.

"The way we just arrived at a sabbatical project—we just kept talking and understanding each other until the subject of ethics emerged. We both recognized that would be satisfying to us and of service to educating students."

I was getting an aspect of nonlinearity now in a way I hadn't before. These words were beginning to mean something personal to me.

WE HAD ALREADY BEEN TAKING steps in all these directions as part of our initial research. Together we had listened to Huston Smith's book on tape, *The World's Religions*, wherein he described the major teachings of what he called the world's wisdom traditions. After a distinguished career as a philosophy professor at MIT, Syracuse, and Berkeley, he had become an icon of the spiritual community known for his teaching and research of comparative religion. We'd read some of his newer books that explored connections between science and religion as well. Eventually, Dr. Smith, some twenty years older than me, became our mentor and guide. At our first meeting, he explained how he and his graduate students had immersed themselves for several years in a particular religion or wisdom tradition, as he called it, taking on its practices and precepts to arrive at an embodied understanding.

I felt comfortable and relaxed as he encouraged us to search beyond western philosophical discourse on ethics and, instead, to turn towards eastern religion and philosophy. He also recommended we investigate Indigenous cultures. His kindness and generosity landed in my heart. At my invitation, he eagerly accepted and gave a lecture on religion and science at a Nuclear Engineering Department seminar and, several years later, delivered a keynote speech at an engineering ethics workshop we'd organized.

"Wow, I am getting excited about the whole project," Gloria said after our luncheon with Professor Smith. "Still, I'm less interested in the content or underlying science than I am in how you and I—and the students— might think or feel about it."

We were already discovering the differences in how we would approach our research plan. Gloria's natural tendency was to consistently step back into context.

"Yes," I retorted, "but we are developing an engineering ethics class, so it also has to include the underlying science and philosophy. It's about the content too. That's what accreditation calls for."

We were heading into a new arena for teaching engineers and, despite some challenges between us, it would turn out that we had the perfect combination of approaches. I was excited to be developing something new. While I had some trepidation about doing research with Gloria, I would never have approached engineering ethics in this way without her encouragement. She was focused on how our studies and immersions might open us up. Rather than "learning about" and "applying" ethics—the old teaching paradigm—we would be pointing towards a process of "becoming" ethical— changing our "way of being."

Gloria had been reading the work of Francisco J. Varela, a Buddhist practitioner and cognitive psychologist whose book *Ethical Know-How* described an embodied ethics—linking Confucian ethics with Buddhist epistemology. Varela's ideas had a big impact on her. I was appreciative and grateful to Gloria for bringing his ideas to me, as they reinforced the idea of bringing eastern ethics into the conversation.

We realized that, while we might not be able to teach engineers to be more self-reflective—as they might become with years of meditation or other practices—at the very least, we could encourage students to understand what drives their decisions. This solidified my commitment to do the same. We were getting to the heart of something we both found intriguing: how does an individual become ethical and apply that to how they live and affect the world?

With that notion, our sabbatical journey was charted. We would crisscross the globe seeking insight into how to shift the mindset of engineers from Descartes' linear-reductionist thinking to nonlinear-holistic thinking. During the course of this journey, the project would become personal, shifting my own mindset. In the process of developing and eventually teaching a course on ethics, I was also addressing the question: how do I become me? Attempting to answer this question would lead me into a new way of thinking, all the while challenging me to expand from the "how this would be presented to my students" position to "how I would integrate this into my being and be myself" with them.

THERE WAS CHEMISTRY between Paul and Gloria when we visited France that summer. She seemed to come alive when they conversed with each other in a way I hadn't observed since our own early days together. I could see in their conversation that Paul had an ability to listen and then reflect and add to whatever Gloria was saying. They almost seemed to be dancing with their words and energy.

Was this the very thing Gloria was wanting from me? If it was — why couldn't I simply learn how to do it?

I felt challenged to up my game.

I didn't have the same ease with Françoise. On the other hand, Gloria felt drawn to Françoise as well. She was widely read on eastern philosophy; she was an artist—ceramics was her medium—and she possessed a spirit of enlightenment.

Paul seemed interested in exploring a relationship that was like what we had with Lisa and Steve, but it soon became clear that, despite her graciousness, Françoise wasn't in alignment with Paul. She made it clear she was only interested in friendship. While I genuinely liked her, I also felt awkward. At some level, I felt rejected. That she didn't want to participate would create a logistical and emotional challenge for me if Gloria and Paul wanted to explore intimacy.

But the plot was thickening, as I too found Paul intriguing and enjoyed his attention as well. That he had a doctorate from a prestigious university meant that he could be an intellectual match for me. He had written his dissertation on the psychological aspects of Jean-Jacques Rousseau's philosophy and had published several peer-reviewed articles on the subject. That was impressive to me. To my delight, he could converse with me on any subject. However, because his years of working with consciousness change meant he had insights into the nature of the mind and the work we were wanting to develop for our ethics project, his knowledge and experience felt a little intimidating to me.

I was conflicted. On the one hand, I was aware that I could learn much from Paul. At the same time, I felt insecure revealing what I didn't know. And I felt a bit of dismay at how he charmed Gloria. Still, my overriding goal of creating the "perfect" course trumped whatever insecurity I felt. Insecurity was a new feeling for me, and I didn't know what to make of it.

We would spend considerable time with Paul and Françoise in France and later in Berkeley, leading to a significant turning point in our own relationship. Paul would also have a major influence on our experiential research for the engineering ethics course, beginning with one of his first recommendations. When he was consulting with a firm in Southern India, Paul had met an Ayurvedic practitioner, Dr. Patel, and he and Françoise had continued to see him every winter for treatments.

"The holistic philosophy of Ayurveda might add an experiential aspect to your ethics research. We can meet you there," Paul said enthusiastically during our first visit to France. "At least you can give Ayurveda a try for your sciatic nerve issue, before you consider back surgery."

"We'll arrange the treatments with Dr. Patel for you," Françoise chimed in, "and reserve a room at the hotel where we will be staying too."

Gloria agreed that this experience might be the perfect way to begin our research project. If it meant I could learn something of what made Paul so attractive to her, despite my trepidation, I was up for another trip to India. Perhaps, if I could truly denounce Descartes' prescription and overcome compartmentalizing where I was all parts and no sum, this might all work for me.

I could become a non-linear human being.

When only two people are involved, it's much easier to have the illusion of causality. But add a third and a fourth, and there is no illusion—chaos ensues.

Was this Descartes' dilemma?

Chapter 15

No-Self

Man was born free, and he is everywhere in chains.
—Jean-Jacques Rousseau

"I'M SO HAPPY TO BE BACK in Mother India," I said as we veered through the streets of Kovalam Beach. It had been seven years, and the sweet memories of our first time there were fresh in our minds.

"She just kind of wraps her arms around you," Gloria replied. "Doesn't she?"

"For sure," I said. "I'd forgotten just how strong a connection and love I have for this place."

We were in one of India's many patched-together yellow and black taxis on our way to meet Dr. Patel. I sat back and took it all in. The gentle breeze off the Arabian Sea, the scent of incense from the Hindu temples, the endless array of coconut palm trees, and the sing-song cry from the women on the beach—"pineapple, coconut, papaya"—seemed to welcome me home. The vivid sense of aliveness and acute awareness I'd felt during our first visit to India had returned in a flash.

A couple of days later, my experiential research for our ethics course began. I found myself lying face-up on a wooden table under a bowl suspended a few inches above my forehead. A small opening at the bottom of the bowl was releasing a steady drip of herbal infused sesame oil that landed exactly between my eyes. Within three or four minutes, I was in a very relaxed state. Despite that, The Professor remained committed to the task.

"How does the *Shirodhara* drip work?" I asked in a voice that sounded low-pitched.

"For your western mind," Dr. Patel said, "the drip relaxes the hypothalamus gland."

"And for your eastern mind, what does it do?" I asked.

"*Achha*, there is no cause and effect," he responded, shaking his head from side to side in that characteristic Indian gesture. "It treats a whole range of systemic issues in your body — physical, psychological, and spiritual — all together. It is very complex. I cannot explain it. It's metaphysical."

"I'm totally confused," I said, although I did remember Vic saying something similar regarding holding relationships metaphysically. Maybe the treatment was allowing me to be forthright in admitting my confusion. "That sounds contradictory to me. If there is no cause and effect, then how could the drip treat certain specific issues in my body?"

He smiled. His kind manner put me at ease as he offered a way of explaining the difference between western and eastern medicine that made sense to me.

"Western medicine is concerned with treating a patient's organs—the heart, kidneys, pancreas—and their physiological systems—digestive, endocrine, and so on."

I nodded yes in agreement as I lay on his wood table, which had at least seven generations of sesame oil absorbed into its micro-cracks and crevasses—at least that is what he had told me.

"That is a reductionistic and deterministic approach to health and healing," Dr. Patel explained. "Eastern medicine is concerned with treating the person as a whole—a holistic and subjective approach to healing. Diagnosis and treatment are open to interpretation by the practitioner, and good health can emerge from an interactive relationship with the patient."

Essentially, he was saying that the human body is greater than the sum of its parts, including a person's energy, feelings, and thoughts, in addition to discrete pathologies. It occurred to me that this might represent another example of emergence that Gloria and I could relate to ethics. Engineering the physical elements of a system—a bridge or even a nuclear power plant—is complicated, whereas assessing the risks and benefits of systems with emergent properties is complex, as in eastern medicine.

As I lay there with my hypothalamus relaxing, I felt my initial confusion subside. Describing the shift from linear to nonlinear behavior when an automobile encounters an icy road is easy to understand—most drivers have had such an experience. And now I had a graphic example of an open living system—the human body—with consciousness as the emergent property. I thought about using these examples as a way to begin integrating complex systems into my risk analysis class and introducing nonlinear thinking in the ethics class.

Imagining how I could teach something is a sure sign I'm getting it. If I get the difference between complicated and complex systems, students probably will as well. And, hopefully, I'll see how that difference applies to me.

While I was taking a baby step in changing my worldview, it felt significant. Maybe I was beginning to see and interpret the world the way Jackie Margoles did—not just as a collection of interacting parts but also as a set of relationships among the parts from which a property of the total system emerged. I was also seeing how this difference might apply to the interactions between Gloria and me. In fact, that is how we had eventually arrived at our sabbatical project.

Following that discussion with Dr. Patel, I started realizing that human consciousness experienced through feelings, thoughts, and physical sensations could also be considered an emergent property of the human organism. I began to understand that consciousness is not located in any one organ or physiological system of the human body but is an emerging phenomenon of the whole body. That worked for The Professor—a nice, clear understanding of the way the mind works. I looked forward to further conversations exploring these ideas with Paul during our afternoon meetings.

"IF YOU HAD TO CHARACTERIZE engineering in a word or two, what would it be?"

That had been one of Paul's first questions to me a few days after we arrived in Kovalam Beach. We had been exploring these ideas during regular afternoon meetings, sitting on the balcony of our hotel, facing the beach along the Arabian Sea.

"Utilitarianism," I'd replied automatically. I didn't need to think about it. But bringing ethics into the equation would require something more than an automatic answer, and Paul's contributions would prove critical in that area.

One afternoon I brought up the insight I had during my discussion with Dr. Patel regarding holistic systems, emergence, and consciousness. I recalled how I translated Patel's explanation of eastern medicine to consciousness as awareness—awareness of self, others, and the surrounding environment via feelings, thoughts, and sensations. Paul added that consciousness was also about making meaning or interpreting awareness by what he called "making up a story," a phrase similar to one Jackie had used. We talked about how humans can cultivate a sufficiently high level of awareness, giving us the ability for self-reflection.

The extent to which I understood that it's all a story—depending on how we draw a boundary—helped me integrate all that I had learned from Landmark, Morehouse, Jackie, and science. The wholistic medicine of Patel, ancient as it was, left me directly feeling the implications in my body. Discussing with Paul how my mind had worked when I was in such an opened-up state was helping me understand what had been sorely needed in my own life, and what Gloria encouraged: why and how to turn inward. Now I was left with the question of why turning inward was so scary to me.

Over the next days, our conversations ranged from the differences and meaning of paradigm, context, and content and how they forge an individual's worldview and how culture shapes a society's worldview. Paul and I relished exploring "distinctions" to increase our understanding of how and why cognitive processes make meaning out of life, thereby giving rise to value systems and ethics. This was exactly what I needed to prepare myself for developing the ethics class.

"Can you make a general statement defining a distinction, as you see it?" I asked him after one of my Ayurvedic treatments.

"A distinction is a linguistic phenomenon that brings something into being as a presence, where previously there was no presence," he began. "When you call some-thing 'beautiful,' something 'not beautiful' comes into existence as well."

He paused to see whether I was following him.

"The front and back of a hand are distinct, yet both are still an integral part of the hand," Paul continued.

"Whether you consider the front or the back, there's still the whole entity of a hand."

From the way Paul seemed to think and the questions he asked me, I began understanding the distinctions Jackie had taught at a whole new level. However, with Jackie I had often felt criticized and like a failure. With Paul, it seemed we were embarking on a mutual exploration. We treated each other as colleagues, regardless of who had more knowledge of a subject. I always felt understood by Paul. My conversations with him were so rich they compensated for whatever discomfort I had begun to feel regarding his flirtation with Gloria. Of course, I had explicitly agreed to this flirtation—so I was surprised when I felt jealous. This was a new feeling for me and one that I tried to ignore and rise above.

Paul, Françoise, Gloria, and I usually took our evening meals together, engaged in light-hearted conversations about our treatments, Indian culture, and our interactions with the local people. Sometimes we spoke about esoteric subjects—mostly about non-duality and how it lived in Françoise—and how these subjects were associated with values, ethics, and morality. We usually ended the day with dessert and a game of Canasta at a coffee shop called the German Bakery. Meeting each year in India for Ayurvedic treatments during winter break became a ritual for the four of us over the next three years.

A few days before Paul and Françoise left India, they introduced us to a European friend of theirs, Martin, who lived part-time in Kovalam. They thought we would enjoy meeting him and that he might have something to offer us in the way of tips for our further travels in India. When we met Martin and told him what we were up to, he suggested we visit his spiritual teacher, Ramesh Balsekar, who lived in Mumbai. His description of Balsekar's teaching felt very relevant to our quest for a more comprehensive approach to engineering ethics. What had been The Professor's quest for excellence in the ethics project was shifting and becoming a compelling quest for self-exploration; something was profoundly shifting in me. Saying goodbye, we arranged to meet Paul and Françoise in France the following summer where they were now living—in the home her deceased father had built—and set out for Mumbai.

"Since I'm an engineer who works on environmental issues, do I have a moral obligation to help clean up the environment?" I asked Ramesh—quite bravely, given what had happened when I asked Papaji a similar question.

Gloria looked at me incredulously, as if she couldn't believe I was bringing this up again.

We were in Ramesh's apartment for the *Satsang* he held every morning. Once again, I was sitting on the floor in front of an Indian guru. Still feeling a little stung and confused by Papaji's admonition to clean up my mind, I was trying again to get an answer, but this time from the ethical perspective that could be useful for our engineering class. I was hoping to receive an example of how eastern philosophy might resolve an ethical issue in the real world. Even more important, perhaps I could get an understanding of what Papaji was trying to get me to see. And Ramesh seemed like someone who could respond to that.

Ramesh had had a professional career in banking, rising to become president of the Bank of India. All the while, however, he had also been a student of Nisargadatta Maharaj, a renowned teacher of *Advaita Vedanta*—the philosophy literally meaning "not-two"—commonly referred to as non-dualism. If I understood Ramesh, it basically means that what we perceive as separate is in actuality the same: Creator and Creation are one. Ramesh had integrated his "worldly" and "other-worldly" life, and when he retired from his position in banking, Nisargadatta had told him to "go teach."

"Consciousness is all there is," Ramesh began, in answer to my question, following with a quote he attributed to the Buddha: "Events happen, deeds are done, but there is no individual doer."

"Does that mean I should do nothing about the environment, then?" I asked.

"No, no, no," he said. "Do your best to clean up the environment. Then stand back and whatever happens—happens. It is God's will."

I was stunned by his answer. My grandfather had said the very same thing to me after my mother's death: it is

God's will. His statement had been the source of my childhood rage towards any form of deity.

Ramesh's words settled deep in my being. Was my mother's death God's will, after all? What about that lingering feeling that I was the cause of her death? Was her death God's fault or my fault? Or was it no one's fault, but rather the interaction of selfless conditions and circumstances, as non-duality might say? Certainly, the way Ramesh referred to God—nothing but the interaction of all consciousness as an entity—differed from my grandfather's way.

I let go of the questions in my mind and came back to the room. In answering me, I believe Ramesh was talking about non-attachment to outcome. This was the opposite of the work of an engineer, in which attachment to outcome drives the process. But Ramesh seemed to be talking about attitude, not product. It was attachment, he was saying, that leads to guilt and shame, or to pride and arrogance, both accompanying a sense of a personal "doer," separate from—rather than embedded in—a network of causes and conditions. I pondered this distinction, asking myself what it would be like to be free of these dualities in my mind.

I was also beginning to understand what cleaning up my mind might mean. In this context it meant, in part, giving up control—or thinking I actually had control—of the events in my life. I might not have caused my mother's death, especially if life isn't causal. It remained an open question for me. While I had certainly responded to her death as if I were the cause—with the accompanying shame and guilt that plagued me and colored my life—I began to realize that life isn't quite so linear. In that way, life is also about being able to course-correct, the same way a sailor maneuvers her boat in the face of wind patterns she cannot change, the same way I'd course-correct driving on an icy road. I was continually responding to circumstances I had little control over.

Ramesh was giving me an important understanding for bringing an ethical approach to engineering students. Science and technology—since Newton and Descartes—emerge from a linear mindset based on causality. The laws of physics are deterministic. Ramesh was saying that human behavior is not deterministic—the outcome you desire or seek is not necessarily the outcome you get. And that wasn't because you made a mistake. I could view his instruction to "stand back and whatever happens, happens" as congruent with the nonlinear nature of the new technologies, such as self-assembly of nano-chips, that exhibit emergent behavior. Unlike the process of building a safe bridge, there could be many outputs for a single input. Similarly, in my profession or in my personal life, attachment to any one outcome made little sense.

I was beginning to realize that my own attachment to outcome was manifest in my resistance to changing personal habits and attitudes. My stubborn defensiveness—trying to control a world that was scary to the little boy who lived inside me—had prompted me to interpret a suggestion for change as an attack. And that had left me unresponsive to Gloria's wants, needs, or desires. I especially reverted to these old patterns under stress.

I understand in retrospect that, for me, non-attachment also meant being open to criticism and change, having tolerance for ambiguity, and developing the ability to course-correct when receiving new information. These weren't necessarily new ideas for me. I'd been introduced to them in studying with Jackie, and even in the sensuality courses. Yet during these days in India, something was shifting anew in me, and I was able to take in these teachings with an open mind.

I wondered whether I might be receiving a transmission from Ramesh—a way of knowing or transmitting knowledge beyond my senses like what happened to me at Muktananda's Samadhi shrine years before. Or perhaps this information pointed to something that couldn't be explained, similar to what Patel told me.

Was this new awareness a story I was making up? Or was it simply an instance of "enough differences that made a difference" allowing for something new to emerge?

In either case, a new awareness seemed to be coming together in my mind. I could see that non-attachment to outcome was very much a part of the consciousness change I needed to integrate for myself and eventually teach. Now all I had to do was incorporate that understanding into my relationship with Gloria.

ONE MORNING ON OUR WAY to Satsang, Gloria and I got into an argument. It might have been about whether to walk or take a taxi, or where and when to have lunch—no doubt triggered by some unexpressed issue lurking between us. Unable to speak about it, we defaulted to the usual attack-and-defend dynamic. Always hopeful that spiritual teachings might offer us a higher perspective, Gloria asked Ramesh about the argument.

"The purpose of marriage is to fight with your husband or wife," Ramesh answered.

We both were a bit puzzled, and I immediately concluded that he just didn't have an answer in the domain of relationship. In hindsight, however, I believe he was echoing the thesis of John Welwood's book—a thesis reflected in our marriage vows—to use whatever issues that come up in relationship as opportunities for spiritual growth and deeper understanding. I now believe that Ramesh viewed the fighting to be about illuminating the patterns that needed to be deciphered. Without this very partner—Gloria—I might never have seen the issue that kept me separate and in that soul-cage Welwood spoke about. I was on the brink of actually understanding our marriage vows.

That night, lying in bed and listening to the sounds of Mumbai outside our bedroom window, I asked myself what I had been protecting in the morning's fight with Gloria. What did my reactivity illuminate about me? I could feel that I'd been defensive but still had no clear sense of why, except for my jealousy. How could I tell her

I was jealous when we'd explicitly agreed to explore with other people? And why was I so attached to projecting an image of being above that jealousy? What would have happened had I told Gloria I felt jealous of her attraction to Paul?

As I tossed and turned that night, I received some surprisingly clear insights. I recognized that I was making up a lot of stories and trying to control a lot of outcomes. While I felt relieved to make connections to the morning's teaching and the purpose of our fight, I noticed a great deal of fear associated with giving up control. I also had a glimmer of how that fear had kept me on the surface of my life.

It would be some time before I realized that Gloria probably would have been thrilled had I told her—thrilled not that I was jealous, but that I would tell her how I felt. I was determined to be a good Morehouse student, "giving her everything she wants." And if that included a man she found attractive, so be it. I didn't realize that what she wanted even more was my truth.

By morning, I had forgotten these fleeting thoughts and was back on the trail of our ethics project. Thus, I missed the opportunity to deepen my connection with my beloved. Still, the spark from these thoughts had ignited a fire within me. So before we left Ramesh's Satsang, I surprised myself by asking a very personal question.

"Why is it so scary for me to turn inward?"

He answered with another question. "What do you tell yourself about it?"

"That if I look inside myself, I won't find anything," I said. "There'd be nothing there."

He laughed with the kindness of a loving grandfather. As he spoke, I listened intently and interpreted what he was trying to tell me.

"There isn't anything to find. But that is good news," Ramesh said. "It's your true nature. It's all about genetics, conditioning, and the will of God. Nothing is solid or set in stone, but constantly in flux."

"Then why am I so afraid of it?"

"You are afraid of the story you make up about what you will find and that illuminates the lesson meant for you to learn: the lesson based on genetics, conditioning, and the will of God."

I was in a whirling vortex. My head and entire being swirled around, attempting to blend all the input I'd received in those six weeks in India.

The interactions I had with Patel, Paul and Françoise, and Ramesh had begun shifting the lens through which I saw and interpreted the world around me. My inner world was now coming into focus and the boundaries between the inside and outside were loosening. My view of a world that had been understood only through a reductionistic, deterministic, and objectivistic lens was slowly changing, like the turn of a kaleidoscope revealing new colors and patterns.

Several months after returning to the Bay Area, when Gloria and I were invited on a trip to the jungles of Ecuador, I said yes. I was ready to try a completely different way to experience consciousness change. Although I couldn't necessarily change my awareness, I could change the story I made up about that awareness.

"DO YOU KNOW THAT MEN have walked on the moon's surface?" one of the members of our group asked the Achuar tribal chief.

Gloria and I were in the rain forest of Ecuador, traveling along an upper tributary of the Amazon River. We were part of an eco-tour organized by the Pachamama Alliance—a non-profit focused on saving the rainforests and learning the customs and traditions of the native peoples. Our leaders were founders of the Alliance. Lisa and Steve, along with several other mutual friends, were also in this group.

As recommended by Huston Smith, Gloria and I had seen this as a chance to gather information from an Indigenous culture as part of our ethics research. And, just as important, it would be experiential research.

We started in the foothills of the Andes mountains, visiting several Quisha shamans along the way, learning about their culture and values. These were ancient peoples who had long been living close to the Earth. After many hops by bus, small airplanes, and longboats, we had travelled from Quito to an eco-lodge built by the

Achuar to earn some funds for legal fees to help them stop oil developers.

The Quishas' presence in the Andes grew out of the ancient Indigenous folklore of the eagle and the condor, they told us. The eagle, representing the mind and technological world, flies in the northern sky. The condor, representing the heart—the intuitive, feeling self—flies in the southern sky. That they fly in separate skies contributes to the mindset that gives rise to the global problems we face. As the lore goes, when the eagle and the condor can fly in the same sky, the world will come into equilibrium. This hypothetical concurrence precisely represented my personal challenge—the integration of my mind and my heart coming into equilibrium.

The Achuar, the indigenous tribe of this region, are a dream culture. They dream at night, sometimes using sacred medicine to enhance their dreams and visions, gathering in the morning to interpret their dreams. They allow their revelations to inform them as to their daily life. We learned that they had had a recurrent dream of a northern woman who would come to help them in their quest to save their land from the oil company. They needed to become educated in the knowledge and skills of the north for that to happen. At the same time, a northern woman, our guide, had been dreaming about them. She would learn their Indigenous wisdom, bringing it north. Their exchange would be the beginning of the eagle and condor taking flight in the same sky. Ultimately, they met, and she and her husband founded the Pachamama Alliance. We were thrilled and inspired by this story. It aligned perfectly with our intention to bring Indigenous culture to the study of ethics.

On our first night, our group was conversing with the tribal chief and elders through a double translation, English to Spanish and then Spanish to Achuar. We were all looking up at the full moon when someone posed that question, wondering whether news about the moon landing had reached what seemed to be an isolated jungle community. After a long pause, the chief had responded with one word: "Why?"

His body language told the story. The tribal chief wasn't looking for a Sir Edmund Hillary answer—climbing Everest "because it was there." Nor was he asking for an answer that justified the reasons for space exploration. As simple as his question was, it was profound. He was asking us to be introspective in a deep way and was making a statement, as we learned later that evening from our interpreter: why bother, when there are so many more important issues to resolve here on Earth?

I began to realize that we in the industrial northern hemisphere lose sight of the fact that, by looking at space exploration or other major scientific advances, we tend to ignore less glamorous earthly problems. It seemed like a call for me to encourage our students to work out our societal and environmental problems before we do things just because we can. The motivation behind developing new science and technology became something I wanted to explore as an ethical issue and provided yet another reason to personally understand my own motivation regarding the problems I worked on.

The chief then told us a tribe living upriver had set nets across the river so that fish—one of their staples—never made it down to their fishing grounds. That afternoon, he had held a tribal council with the village elders to decide whether to send a war party to fight or a peaceful party to negotiate with this tribe. My understanding was that the elders came to the meeting without any preconceived ideas of how to proceed, were open to all options, and continued to raise questions and give answers until consensus emerged. It was a holistic and emergent process—not unlike Jackie Margoles' process—an extension of the nonlinear physical processes I had been studying and slowly integrating into my teaching and research. Apparently, the elders discussed as many different scenarios as they could imagine—something we engineers would call "realizations" in a risk assessment study—until a course of action emerged.

As a result of their meeting, the tribe had chosen to negotiate. The chief and village elders had been introspective, seeming to carry out a risk-benefit analysis. I thought about the conflict on the India-Pakistan border with nuclear weapons at the ready, analogous to the spears and poison darts in Amazonia. The Achuar had confronted the universal issue of war or peace in a collaborative way. Our group would leave before the negotiating party returned, but we later learned that the conflict was resolved peacefully.

On the evening before we left the Achuar village, as part of a shamanistic ceremony, each member of our party was invited to lie down on a big banana tree leaf in the middle of a jungle clearing that was used as a runway for small single-engine aircraft. As I lay there, having taken the chief's sacred medicine—ubiquitous in the Amazon and becoming well known in the north—I could hear the jungle: the rustling of palm trees in the slight breeze, the howling of monkeys, and the cawing of birds, large and small. As daylight turned to dusk and then nightfall, I had an epiphany—the jungle flora and fauna and I were one and inseparable. There was no boundary between my body and the Earth's body—no boundary between my essence and the Earth's essence. The jungle was alive—as alive as I was. It was a profound lesson for me—a shift from learning about the environment to becoming part of the environment.

I had been thinking about what a shift in consciousness from a linear, reductionist mindset to a nonlinear, holistic mindset might be like. Here in the jungle, I actually experienced such a shift. It was a felt sense or embodiment of the holism of everyone and everything. Boundaries dropped away. There was no me. The trees and sky and all the creatures were vibrating a form of energy without boundaries or classifications. Rather than a separate being with a distinct boundary, I was pure light or nothingness, as I became one with the jungle.

This epiphany was also a breakthrough for The Professor. He understood—intellectually of course—that if the environment was healthy, I would be healthy; if the environment was damaged, then I would be damaged. He couldn't quite grasp it the other way around—if I were healthy in mind and spirit, the environment would be healthy. Over time, he would see that mind and spirit health would invite action, to do something that would affect that alignment.

In the days after that experience in the jungle and integrating that epiphany, I began feeling the connections amid all I had learned from the experiences and teachings I'd encountered during the previous few years.

My sabbatical was nearly over. Looking back on it, I realized that my mind had been getting cleaned up, as Papaji had suggested. Now all I had to do was create a syllabus and a course proposal—and integrate my new awareness into my relationship with Gloria.

Meanwhile, our relationship with Paul would continue to deepen as he increasingly became part of our research in creating the pedagogy and content for the course. The price I would pay for my intellectual enrichment with Paul would be the pain of feeling Gloria's increasing connection with him.

Chapter 16

Freeze and Flee

Everything that irritates us about others can lead to an understanding of ourselves.
—Carl Jung

"W"HAT'S THE DIFFERENCE BETWEEN resonance and coherence?" Paul asked me. "Can they be used to describe a group dynamic that achieves that elusive Aha moment?"

Paul and I were meeting in France, this time at an outdoor café in Aix-en-Provence, a beautiful walled city twenty miles from Marseilles, where he and Françoise were living. I'd been invited to give a series of lectures on reactor safety to a group of young scholars at Cadarache, the French nuclear research laboratory just north of Aix. This was a welcome chance for me to pick up the conversation he and I had started in India.

Paul always asked me great questions, mostly soliciting distinctions from me that I hadn't even thought of before, especially regarding a range of scientific and technical phenomena. He was one of the few men I'd ever met who wanted to know what I thought and how I felt about science and technology—and how both affected the natural and social worlds. He was the only person I'd engaged with who was attempting to translate my scientific and technologic acumen as a context for how individuals and groups process information—and he was including me in that exploration. While Jackie had also attempted to make bridges between her communication model and science—but on her own— Paul wanted my input to formulate his thinking. The collegiality was compelling. And he wanted to know me personally. I can't recall ever having that kind of relationship with a man, except perhaps with my college roommate. Paul and I were learning from each other— something that fed my soul.

Answering Paul's question led us to a discussion about how the concepts of resonance and coherence are often used interchangeably, although they are different physical phenomena. I explained that resonance had to do with exciting an object in its natural frequency, like Ella Fitzgerald singing a note that can cause a wine glass to vibrate and shatter—as seen in that TV commercial. Coherence has to do with the phenomenon that causes a photon beam to lase, wherein the stimulated emission of electromagnetic radiation, namely light, becomes a unified whole in space and time—the photons don't scatter. Paul understood my explanation, although I cannot recall which phenomenon best illustrated the Aha moment he was wanting to describe.

Paul had what I had considered a remarkable ability not only to understand himself but also to know others through his curiosity and patience. The more specificity he garnered by asking questions, the better he understood the person he was relating to. In fact, I hadn't realized that, before meeting him, I'd been habituated to providing information rather than questioning people and learning to understand them. As he'd been a transformational coach and trainer for more than forty years, he was a master at asking "interested" questions and getting to know people. Paul was becoming a role model for me. I was beginning to appreciate that the notion of consciousness change was also dependent upon being open and responsive to new concepts, ideas, and especially people and their way of understanding the world. No wonder Gloria was drawn to him.

Not only did Paul ask me questions about science, but he was also very interested in what I had learned from Morehouse and Vic, who he knew about from having lived in the Bay Area and whose teaching circles overlapped with his. He wanted to know about Gloria's and my relationship with Lisa and Steve—how that worked and what we got out of it. Paul also wanted to know how couples negotiated such relationships. I found his inquisitiveness illuminating.

ONE DAY I ENDED UP IN PAUL'S study while he and Françoise were discussing the possibility of having an expanded relationship with Gloria and me. It seemed that

Françoise wasn't interested in such a relationship. The question they were arguing about was whether they would open their relationship, at least for Paul. As they went back and forth, their emotions intensified.

"I don't want to be controlled," Paul said at one point.

I felt genuine compassion for them, as difficult discussions between Gloria and me often ended up with intensified emotions. "I can really feel how upset you both are," I said.

Taking in my response, Paul motioned for me to stay. He took a deep breath and, with a sigh of relief, turned to Françoise.

"Something you said obviously triggered me," he said. "I'm sorry. Give me a few moments."

As he sat down, I could imagine him looking inside himself. After several minutes of silence, he turned to Françoise. "Oh yes, of course, it was the look on your face that reminded me of my mother when she was angry with me."

Françoise smiled.

"Even though I know you weren't angry," he continued, "I can see how I reacted to you as if you were."

Françoise was relieved. Paul's noticing so quickly what had triggered him made me think of the time Gloria and I were arguing in the kitchen in Berkeley, and I had realized for the first time that something she said had triggered me, reminding me of my father's criticism. I had recognized that projection had been a one-off event for me and had left me embarrassed that those kinds of projection persisted. Now, seeing a projection happening for Paul—a man I assumed had great skill at sorting out others, yet finding himself in a similar predicament and observing the ease with which he opened to himself—was comforting to me. Watching Paul and Françoise have issues in their relationship despite years of self-exploration was also a relief to me. What struck me most was Paul laughing at himself as he took complete ownership of his reaction. It was a great lesson for me. I felt newly motivated to turn my attention towards my inner world too.

He made it look so easy.

Paul's pausing to look inward and then report what had triggered him exemplified the kind of quality Gloria regarded in him as vulnerability. It seemed he was not attached to how he looked or to some image he had of himself. I began to question why I was so reluctant—consciously or unconsciously—to reveal my own vulnerability.

How had I come to believe that such revelations were a sign of weakness?

Ultimately, Paul and Françoise arrived at an agreement to open their relationship, at least for him. Meanwhile, I was seeing my wife being drawn to this man, partly because he could be self-revealing and vulnerable. In much the same way I was traveling with Paul through the twists and turns of science and technology, and even the pitfalls of relationship, Gloria began taking similar journeys with him in conversations related to spirituality, psychology, and—no doubt—sensuality. I observed that he was just as curious with her sensually and energetically as he was with me intellectually. The questions he would ask her were more penetrating than any that occurred to me, and she loved it.

Now I can see what she was wanting. Why have I been so defensive?

While being defensive was troubling to me, I asked myself why I wouldn't or couldn't give her that kind of attention. The answer, once again, was that stubborn streak covering my insecurity and my fear of incompetence. I told myself that I refused to compete with Paul because of the incompetence I felt in this domain. But at the same time, I also enjoyed having him alleviate the pressure on me to satisfy Gloria's need for this kind of intimacy, leaving me to engage with her in the ways I did feel competent. So at first, having Paul in our lives was a relief. Now he could give her something she wanted. But before too long, this dynamic would become deeply troubling.

"I CAN'T TELL YOU WHAT I WANT," Gloria yelled at me. "Whenever I tell you what I want, you disappear. Don't you want to know me? I'm frustrated. No, I'm desperate."

I was quiet. I cringed. I was ashamed, and I was angry. Rather than follow the example Paul had displayed in his office with Françoise, calmly looking within, I turned to stone.

"How come Lisa can tell you what she wants, and you take it in?"

"Because she tells me how great I am," I responded in as calm a voice as I could.

Gloria glared at me.

"She makes me feel like a man. You just belittle me." My voice was slowly rising. "I can never win with you. Lisa always has me win, no matter what I do."

"Well then, I'm fucked." Her face had turned beet red. "Sure—when it's all about sex, you're attentive. Lisa knows how to sweet talk you. Of course you can hear her. She doesn't have to live with you and your damn stubbornness."

We were back in Berkeley after our trip to France, and at a low point. All the strategies we knew were failing us despite deeply caring about each other. I had retreated, hiding behind a distant wall. I knew this wasn't what Gloria wanted. It wasn't even what I wanted, but I felt powerless. Like an electric guitar played too close to a microphone, we were in a positive feedback loop that I couldn't change. Even if I had wanted to—and, at that moment, I didn't—I couldn't reach her. As usual, Gloria's thoughts and feelings had come at me faster than I could've taken them in. I couldn't keep up with her. In my mind, I was standing on the 77th Street subway station platform in Manhattan waiting for the local train, and the Lexington Avenue express had just roared by.

I was emotionally disappearing. The feelings in my heart were intense, and yet I didn't know—or couldn't express—what I felt. All I could do was blurt out, "I'm flooded"—a typical phrase Jackie suggested using when unable to take in any more information, but a phrase that tended to frustrate Gloria. She assumed that "I'm flooded" was intended to cut her off when I couldn't connect with her or didn't want to hear her. She was right. The combination of stubbornness, habit, and emotional illiteracy had raised its ugly head again.

"I'm finally learning to ask for what I want," she yelled, "instead of catering to a man or managing an irrational mother—and I need to shout it out—I need to say what I want, damn it! I want to say how I feel. I want you to be interested in what I want and not stonewall me. Why can't you be more like Paul?"

She later claimed that wasn't what she had said, but that was certainly the way I heard it. In either case, the comparison to Paul landed like a punch in the stomach.

Is my soul drawing me to this situation again to teach me something? What is the lesson? Did I not learn anything the first time around?

On two occasions, my first wife had become emotionally intimate with two men in succession. Even though their relationship had not been physical, these affairs of the heart cut into me perhaps more deeply, as they struck into the deficiencies of that motherless boy who had determined to protect himself from feeling pain. I seem to recall her telling me these men could listen intently to what she was saying and could reflect back to her what she was feeling.

They were always complementing her on her dress, her looks, and her views on life. They were romantic, and she felt "penetrated" by them, something I was now beginning to hear Gloria say about how she felt with Paul. I had been too shy to talk to a woman that way. I was not a charmer.

It had been easy for me to be romantic in my early days with Gloria. I now wondered what changed after we married. I remembered words I said to her at our wedding—words I felt perfectly comfortable reciting to her in front of our hundred or so wedding guests as I gazed deeply into her eyes: "I love you because you are real, acknowledging and unafraid of your past, strong enough to question the future. I love you because of your intuitive sense, always in the present with me, and always willing to confront our demons and shadows."

What happened to the courageous man who spoke these words?

Gloria's question prompted a painful reminder of the phrase I heard many times during my previous marriage: "Why can't you be more like them?" Now Gloria was charging me with the same deficiency, and I had no idea how to correct it. All the communication skills and sensual techniques, the journeys through the Amazon and India, and the sessions with enlightened masters hadn't been able to shift my tendency to freeze at the first sign of criticism or to ensure my ability to maintain an energetic connection with the woman I loved. While I could tell myself that I truly didn't know what I felt and that emotions were not this engineering professor's area of expertise, in fact, the way I simply gave up was The Professor's way of protecting me—by stonewalling my beloved.

Gloria's voice trailed off as she stormed out of the room—a move she'd often make when she was exasperated with a conversation. Our attack-and-defend dynamic had devolved into a freeze-and-flee dynamic: me freezing emotionally and Gloria fleeing, physically— literally—and emotionally, into the arms of another.

This freeze-and-flee dynamic had also been described in Dr. Johnson's book, *Hold Me Tight*, along with our attack-and-defend dynamic. According to Dr. Johnson, these two strategies, along with the blame game, are indicative of the most prevalent dynamics that therapists encounter in couples' work. Gloria and I would continue to step back emotionally or physically to escape hurt and fear and, before too long, while we didn't leave our marriage, we both looked to other partners for a solution.

"I'VE RUN INTO A BIG DILEMMA," I sorrowfully confessed to Fred and Mable. "Gloria has fallen hard for Paul."

Gloria and I were at the wedding of some mutual friends, and I was relieved to see my ESP guides from Morehouse, as I knew I could confide in them. When I explained the situation between Paul and Gloria, they began heaping praise on me: I was giving Gloria everything she wanted. Because the good boy alive and well in my unconscious had a high tolerance for pain when he thought he was doing a good job, their praise temporarily ameliorated the anguish I was feeling in my heart.

"But without Lisa in the picture," I said, "I feel terribly left out."

Gloria had been honest with Lisa and Steve about her feelings toward Paul when we returned from France. It wasn't appropriate for her and Steve to continue their physical intimacy—we had been in a STD-screening pod—now that she was intimate with Paul, which changed everything for them. So my relationship with Lisa ended too. Mabel had an immediate response when I explained this situation.

"It's simple," she said. "You need a new girlfriend. And to form a new screening pod."

That felt good. They always seemed to come up with workable and enjoyable solutions.

"Of all the women at this wedding, who would you pick?" Fred asked.

Precisely at that moment, Julianne appeared in my field of vision. Tall, sensual, recently single, a bodyworker with a master's degree in engineering, and Gloria's best friend—the friend who had taken the Forum and Morehouse courses with us. I looked into Julianne's eyes as she approached us and, before I even thought about it, I pointed my finger and the words rolled out of my mouth.

"I want her."

It didn't take long for Julianne and me to develop an intimate relationship that was exciting, satisfying, and a lot of fun. Still, during Paul's visits, I often felt parked with her. Even though she was beautiful and sexy, I was in pain. Many years later, a friend who had also been in the Morehouse program would remind me about the corollary to giving a woman everything she wanted, which, apparently, I had missed: "If giving doesn't feel good to you, don't give." But I didn't understand the nuance at the time. And despite the difficulties in our marriage, I loved Gloria and didn't want to lose her. I was thoroughly confused and conflicted, and I was living out yet another dichotomy.

Of course, I tried to deny the pain. After all, I genuinely enjoyed my own growing connection with Paul and with Julianne, and I was getting accolades from my teachers at Morehouse for being so adept at an expanded relationship that gave Gloria what she wanted—all of which made it nearly impossible to say no and perhaps be seen as a failure. During Paul's visits, I'd spend afternoons shopping, running errands, or attending to my academic affairs. Most evenings were spent with Julianne, but I wanted to be with Gloria and Paul, and I increasingly felt left out and insecure. A crack in The Professor's armor was growing—a crack that frightened me.

Before Paul, I had grown to take Gloria for granted. Now that had changed. I coveted and protected the time I had alone with her. Rather than pour my heart out to her — telling her how much I appreciated her and why — I played it safe, focusing on our ethics project. But even there, I didn't tell her how much I valued her input in bringing the course together. Somehow, thinking it was obvious, I didn't tell her that I admired her mind and her creative ideas. It seemed to me that our travels had brought us closer together in the rational and spiritual domains and that, despite our difficulties, we had become better communicators. But I didn't dare ask her whether she felt the same way. We were more compassionate and kinder to each other but, when we fought, we were also more triggered. Oddly enough, I became more comfortable with the fights, as they seemed to clear the air.

In reality, I was falling in love with Gloria all over again — but I neglected to woo her all over again. At the same time, however, Gloria would begin anticipating Paul's next visit in the weeks before he arrived, and she would feel saddened in the weeks after he'd left. During those periods of time, I felt as if I had lost her.

PAUL WAS VISITING AGAIN. "Bill and I have been talking about shifting engineering ethics education from learning about ethics to become ethical," Gloria said. "What do you think are the attributes that could enable an engineer to become ethical?"

"That's a great question," Paul responded.

"We've also been talking about an ethical approach that's congruent with the characteristics of nonlinear or complex systems," she continued.

"So, let's begin with the three characteristics of nonlinear systems," I said, "holism and emergence, stochastic or chaotic behavior, and subjectivity."

We were off and running on what would become a unique way of introducing ethics into engineering programs. Despite—or in addition to—Gloria's attraction to Paul, he had become an integral part of developing our engineering ethics course. In working together, I disregarded my own feelings of insecurity, jealousy, and pain. Instead, I focused on the intellectual connection we three shared and the personal satisfaction of creating an innovative course. And we were having fun. This kind of relationship was certainly gratifying for The Professor. He knew how to help me overlook the things that tugged at my heart. After all, he was experienced at it, having allowed me to stay in my first marriage long after it had ceased to be viable. There should have been an alarm alerting me not to be so willing to sacrifice what my heart wanted for the sake of what my head needed. If such an alarm was sounding, I couldn't hear it—yet.

Over the next few months, the three of us wrote the context for an engineering ethics course based on our collective life experience and the sabbatical travels Gloria and I had made to the Amazon and India. After hours of rich and deep discussion and many email exchanges, an integration of our ideas emerged. Ultimately, we were able to define three distinctions that we believed might enable the change in mindset we were after: holism, transparency, and responsiveness. Having agreed on this foundation, we began to envision giving students a sense of how to experience the meaning behind each distinction.

The first distinction, holism, recognizes that the practice of engineering and the development of technology do not occur in a vacuum, but rather within a social, economic, political, and cultural milieu. Assuming that is so, the second distinction, transparency, requires engineers to make explicit to that milieu, via self-reflection and dialogue, their engineering judgments, and technical processes. And these two distinctions led to the third distinction, responsiveness. Being responsive means being in a feedback loop with the milieu and includes the ability to remain provisional as more information becomes available via feedback from the milieu. Responsiveness concludes with an understanding that ethical thought and action emerge out of an integration or convolution of these three distinctions and the technological system under consideration.

Personally, these distinctions were giving me a map for our course and, more importantly, a map for my own life. I'd had a visceral experience of holism in the Amazon—participating in the shamanistic ceremony when my sense of individual self had disappeared into the oneness of the natural world. After that experience, I'd started realizing that I had been approaching my life in the same way I had been approaching engineering problems—with blinders on—focusing on the issue at hand without seeing the larger picture. Similarly, at home, I focused on my work, leaving my wife and my heart behind. I needed to be able to hold my personal and professional domains "metaphysically" in the way Vic had suggested I attend to Gloria.

My view of transparency had coalesced after my discussion with the Indigenous chief I'd met in Ecuador in the context of my extraordinary soul-opening experience. The inclusive group consensus process he and his tribe had used to reach an agreement seemed to be at the core of human resolution, imbedded in the natural way of things. At the same time, listening to Paul and Gloria share their inner process made me deeply appreciate the need to be personally self-reflective—to know myself—and to bring my own internal process forward. I needed to make my internal reality transparent to Gloria in a way that felt real to her. However, self-reflection became real to me only when transparency was translated into an ethic. And still, often, when I felt deeply emotionally charged, I would freeze, unable to recognize what I was feeling.

My view of responsiveness had coalesced with our visit to Ramesh and the discussion of non-attachment to outcome. I began to realize that, in being attached to outcome, curiosity is lost, and that sustaining curiosity is what allows engagement in dialogue—wherever it takes one. Responsiveness allows new ideas and possibilities to emerge in a non-linear way. If engineers could grasp this shift in mental processing, it would enable them to be more creative and to stay open to the possible unintended consequences that technologies might bring, and that might eventually lead to change.

Personally, this view meant remaining open to and curious about Gloria—expressing my desires, being responsive to her desires, and engaging in a dialogue leading to a way of being together that worked for both of us. The intimacy between Gloria and me had been deepening. I wondered if this was happening because I was feeling more vulnerable and responsive. Perhaps she could feel it.

Our goal in developing an ethics course was to give students an experience of becoming ethical, beyond just learning about ethics. But how could I offer this to students before I had made that shift in myself? As I was a long way from incorporating these distinctions seamlessly into the fabric of my being, I was naïve in my thinking. The question remained also of how to engage students in a classroom setting in ways that would make ethics relevant. Resolving that would take several years.

We had immersed ourselves in the practices of various traditions that had left me more open, intuitive, and better able to sense and feel an expanded version of truth. The realizations I'd had of the need for change were now part of my being. Eventually, I hoped to inspire students toward that end: that it would no longer be necessary for them to rely on rules and principles to analyze right and wrong or good and bad, but instead to incorporate the three distinctions evincing a sense of ethical know-how in the same way an experienced driver knows how to navigate an icy road. But how could I give the students in a classroom a taste of those experiences? I knew what to point them towards, even if didn't know how to take them there.

In hindsight, I can see that a shift from learning about ethics to becoming ethical was also about a personal shift from learning about me to becoming myself. Like the novice who must learn the rules and principles of the chess game before becoming a master player, becoming myself would require knowing about me first. It would require a shift from relying on rules and principles to guide my life to being informed by my life—living moment to moment—changing the course of my life as I took in, digested, and metabolized new information. I'd be letting life find me.

My relationship with Paul was imprinting something new for me. The price I paid was the pain of sharing Gloria. It was difficult for me to admit that I wanted to learn how he could satisfy her in ways I couldn't.

Chapter 17

The Gap

It is true that we think of teachers teaching students, but it is also the case that in an interactive environment the students teach the teachers.
—Hubert Dreyfus, On the Internet

Our course launched in the College of Letters and Science for the spring semester of 2002 as Ethics and the Impact of Technology on Society, upon the recommendation of my dean and approval by a committee of the Academic Senate. It was quite rare for a husband and wife to teach a course together, nepotism being an issue. However, Gloria and I weren't concerned with nepotism—we were facing other challenges. During the months of preparation before the launch of our course, we faced the question of how we would implement our original idea about a shift in pedagogy from learning about ethics to becoming ethical. It was a shift that proved to be elusive, especially for me. And even though I was planning several lectures on non-linear systems using the automobile on ice example, developing a process for shifting the students' mindset from linear to non-linear thinking was daunting. Practically, though, we were facing something more basic: learning to integrate our different goals and approaches to teaching the course material.

"I know it will be very difficult to help students think non-linearly, given what it took to do it ourselves — to whatever extent we actually have succeeded. Still, don't we need to challenge the students to, at least, get 'meta' to their thinking and to question it?" Gloria asked. "If they could understand that their assumptions, values, and beliefs are essentially stories they make up, wouldn't that help change what they think are fixed truths? Wouldn't that be amazing?"

"I just don't see how we could do that in a class of a hundred and twenty students," I responded. "I'm sorry, but the class is going to be too big. We've got so many topics we want to cover, including eastern philosophy and religion."

"In the Forum, there were more than three hundred people in the room," Gloria said. "We could work with a few students on any given day, as an example. I know it would be challenging, and a new way for them to learn."

"It's not part of the course description, nor what the University is expecting from us," I struggled to add, noticing that I was disappointing her.

"I still think the first step on the path to becoming ethical is a growing acumen that comes from looking inward."

After thirty-five years in academia, I had been recognized nationally as an innovative teacher by my peers, having been awarded two distinguished teaching awards. Moreover, I had developed a style of lecturing, creating exams, and grading that I was comfortable with. I'd even developed a dozen or so new courses over the years as my interests changed. But the formula I used never changed. My approach had been to develop the course material first—the content—and then, as I became more and more knowledgeable in the subject material, I developed the context. So my practiced approach to teaching students utilized the same formula—beginning a course with the content and then letting the students draw their own conclusions about context.

Gloria's vision for teaching the course was very different from mine. Since she had learned inductively using the Socratic method in law school, she envisioned something similar for our ethics course.

"Isn't the purpose of the course to teach students critical thinking about their own arguments and those of others?" she asked.

I nodded yes.

"The method they used in law school seems to easily lend itself to teaching ethics," she explained. "It requires students to articulate, develop, and defend how they would resolve an ethical dilemma that may be, at first, an imperfectly formed intuition. We can help them explore how they arrived at their conclusion by diving into their mindset and contrasting their ideas with the theories we're teaching."

"But this is not the way I learned engineering—or have ever taught it," I said, cutting off her enthusiasm. "I've been at this for a long time, Gloria. You're being idealistic."

Changing my approach to teaching would have challenged me to try something new. Change had always been difficult for me. I realized that a big part of Gloria's motivation for the whole ethics project was personal—for us to understand ourselves better. It was mine as well. But I was already challenged, teaching a new subject. My need to master the content took precedence over using the course as grist for the mill of personal growth.

Although I tried to give Gloria's ideas credence, I silently justified my rationale based on her teaching inexperience. While I knew what worked and what didn't work in the classroom, I did appreciate her novel ideas. To my surprise, I judged myself in equal measure for something I couldn't admit: that I didn't know how to execute her ideas.

In hindsight, all she really wanted was for me to be able to expose my vulnerability to her. Admitting my struggle would have actually connected us. Instead, like a true patriarch, I just told her what we were going to do, which, of course, created more distance between us.

However, during our preparation for the course, I received a Call for Proposals from the National Science Foundation offering $25,000 grants to develop full proposals focused on innovation in engineering education. Deciding to apply for the funding, Gloria, Paul, and I put our heads together and proposed a workshop—one that would delve into the very things that Gloria wanted to do: change the thinking of engineers through engineering ethics education and explore a more inquiry-based teaching style. The time spent on writing the workshop proposal would negate the question of designing a new approach for our upcoming course. But writing the proposal would give us a definite project to work on with Paul that would pay for his travel and his efforts.

When we began teaching—despite the fact that we had decided to stick with my format—I was still challenged sharing and negotiating my autonomy in the classroom. I was caught in a familiar dichotomy: not only did I judge her performance, but I was insecure that she would see things that eluded me in a similar way as had happened when we were with Papaji in India.

Gloria *did* see things that eluded me. And, while I had gladly given her the job of informing me of new ideas early in our relationship—and loved her for it, this was different. Now, when her ideas seemed to challenge mine, I resented her for it. Combine that with my concern that she would explain things similarly to the way Jackie did when trying to elicit a non-linear response, I was in a quandary. If those complex ideas were over my head, I worried that the students wouldn't get them either. My growing resentment created another wedge between us that I hadn't anticipated. The excitement of working together became a struggle for me and, rather than using that struggle to enlighten myself or us, I tried to solve it.

On our first course evaluation, a student made this comment: "I sometimes got the feeling when you guys were lecturing that I was home having dinner with my mom and dad, witnessing an argument between them." In our joint teaching experience, it wasn't unusual for me to ask Gloria to comment after I explained a subject. She might use the opportunity to demonstrate a mindset difference by saying how she viewed the subject another way. We'd go back and forth with each other in front of the class, so I could see how the student could have imagined bickering parents.

It was difficult enough for me to navigate our differences at home. I refused to put the students through it with us and expose our foibles.

While the course evaluations were good in general, they were not as good as I was accustomed to. I had been right that some of the students didn't understand what she was trying to get across, in much the same way that Jackie couldn't get her ideas across to me or to my colleagues.

Gloria and I ultimately recognized that trying to combine our teaching styles was too distracting for the students. We simply had to split up the lectures, as I'd done with colleagues when we team-taught a course. One of us would sit down while the other ran the class, giving each other a chance to comment at the end.

For future offerings of the class, we followed this formula. The reviews proved that was the easier method for the students — although not necessarily for us.

SURE ENOUGH, I WAS AWARDED the funding from NSF. Supplemented with funds from my dean and my endowed chair, we invited about fifty individuals to participate in the workshop — scholars and practitioners from a variety of disciplines: western and eastern philosophy and religion, psychology, social science, and, of course, engineering. Included were also a Native American tribal member and a Sufi Master. We assembled at an off-campus center in April 2003 for several days to explore a set of questions Gloria, Paul, and I had determined would give us the kinds of responses we would need to write the full proposal for teaching ethics in a newly proposed context. I opened the workshop with some welcoming comments and then proceeded to introduce the subject matter.

"We are entering a new millennium with emerging technologies that pose ethical dilemmas far beyond what conventional wisdom can offer in resolving them," I said.

I went on to explain the complex nature of these technologies and offered a sampling of the ethical dilemmas we, as a society would be facing. Gloria spoke briefly about mindset change and the question of shifting from learning about ethics to becoming ethical, and how engineering curricula, as structured, hadn't changed much in sixty years — since the end of World War II. Paul concluded the first session by stressing the need for change, defining mindset and consciousness change, and masterfully facilitating the remainder of the session as the participants spoke about their interests, backgrounds, and what they hoped to contribute to our task.

Over the next few days, we organized several breakout groups that considered and answered our questions and, after each breakout, reported back to the group at large. It was a rarified experience hearing the creative ideas of a dynamic, well-informed and intentioned, cross-disciplinary, and cross-cultural group.

"After taking in all of your wisdom—your advice, suggestions, and proposals," I said at the closing, "I believe we not only need to recontextualize engineering ethics education itself, but perhaps we need to recontextualize all of engineering education as well." After a brief pause, and almost as an afterthought, I said, "Maybe all of higher education too."

To this day, I don't know where those statements came from, because they were not in my prepared closing remarks. It seemed as though they were channeled through me.

When Gloria, Paul, and I went to dinner that night, we were flying high: they marveled at my vision; I was extremely satisfied with the skill and presence that Paul generated in facilitating the workshop—I'd never witnessed him in action; and Gloria seemed thrilled being with the two of us. The "three-body problem" of classical physics, while it leads to chaos for most initial conditions, at this point for us seemed to be creating a level of stability and creativity that none of us could have brought about alone. We were quite the threesome.

In hindsight, the proposal we prepared and ultimately submitted to NSF was audacious. Our project, if successful, would change the so-called Science-Based Engineering Curriculum—a curriculum that had led to landing men on the moon, inventing the Internet and wireless communication, and, of course, building nuclear power plants—to an Ethics-Based Engineering Curriculum focused on social responsibility and engineers' inner awareness. This change, we hoped, would be accomplished by integrating experiential learning with didactic learning—introducing the concept of *praxis:* a set of personal and professional practices with the goals of enhancing self-awareness and embodying the complexity, uncertainty, and ambiguity inherent in the emerging technologies. It was a big idea. We crossed our fingers.

NOT SURPRISINGLY, EMOTION became an important consideration in our ethics course. It wasn't something we included in our workshop, course material, or even in our NSF proposal, but it kept coming up in our research. Emotions were often portrayed as subjective judgments that posed a threat to rationality and morality. Accordingly, for engineers in general, and me in particular, being rational usually meant sequestering emotions that might bias analyses—indeed, good reasoning is tied to quantitative analysis.

Traditional moral approaches have emphasized that rules, principles, and laws must govern ethics, whereas emotions have been portrayed as more primitive and less reliable than reason. Inherent to this view is the reason-emotion dichotomy—the notion that emotion and reason are two distinct kinds of things. In contrast, I found a growing scholarship suggesting that separating emotions and reason is a category mistake—that they are, along with sensation, aspects of consciousness. Emotions are not positive or negative, or good or bad. It's the context within which we are emotional—how we interpret or react to emotion—that gives them meaning.

The importance of emotion was also evident regarding our students. It became clear to us that students came to the study of ethics with some already solidly established values, assumptions, and beliefs to which they were strongly attached—knowingly or unknowingly. This meant that our class discussions often devolved, or evolved, into emotional reactions to ethical issues rather than following the guidelines of moral reasoning that is classical in a typical ethics class. We began to see that students could open to a new kind of understanding only after expressing their feelings about an issue. In truth, that was the way I needed to compartmentalize as well.

A perfect example of this came up in 2003 when Proposition 54 was placed on the California ballot which, had it passed, would abolish the Affirmative Action policy for admission to the University of California. It became a hot topic on campus and led to several student protests. I thought it was a ripe subject for discussion in an engineering ethics class.

During one discussion section, I raised the following question: "Is affirmative action a moral admission policy for the University?" I had anticipated hearing some discussion following the values and ethical principles we were trying to instill, such as humility, fairness, and the common good. Instead, students' reactions seemed entirely fueled by emotion—their immediate gut reaction.

I had invited two students with opposing views to the front of the class to explore how approaching the issue with moral reasoning might apply. As it turned out, I had to place myself between these two male students, both about four or five inches taller and thirty pounds heavier than me, fearing they would get into a physical altercation.

"Students should only be admitted to the University based on their high school grades and SAT scores," one vehemently declared.

"But don't the parents of the economically-disadvantaged and underrepresented minorities pay their taxes and support the University that their kids can't even get into?" the other young man responded loudly. "They need special treatment."

"So you're advocating a strict meritocracy," I said to the first student. "And you," turning to the other student, "are an advocate for social justice."

They both nodded their heads in agreement. Then I asked each of them how they came to their conclusions.

"From my father," the advocate for meritocracy said, "I grew up in Orange County."

"From my mother," the advocate for social justice said. "I grew up in San Francisco."

As the students agreed to disagree, shook hands, and walked away from the discussion section, newly understanding something about their mindset, I wondered: Was this the kind of approach that Gloria had in mind in the first place? That might have been the case, but I was discovering something even more profound for myself about the importance of emotion as an antecedent to moral reasoning and decision-making: how a particular emotional response was influenced by family-of-origin psychodynamics and societal milieu. It was also dawning on me that emotion was an antecedent to risk management. All of this constituted a big Aha for me.

Meanwhile, as she was combing the literature on emotion and ethics, Gloria began pondering the question of consciousness change from the angle of emotion: could emotion be a pathway that might lead to consciousness change? This was an important question to answer, not only for the two of us becoming more vulnerable and skillful, but in relation to a more expansive, holistic, and compassionate mindset.

As a result of her search, I became intrigued by Antonio Damasio's book, *Descartes' Error: Emotion, Reason, and the Human Brain*, and his critique of mind/body dualism: "the separation of mind and body, rationality and emotion." Based on his medical practice as a neurologist, instead of the presumed separation, Damasio proposed "a mechanism by which emotions guide (or bias) behavior and decision making ..." This certainly described what I was experiencing in the classroom with the students and outside the classroom with Gloria. Once there was a strong emotion present, resorting to reason and logic didn't work.

Was there a shortcut to solve this conundrum? Could I gain some traction out of the trap of linear causal thinking that would bring us the closeness and understanding I so desired?

It seems I was teaching what I needed to learn—and learning what I needed to teach. From early on in my relationship with Gloria, we had spoken at length about the impact our parents had had on us and how those impacts had led to our current-time projections. I also recognized my belief that emotions only got in the way of solving problems; I hadn't realized emotions were perhaps the key to unlocking the solutions. We became intrigued with understanding the role of emotion in conflict—and maybe even consciousness change.

What would this mean for us?

"BILL, YOU SEEM SO ANGRY and distant. What's going on?" Gloria asked, clearly distressed.

Paul had left that morning, returning to France after an extended visit with the two of us. Gloria had asked me how I could find the funding to bring him back to Berkeley to revise the curriculum proposal, based on the

NSF reviewers' comments. Their comments were very positive overall; however, they required we address the question of how we would evaluate the success of the program and we didn't yet have an idea of how to do that. Of course, I wanted to work on this with Paul. Still, rage was boiling up in me.

Instead of confessing my rage, I absolutely froze, as usual, in response to her question. As always, I had greatly enjoyed my in-depth conversations with Paul. I loved working with him and getting to know myself in relationship to him. It made me feel bigger and more expansive. But our connection was also confronting me with major feelings of inadequacy in the personal domain. I feared that it was he—not I—primarily satisfying my wife's emotional needs. But I couldn't find the words to say what that meant to me or how I felt. Before I had a chance to turn away, Gloria continued.

"This friendship with Paul and Françoise was supposed to bring us closer, but you feel farther away than ever," she said. "I don't know how to bridge the gap. I don't know how viable this is for us anymore. Or, for that matter, for them. I'm sensing this is becoming very difficult for Françoise and that doesn't feel good."

I didn't know how to bridge the gap either. I wondered how we would ever find each other again.

Did I want to be found? Did I want to find Gloria?

During his visit, Gloria and Paul had spent long afternoons together while I sat alone in my office on campus trying and failing to concentrate on a research paper about nuclear reactor safety, aware that Gloria might be getting from Paul the heartfelt connection I wanted with her. And I was beginning to realize that Gloria's relationship with Paul was becoming painful for me. I was still seeing Julianne, but was that what I really wanted?

Still, Paul's friendship and partnership were very important to me. He felt like the brother I never had, which made my internal conflict even more confusing and irreconcilable. Though I wasn't able to express it, I was consumed with pain—the pain of remembering my mother's directive to take care of my father, the awkwardness of arranging Paul's travel, the anguish of sharing my wife, and the pain of possibly losing a friend and brother.

Now our three-body problem was becoming unstable; the initial conditions had changed. I felt the gravitational pull strengthening for Gloria in Paul's direction and weakening in mine. Adding a fourth person—Julianne— might have provided stability but, more often than not, it didn't; the system was chaotic, the motion unpredictable. As long as Gloria and I remained intimate with other partners, nothing in the system seemed predictable. We had experienced creative highs and moments of deep intimacy. Now, something was amiss. While Gloria and I had believed we were on the cusp of a new way of living, our marriage within the third and fourth body of expanded relationship was not only becoming unstable— I felt it was flying apart.

IN THE MIDST OF ALL THIS, GLORIA'S mother died. That loss, along with the chaos of our relationship, left her feeling adrift in a sea of emotion. Hoping to sort things out, deal with the impact of her mother's death, and get back to her "core," she decided to go on a ten-day silent meditation retreat at a center north of San Francisco. This was something she had done several times before and had found the process clarifying.

While Gloria was away, I did some of my own introspection. Something had to change. The Professor's armor was cracking. All his life, he had been building layers of confidence to cover insecurity, and the strategy was no longer working. Opening our relationship to Paul had become grist for the mill in helping me make a change in consciousness, causing me to look inward instead of continually looking outward. Even the process of adding a level of complexity in my relational world had loosened my embeddedness in linear thinking. Paul had modeled for me a level of openness, but now I would have to act on that.

Could I?

I thought a lot about Gloria and our life together, especially as I lay in bed at night. In that stillness, I would reach out and feel the empty side of the bed. Touching her pillow, I imagined her there. I missed her. I wasn't just missing her company or even having her warmth beside me. I missed the promise of what we once had with each other. I wanted this woman. I didn't want to share her. And, I realized, alone in the dark, that I didn't want to share myself with Julianne. I wanted to be with Gloria. I asked myself why I couldn't have told her before she left what made it so hard for me to show my vulnerability. It had once been so easy to say, "I love you." Why, now, couldn't I simply tell her that I was hurt sharing her with another and that I felt insecure being compared to him?

Because I didn't display jealousy, she assumed I didn't care. Worse yet, she thought I didn't feel. The real problem was that I felt too much. Instead of simply telling her how I felt, I had angrily pushed her away.

What happened to the joy we'd felt finding each other — revealing myself to her and feeling her love?

Now I didn't know if I could ever figure out how to satisfy her. I wasn't sure she would even come back.

But she did come back, and I was glad to see her. She was quiet and somber as we sat down to dinner. Before she had a chance to say anything, I mustered all my courage and reached across the table to take her hand. There had been so many times in recent years when I reached for her like this and she'd have something on her mind or something unspoken lay between us, and she'd snatch her hand back. But not tonight. She seemed to gladly give it to me. I looked into her eyes. She looked back and began to speak.

"Bill, I did a lot of thinking ..."

I stopped her. "I'm so sorry I haven't been honest with you." Without waiting for her reply, I continued. "I love you and I missed you. I was hurt and insecure ..."

She interrupted me. As she began to speak, I held my breath, not knowing whether she was trying to be gentle as she delivered the final blow that would mark the end of our marriage.

"I can't do this anymore," she said.

My heart sank. This was it.

Her next words changed the course of our marriage.

"I can't be in expanded relationships anymore. Sometime during that retreat, I reconnected with my deepest truth, as I did at the very beginning of our relationship. I found you there. Deep in my heart, Bill Kastenberg. I want you and I love you."

I could hardly breathe. My heart was pounding.

"I made a commitment then to go as deeply as I could with you," she said. "Maybe we've gone as deep as we can. Still, I want to try harder. I want to be with you. Maybe I am deluding myself, but at least then I would know the truth. I don't know how you feel about Julianne, but I simply know that I can't go on anymore in this way. If that means losing you—while my heart will be broken—so be it."

"My heart is with you, my darling," I said, as I began to cry. "I'm yours."

I was relieved—and also terrified. Would I be able to satisfy her emotionally now that she's had this experience with Paul? Could we remain friends with Paul and

Françoise, and would those friendships remain rich and vital? Could we still be friends with Julianne?

And what about emotion? Could that be the key to unlock the door between The Professor's head and his heart?

Right now, though, none of that mattered as I took my beloved into my arms.

Chapter 18

Emotional Congestion

Limbic resonance supplies the wordless harmony we see everywhere but take for granted between mother and infant, between a boy and his dog, between lovers holding hands across a restaurant table.
—Lewis, Amini, and Lannon,
A GENERAL THEORY OF LOVE

GLORIA AND I WERE SITTING with Paul and Françoise in our living room with its big picture window facing the San Francisco Bay and the Golden Gate Bridge. It was June 2004. This was their first trip back to the Bay Area since it was decided that he and Gloria would no longer be intimate. This adjustment had opened the way for the four of us to have a new kind of intimacy—one in which I felt much more relaxed.

I poured the four of us a glass of Prosecco and, with a slight nod, held it up in a silent toast, welcoming Paul and Françoise to our home again. They had introduced us to Prosecco the first time we'd visited them in France, and this apéritif had become a ritual whenever we met.

"We are so grateful we've survived our years of sexual exploration and are still together," I said.

"And I want to appreciate you, Françoise, for your spaciousness during these past years," Gloria added.

"Thank you," Françoise responded, emotion in her voice. She and Gloria lingered a moment, gazing into each other's eyes.

Gloria reached out and took her hand. "It's really wonderful to have you both here with us in our home again."

Smiling in agreement, Paul asked, "How's your course and research going?"

"I'm fascinated by Damasio's work linking emotion and consciousness," I answered. "We also read Daniel Goleman's book, *Emotional Intelligence*, but I don't see any practical application of the work."

"They do put emotion on the map as critical to understanding cognition and its value in intelligence and consciousness change," Gloria said.

"I'm exploring emotion, too, in my consulting business regarding organizational change," Paul responded.

"I can't help wondering about the potential of emotional awareness — that it might be another key, short of meditating on a cushion for seven years," Gloria said. "We're interested in something useful for our class — even more important — for us."

Paul and Françoise were listening intently.

"You've witnessed our dynamic," I said with a big sigh. "It still persists. Even today, before you arrived, I found myself relating to Gloria as if she were my father. Although I caught it quicker and was able to find my center, it's still disconcerting that, after all these years, the pattern persists. It grabs me and I'm lost."

I discerned the sympathetic looks on our friends' faces.

"I understand. Françoise and I have a similar dynamic."

Indeed, I had witnessed that interaction between them during our visits to their home in France, but with a difference: they somehow knew how to address openly and honestly what was happening and quickly move back into connection.

"When Gloria becomes alarmed at my reaction," I continued, "I retreat into myself and become withdrawn. And that only exacerbates the situation."

"I can't read him," Gloria said. "I get frustrated—I make up a story and we spiral. You know the dynamic. It's still there. I can watch it but ... what if there were something else that could actually ... I don't know ... maybe heal it?"

With that statement, Gloria excused herself to continue preparing dinner and Françoise joined her in the kitchen. Paul and I sat for a few moments in silence. He knew us well: our histories and the seminars and workshops we had attended—including the processes he'd led for most of his career.

"Most of the work I've done seemed mental, strategically-based," I continued.

"What about the sensual work?" Paul asked.

"I'd get out of my mind and lost in my body, of course, but the communication techniques are just that — techniques. They were essentially strategic. Mental."

Paul nodded, listening deeply.

"While I've become more sophisticated in my strategies, I still get triggered. I've learned now to go into my head looking for a strategy," I said with a bit of sarcasm in my voice. "But I can't seem to think my way out of it. Maybe emotion is the key for Gloria and me."

Paul looked at me, astonished.

"You must have read my mind," he said. "You know that Françoise and I still have areas that trigger us in much the same way. You've been with us when it's happened."

I nodded my head in agreement.

"This is exactly what I wanted to talk to you about. Françoise and I met an American spiritual teacher at a seminar in Italy who I think might have something to offer. His name is Vincent Gray."

He paused, perhaps to gather his thoughts, and took another sip from his glass of Prosecco.

"Vincent has a way of healing childhood emotional traumas or wounds that continue to persist through adulthood," he continued. "These wounds prevent us from becoming authentic in our intimate relationships — in fact, in all of our personal relationships."

I glanced out the window for a few seconds. So did Paul. The sun was setting over the Golden Gate Bridge, turning the sky orange and then pink. I took in the expansive view, contemplating what Paul had just said. But something was niggling me.

"From my limited experience with psychotherapy," I said, "I'd always thought that therapy enabled an individual to cope with childhood trauma. This sounds different. How is it possible to heal our childhood conditioning?"

Without missing a beat, Gloria asked as she and Françoise returned to the room, "The original est and the Forum got at some of our conditioning, but isn't it mental too?"

They had no doubt been talking about the same thing while together in the kitchen.

"It just seems that identifying and tracking a person's racket—and all the other strategies they've come up with—help but don't seem to get to the heart of it."

"The *heart* is at the heart of it," Paul said. "Vincent has identified something he calls the 'emotional body' that is as real as the physical body. And he's developed a way of working with it that is user-friendly. And it's all about the heart."

Paul shifted in his chair, gazing through the window at the fading light, and then looked directly at Gloria and me.

"Françoise and I have started to work with him," Paul said. "I think you'd find his work helpful, both personally and professionally. He lives in Grass Valley. Just a three-hour drive from Berkeley. I could arrange a meeting with him for you two. Of course, we're working with him in Europe where he's got a following. He doesn't have much of one here in the U.S."

"How is it for you, Françoise, to work with him?" Gloria asked.

"I too believe he's onto something," she answered. "He claims to have had a non-dual awaking earlier in his life. I can sense some truth in that; however, his childhood emotional baggage remained after enlightenment."

Françoise then told us that, while his enlightenment had allowed Vincent to transcend his childhood wounding, he wasn't happy with that outcome because his early emotional baggage still leaked into his adult behavior. He reasoned that the awakening had impacted his mind, and that what persisted was primarily emotion. Believing that his emotional body had to be enlightened also—to heal the patterns rather than transcend them— he worked with a Jungian therapist to develop a protocol for doing just that.

"His story and argument are very compelling," she concluded.

Françoise seemed to have easy access to non-dual awareness, like the awareness we encountered in Papaji and Ramesh. Her recommendations, as with Paul's, had always carried weight with both of us.

"Vincent seems to be doing for the emotional body what Werner Erhard did for the mental body," Paul added. "He's simplified his understanding of emotions and how to work with them."

I went blank for a minute in a mysterious way that reminded me of being at Muktananda's Samadhi Shrine. I noticed my moist palms and sweaty armpits. Gloria and I had engaged in many heady conversations with Paul and Françoise about philosophy and ethics and other subjects of mutual interest. But this was different. The whole idea of opening childhood wounds made something inside me churn. Perhaps it was the remembrance of my mother's coffin being lowered into the ground or my father's constant pressure for me to succeed.

"How does it work?" Gloria asked.

A look of enthusiasm came over Paul's face as he turned to answer her. He was excited about their new discovery and eager to tell us about Vincent's work.

"Vincent starts with a premise that completely coincides with the latest research described in Damasio's book on the primacy of emotion that you read about: that we are developmentally and psychologically emotional beings before we are mental beings."

We'd used Damasio's book as a reference for our engineering ethics class. I had appreciated his work intellectually but hadn't considered its relevance to me personally. I suppose that was the bridge The Professor was now struggling to cross.

"Vincent takes it a step further and explains that the imprinting we get from our parents as infants lays down the emotional patterning in our subconscious before the neo-cortex develops mental capabilities," Paul continued. "And those patterns follow us through life."

This was becoming a compelling conversation.

"We have observed a similar pattern in our ethics class," Gloria said. "Students have an emotional reaction to difficult ethical issues before they can logically resolve them."

"Yeah," I jumped in, proceeding to tell them about the two students who responded to the affirmative action ethical dilemma in class one day.

"We saw that happen over and over with our students and, of course, with ourselves," Gloria added. "That's why what you're saying about the primacy of emotion seems so relevant, Paul. Let's keep talking about this. And now, dinner is ready."

WE MOVED TO OUR DINING room table. I sat opposite Françoise, and Gloria sat opposite Paul along the length of our wooden table. Through the large dining-room window we could see twilight set in and the lights across the Bay in San Francisco begin to twinkle. The conversation we'd started in the living room was stirring up something inside me.

"My recollections of childhood trauma are still vivid," I said at some point, "there is no doubt that the emotions I felt at that time remain unresolved."

At that, a wave of sadness crashed over me. Tears trickled down my cheeks. I took a deep breath and then blew it out, trying to regain my composure. I certainly wasn't used to suddenly crying like this, but I was with the three people I felt closest to, and we seemed to be touching on something I wanted desperately to heal. Paul turned to me with a knowing in his eyes.

"It's not the trauma of childhood that becomes the issue," he said softly. "Rather, it's that we were alone with the emotion we were feeling, and not getting what we needed in response to it from our parents."

I laid down my knife and fork, fully attentive as Paul described how a kind of "emotional congestion" forms in a child when their parents do not "feel them," as he put it. That unhealed congestion gets carried into adulthood.

"Feel them?" I asked.

The idea of being felt, he told us, came from Daniel Siegel, the noted UCLA psychiatrist and theorist in the field of interpersonal neurobiology.

"The capacity to share deep emotional states is connected with the brain's limbic system," Paul explained. "When two people are sharing an emotional response, the sensation of being felt is what is called resonance. Being felt acts like an over-the-counter decongestant."

My chest tightened, and I slumped into my chair.

"My father surely didn't feel my pain after my mother's death," I said woefully. "And I have no way of knowing if my mother felt me when I was an infant or before she died."

Several seconds of silence passed. Needing to break the conversation for fear of falling down that emotional black hole I had encountered as a child, I busied myself refilling our wine glasses. Gloria, feeling my distress, sat there with me, silent but present.

"Thank you," I murmured. I felt her full attention and—dare I say, her heart—as she looked into my eyes.

"I'm okay," I said to her. As if knowing that I needed a moment of quiet, she squeezed my hand and went to the kitchen to retrieve seconds for our meal.

When we were all seated again, Paul continued.

"It's this congestion that's the issue. That's what Vincent is working with. We keep trying to 'get felt' by those we are in relationship with, repeating the scenario of our childhood wounding in an attempt to get the response we needed but didn't get from our parents."

"That surely describes what's happened to me in relation to Gloria," I carefully admitted, "and Gloria in relation to me."

I was beginning to understand the implications of Paul's words. I had been trying for a long time to comprehend the emotional wounds caused by my mother's death and my father's criticism and had realized that these wounds constituted part of what was standing in the way of an authentic relationship with Gloria. Maybe there was a ray of hope in what Paul was saying. Gloria was clearly interested as well.

"I can set up a meeting for you both," Paul offered. "Would you like that?"

There was a moment of silence.

"But be aware," Paul added. "While Vincent is brilliant, charismatic, and a bit of a genius, he may appear arrogant and eccentric. His work is worth it, but it would be helpful to keep it in mind that he is—what shall I say?—different. I'm telling you this so you won't be surprised."

Gloria and I glanced at each other. I started to smile. Then, ignoring Paul's warning, we both nodded yes.

Chapter 19

Emotional Decongestion

*"Oh, I know all about my mother and me," you may say. "All that
business with my mother was over years ago." You don't and it
wasn't.*
—Nancy Friday, MY MOTHER/MY SELF

"How can I serve you?" Vincent asked as he
greeted Gloria and me at the front door.
He had a pleasant smile and welcoming
demeanor. I immediately felt relaxed.

Here we were, two months after our conversation
with Paul and Françoise, at the meeting Paul arranged for
us with Vincent. During the drive to Grass Valley, Gloria
and I shared our hopes and excitement about this step we
were taking together.

Vincent was dressed in black yoga tights and a long-
sleeve polo shirt that draped down to the beginning of
his crotch, which seemed a bit strange to me. However, I
remembered Paul remarking that Vincent was odd, and I
let it go. This attire, we would come to know, was his
signature way of dressing. I don't ever recall him wearing
regular pants or shirts. The tops he wore were always in
subdued colors—dull lilac, athletic grey, sometimes

white. He seemed to be in his mid-fifties: well-built, with a youthful, vibrant look that we later learned belied his true age. His hair appeared to be dyed dark brown. Later, when we got to know him fairly well, he would tell us, "If I didn't dye my hair, it would be almost pure white." He looked not at all how I had imagined a non-dual teacher. He had a prerequisite: he wouldn't give anyone instruction regarding non-duality until they had completed their emotional work.

Settled comfortably in the living room, Gloria and I listened intently as Vincent described his work, which he called The Project.

"I've developed a self-to-self deconstruction process based on the architecture of the emotional body." That's exactly how he described it.

"The first time I heard of the emotional body," I said, "was when Paul told us about your work. Can you elaborate?"

"Imagine that the emotional body is like a ball of yarn made of many different colored threads with each thread representing a different primary emotion: hurt, anxiety, rage, control, depression, and shame," he began. "When you are emotionally triggered by some distressing or disturbing event that unconsciously reminds you of a childhood trauma, different colored threads become more prominent."

I nodded my head, indicating that I was with him.

"We build mental body stories associated with the events that correlate to these different colored threads as they become more prominent."

"Okay," I said, this time with hesitation in my voice.

"What if," he continued, "you just deconstruct the mental body stories but not the emotional trauma that underlies them? It could happen that, because these colored threads remain so intertwined, they can't be distinguished from each other. And so, each time you pull on one thread, the others tighten. It almost seems hopeless to pull apart the entangled threads in that ball, especially at the level of the mental body story."

His speculative statement, beginning with "what if," resonated with me. I was quite familiar with that way of introducing new ideas. I had used it many times myself when introducing new scientific theories and technical ideas to my students and colleagues.

I closed my eyes. The hopelessness he was speaking about felt very real to me. I had begun to wonder whether Gloria and I could ever resolve what was going on between us. I noticed my palms getting sweaty. Anxiety was setting in. Somehow, the balled-up mental body metaphor felt extremely important to me.

"I sometimes feel my emotions are knotted up just like that the ball of yarn you describe, Vincent," I said.

He nodded that he understood.

"We compensate for the intensity of these tangled emotions with mental and physical strategies. You can call them addictions," he continued. "These addictions run the gamut: making judgments about other people and, especially, about ourselves: medicating ourselves with everything from alcohol to drugs, from work to exercise, or even to sex."

I recall a certain excitement in his voice as he spoke, as if he were telling us about a new discovery. Little did I know at the time he was purposely describing The Professor's role in protecting me from being emotional. He'd heard about my academic achievements from Paul and assumed correctly my heady-ness.

"I probably rely on my intellect and my constantly striving for achievement and perfection to compensate for my pain," I said, my voice deepening and speeding up. I too was excited, as I started to catch on to what he was saying.

"Yes, that feels right," he said. "This striving for achievement essentially keeps the ball of yarn even more knotted and protected."

He is clearly describing my emotional distress, I thought. "So how is this metaphorical ball unknotted?"

He looked at me and pushed both sleeves up to his elbows, indicating that he was ready to get to the meat of his presentation. It was a gesture he made that I would witness many times at crucial points during seminars and retreats. This was especially the case when he was about to make a special pronouncement regarding someone's work—including Gloria's or my own.

"I've developed a systematic process, beginning with writing assignments that you complete and are read in one-on-one sessions with me. They are designed to help untangle the ball, so that each thread can be separated or differentiated." He took a breath and continued. "Once the threads are separated, I can feel each of your emotions deeply and completely."

There was that concept of "feeling felt" that Paul had told us about. I found it both intriguing and a little uncomfortable. Feeling felt would make us aware of each thread in that tangled ball, so that we could address them and be released from unconsciously trying to compensate for an undifferentiated tangle of emotions. And as a result, he explained, we would be "reparented," leading to a more wholesome, self-assured, and fulfilling experience of life.

"Feeling felt," he said, extending Paul's analogy, "is like taking an over-the-counter decongestant!"

"Decongestant?" Gloria asked.

"To use a different metaphor, imagine this simple progression describing a child's development as it relates to the emotional body. Consider that, when an infant is born, the mental body is primitive, but the child remains connected to the mother through an emotional bond or umbilicus that remains after birth."

I had raised three children, but I'd never thought about this. How insightful of him.

"At some point, the child will experience an emotion that the mother or primary care-giver doesn't feel, and the connection is disrupted, causing a kind of hurt that oftentimes would be called 'pain' or 'distress.' To whatever extent the child's hurt isn't felt, that emotion congeals into the thread corresponding to hurt that I just described. And so it goes with the other primary emotions too, as they congeal and become tangled and interrelated to each other."

He paused, perhaps to see if we were still with him. My mind wandered back to Paul's explanation of being felt as an aspect of limbic resonance. In engineering, determining the frequency at which systems are resonant was a phenomenon I was very knowledgeable about. I could extrapolate from that to imagine the link between my having an emotion and Vincent resonating with that emotion in much the same way that I had explained to Paul how the frequency of a particular musical note can shatter a wine glass.

"Being felt by your parents could not have happened because they probably hadn't healed their own emotional wounds," Vincent continued. "The outcome of not having been felt is emotional baggage, or what I call congestion."

The notion of a systematic process that led to a certain outcome was very attractive. Vincent seemed convincingly sure about how things operated in what were, to me, the uncertain aspects of life. He was answering questions about life that no one had ever answered for me before, and with clarity that I found reassuring. And yet he was couching his answers provisionally in a way I found familiar and appealing. His process and way of explaining emotions was making sense to me in a way nothing I'd ever read about or tried before had.

"You mean I can release the guilt I have felt about my mother's death?" I asked.

"Correct."

"And the anxiety about feeling like an orphan, with my absentee father?"

"Exactly right."

"And my rage about having to say the *Kaddish* for eleven months? And God taking my mother from me?"

"Yes and yes," he said.

He actually spoke like that.

"The writing I'll assign will eventually lead you into regressed emotional states where healing the trauma can begin to take place," he concluded. "You will feel felt by me and, with that, compensations can dissolve, and more authentic relationships can take place."

I appreciated the economy in his words, the certainty in his demeanor, and the exactness in his description of outcome. I was taken by the scholarly tone of his presentation, by his welcoming voice, by his promise of release from the pain I was in. As Gloria and I would get to know him, we would be continually impressed by his extensive knowledge of psychology, philosophy, religion, and science, in addition to current events shaping the world. Our association with Vincent would be alluring and seductive.

As our meeting was drawing to a close, Gloria got to the core of our shared concern. "What does an authentic relationship look like to you?" she asked.

"If I can use another metaphor," he replied, "imagine that your defenses create a steel plate that randomly moves back and forth across your chest, letting you feel others when the heart is uncovered. Now imagine that is operating inside you. There are moments when the heart is uncovered for both of you and your hearts can touch."

"Yes," Gloria broke in. "That's happened to us in those special moments when we were falling in love."

"That's right," he continued. "The problem is that you can't achieve that at will—only quite by accident. When the emotional congestion is digested and the compensations dissolve, the heart is unshackled from the steel plate, and you can receive as well as give love—unfiltered and whole."

This was the crux of his message. His process would allow us to not only access our emotions but also to release them. At some point during our work, he would also ask us to "de-med" from our addictions or compensations, thereby letting us feel the pain buried in our hearts, release it, and experience a freedom we'd never felt before. Gloria and I could then begin to have a more honest, whole, and transparent relationship. Holistic and transparent—exactly what Gloria, Paul, and I had believed were necessary in engineering ethics education—the very things that I somehow couldn't embody personally.

"Why do you want to work with me?" Vincent asked.

"I want Bill to penetrate me!" Gloria burst out.

She had said that very thing to me in couples' workshops and seminars, and I hadn't a clue as to what it meant, nor how to respond to it. Vincent looked at both of us for a few seconds.

"The reason Bill can't penetrate you," he gently said to her, "is that you're too busy trying to penetrate him."

Finally!

It would take months of work with Vincent deconstructing the tightly knotted ball of emotional yarn before I would understand that Gloria was wanting a partner who could actually feel what she was feeling—or at least sense that she was feeling something. As long as I hadn't healed my own emotional trauma, that couldn't be possible. And I would come to understand that each time Gloria had tried to teach me something about how to be with her, as she had done with her mother, I would hear it as criticism—telling me what to do because I couldn't figure it out on my own—a surefire way to shut me down.

"Are you willing to risk your marriage?" Vincent asked us. "There have been other married or committed couples who have gone through the deconstruction process and found the unhealthy emotional truths in their relationship. But instead of working with them, they either separated amicably, or they stayed together in an unhealthy fashion after leaving The Project."

I surprised myself with my excitement: "I want to know the truth of our relationship."

Gloria nodded in agreement. "It's a risk I want to take," she said.

We had at last met someone who could succinctly describe what might be under our attack-and-defend dynamic, and he claimed to have a process for resolving it. I sighed with relief, and I saw Gloria do the same. I'd found someone I could trust to facilitate my journey of self-exploration and discovery. The hook was placed.

"Sign me up," I said.

Chapter 20

The Turning

I have already lost touch with a couple of people I used to be.
—Joan Didion, SLOUCHING TOWARDS BETHLEHEM

"AUNT FAY TELLS ME you are a good boy, and you listen to her," my mother had written in a letter to me from her hospital bed a week before she died. "Do your homework and study what you have to. Give Daddy my love and also you."

My hands were trembling as I read the letter. Gloria and I were in Vincent's living room, sitting on a small sofa, about a year after our first meeting. He sat cross-legged on a floor cushion facing us. By the time I finished reading, I was overcome with emotion and could no longer speak.

He turned to Gloria and asked, "How did his mother's letter land for you?"

Vincent sensed that I was not present to her answer. He turned his attention back to me. "Where are you now? Where did you just go?"

I was falling through time and space, accelerating into that emotional black hole I had long feared.

"I'm standing in front of my mother's grave. They are about to lower the casket."

"Okay—okay!" he exclaimed eagerly. "What do you see?"

"My father is standing next to my uncles—his two brothers. The three of them have somber looks on their faces. My grandfathers are *davening*. They are rocking back and forth, murmuring prayers in Hebrew. My grandmothers are wailing in Yiddish, 'Lillie is dead, Lillie is dead!'"

"Where are you?"

"Standing next to my father."

"How do you feel?"

"Alone, terribly alone. My father is there and not there."

"What does that feel like?"

"Dark, black, a pain in my chest. My heart is burning."

"What else do you see?"

"I'm in a dark hole. It's pitch black. I see nothing. I'm falling into it. I'm spinning faster and faster. I'm alone, depressed."

Vincent's voice slowly became my father's voice. I had become Billy.

"And what do you say, Billy?"

"Help me, Daddy! Help me, Daddy!"

I fell into Vincent's arms, sobbing. "Mommy, don't go! Mommy, don't go!"

It had taken me more than fifty-five years from the time of my mother's death not only to say those three words, but to express them in an emotionally visceral way. Words that had been stuck for over half a century in Billy's throat—no, stuck in *my heart*—had finally been released.

With those words, I could finally begin the process of feeling the shame and letting go of the grief of my mother's death. It was counterintuitive; Billy begging his mother to stay allowed Bill to begin letting her go. Something had shifted. What that was would reveal itself within a comparatively short time.

"YOU HAD A HUGE OPENING. Still, there is another step required for you to fully feel the core-unworth lying under that shame and guilt," Vincent said at our next session. "Core-unworth is an existential version of shame. Once you can feel it and have this aspect reparented— when you experience a 'surrogacy'—then deeper healing can happen."

By now, we had been traveling to Grass Valley every month for two—sometimes three—full days of facilitation for well over a year. We had completed our writing assignments and identified and "dropped into" the six basic emotions that Vincent identified as making up the colored yarn threads he had described in our first meeting: hurt, anxiety, control, rage, depression, and shame.

"That you can feel the shame and grief associated with your mother's death is essential for further healing your childhood trauma. However, the only way you'll be able to feel the depth of core-unworth is a 'de-med' from one another," he continued.

I looked at him with dread. I knew that a so-called de-med was one of the hallmarks of Vincent's deconstruction process.

"What does that entail?" I asked reluctantly.

"You two will need to separate," he said in a quiet and sympathetic voice. "I have no idea if it will be permanent. Perhaps, after you heal the core-unworth, the reasons you came together in the first place won't be there anymore, and it will be a natural break. I've never had a couple get that far and stay together."

Although he had told us the same thing when we first met, it came as a shock: it was now personal and not just hypothetical. Even though Gloria and I were still finding ourselves experiencing the same rub that had plagued us throughout our relationship, I was allowing more vulnerability at this point in the process. Being more tender-hearted made those altercations all the harder for both of us. Still, we both clung to the hope that we would stay together.

Vincent looked at us. "If you knew then what you know now about one another, would you still have gotten married?"

I felt my fear, and my voice quaked as I gave my answer. "Right now, I love Gloria, and I can't imagine life without her. Yet, no, I wouldn't."

Gloria, visibly shaken, echoed my answer.

"Can you identify how you are behaving for fear of losing her?" Vincent asked.

With trepidation, I described the behavior I'd acknowledged before. "I freeze rather than tell her the truth of what I don't like about her," I said. "And you've identified that behavior as my caretaking — a strategy that has become an automatic way of trying to keep her from getting angry that, of course, has the opposite effect."

He turned to Gloria. "What do you make of his caretaking? By caretaking, I mean something unhealthy, where the purpose is to satisfy his own needs rather than giving a genuinely caring gesture."

"Okay, here's an example," Gloria answered. "Bill is always ready to drop anything he is doing to take me to my medical or dental appointments — or any place I need to go, for that matter."

She looked at me and I nodded yes.

"At first, this felt like a kind gesture. And I believe it is intended with kindness. But something feels off to me. He says he 'just wants to keep me company.' I'm a grown woman and can do this on my own and I'm starting to feel smothered."

Vincent looked at me.

"Well, Gloria not only cooks all my meals, but is always concerned with what I eat," I said. "She gets really upset if

I have a sweet roll with my morning coffee or a Diet Coke in the afternoon to keep me awake."

"So you're both trying to save one another," Vincent said. "I can feel the edge in how you guys describe your experience. You'll have to separate. Once you do, we'll wait to see what else is revealed."

Feeling agitated by the idea, I raised an objection. "But we're still teaching our ethics class together."

He thought for a moment and then made a suggestion.

"You can teach the ethics course separately. Don't go to each other's lectures," he said. "And you can live separately in the same house. Bill, you can either do your own cooking or eat out alone. Create a schedule so you aren't in the kitchen at the same time. Gloria, you can do everything you usually do with Bill by yourself. Separate your finances as well. You must do it with the sense that you will never come back together again."

"We can do that," I said cautiously.

"Keep a journal of how you feel. That might help you uncover other co-dependencies. Remember, we're trying to sort out where you are using each other to satisfy childhood needs in an unhealthy way," Vincent concluded. "The key isn't the behavior itself, but rather the unhealthy relationship with the behavior—clinging to it in a way that keeps you stuck emotionally."

As I took in everything Vincent was prescribing for us, I felt my chest tighten and a clenching sensation in the pit of my stomach. Still, Gloria and I resolved to follow his instructions faithfully in hopes of being able to take the next step in our process.

All through my adult life, I had avoided eating alone. Yet now, as I started eating out without Gloria, I could clearly feel Billy—the orphan still alive in me—each evening as I sat amongst couples and families in our neighborhood restaurants. Sometimes my eyes would water as I felt Billy's loneliness after a lifetime of having buried it. On my return home, Gloria was often in the guest bedroom, reading with the door closed. She had naturally mothered the lonely boy who she felt living in my heart, never having had her own children. Now she was no longer available to provide the consolation Billy craved.

While that separation was difficult and painful, Vincent was preparing us for the next phase of our work, which would be guided by this hypothesis: the more Billy came into focus, the more likely he could be reparented by a loving and present "mother figure" outside of the marriage. According to Vincent, and resonating with both of us, was the notion that there were unhealthy aspects of our marriage that were masking the deepest wounds of shame and core-unworth still alive within the heart of Billy. It was this aspect of Billy that drove the unhealthy strategies locked into the painful dynamic between Gloria and me. Until that pain was unmasked and felt, and Billy essentially reparented by a loving surrogate mother—while I was totally dropped into it— I'd never be able to have a healthy relationship. Healing

Billy's pain and transforming it to what Vincent called core-goodness, even if it meant losing our relationship, became the motivation that pushed me forward without hesitation, despite the risks it posed to both of us.

A few days before our next scheduled weekend with Vincent, he asked to have a conference call with Gloria and me. We were a month into the de-med.

"How's it going?" he asked us.

"The pain is horrible," we said, almost simultaneously from our separate locations in the house.

"Stop it," he exclaimed, referring to the de-med. "You've done enough for now. I'll see you both this weekend in Grass Valley for your next session."

DURING THAT WEEKEND, Vincent prescribed the anticipated second stage for the de-med. Gloria would move to Grass Valley to live entirely separate from me. As we expected, with this new, more distant separation, our process went deeper. Old memories laced with fear and terror emerged for her, going so far in a process that she experienced pre-birth memories of being in her mother's womb and feeling her mother's grief over the stillborn child that came before her.

After several weeks in Grass Valley, Gloria went to Europe for an extended stay, partly to continue the separation and partly for reparenting the inner child associated with her core-unworth. She lived with an older mother figure: a facilitator trained by Vincent. Gertrude had been a teacher of non-duality, with a substantial following before cultivating her own emotional life. Her non-dual access—where the state of "I-other" was transcended—created a distance reminiscent of Gloria's mother's coldness. However, Gertrude was also a very affectionate being who could give Gloria's inner child the love and care she so needed.

During the time Gloria was in Europe, I traveled to Grass Valley so Billy could experience a surrogacy with a facilitator named Elizabeth. Beth, as she was called, had been married to an internationally-known spiritual teacher, had taught Satsang herself, had raised two sons, and was also a kind and loving being. She was the perfect mother surrogate for Billy.

In preparation for my reparenting experience, Beth asked me to write to Billy. The act of writing helped me move emotionally into a regressed state of childhood, recreating the trauma of his mother's death.

"Where did my mother go? And why?" Billy asked Beth, weeping uncontrollably as he fell into her welcoming arms.

"Her soul left her body and went back to the angel realm," Beth answered.

"And then what happened?" Billy asked.

"She told the angels about this lifetime, and they made preparations for her next lifetime."

Until now, Billy had never been able to weep into a woman's arms and grieve his mother's death. Doing so with Beth was cathartic as well as astounding. Beth's explanation comforted Billy. He could finally relax and begin the process of letting go of the trauma and his fear of death.

After Gloria and I had both completed our surrogacies, we both attended a seminar Vincent was offering at a retreat center near on Lago Maggiore in Italy. It would be the first time in several months we'd be together.

Despite my high expectations of a romantic reunion, we were shy and couldn't quite connect emotionally in our new, more vulnerable configurations. At the retreat center, we began the slow dance of finding each other and discovering who we had become.

During our first joint session with Vincent at the retreat, he asked Gloria and me a point-blank question: "Do you want to go back together?" Our response was almost immediate and in unison: "Yes!"

We explained our difficulty adjusting to a new, more tender-hearted way in which we could relate. Vincent found this encouraging; to him, it signified that we were both more vulnerable, and that we were landing in a new place.

Even so, Gloria responded to Vincent's assessment by beginning to pour her heart out. Distressed that we didn't automatically click, she said, "Okay, that may be true. Bill is more vulnerable, but ..."

Vincent cut her off. "You've had a year of focusing on the unhealthy aspects of your relationship. Now it's time to focus on your love and what is good about your relationship. Focusing on the shadow itself can become a bad habit—a new addiction."

This was a big shift in perspective, and we got it. He was telling us that we could now begin to feel our core-goodness and stop plumbing the shadow.

"I have a revised prescription for you," Vincent said to Gloria, authority in his voice. "Go back to your marriage and stop complaining. And give up pushing Bill to change. If you want to stay together, take Bill and the marriage exactly as it is."

He then turned to me. "And Bill, stop trying to change who you are. Let's see where that takes you. Sometimes striving for change, in itself, is a medication."

"GLORIA AND I HAVE BEEN offered a puppy. What do you think?" I asked Vincent at our next weekend session.

"We've both had dogs long before we met each other," Gloria explained. "And Bill's cousins are getting one from a breeder. We thought it might be fun if we got one, too, and raised the two puppies together. They showed us pictures of the litter and we're excited."

"Excellent idea," Vincent said, much to our surprise.

Vincent reasoned that this would be the next step in our process.

"You can focus your caretaking on the puppy, Bill, instead of on Gloria," he reasoned. "And Gloria, you can put your mothering instinct on the puppy, instead of on Bill. The little boy has grown up."

Max chose us as much as we chose him. Gloria and I were lying on the floor waiting when the dog breeder let six fluffy white Maltese puppies loose in our presence.

One of them jumped on my chest, peed on me, then jumped on Gloria's chest and licked her nose.

"I guess he wants to come home with us," Gloria said.

"Yes, I've been anointed as his master," I laughed.

Indeed, we raised Max as if he were our child. Max attended puppy school, advancing to middle- and then high-school levels. We almost never left him alone—he accompanied one or both of us wherever we went, and we had a dog-sitter for those events he couldn't attend. As a puppy, he sat on a desk in a Berkeley classroom while the students in our ethics class took their finals. Many of them petted his head for good luck as they handed in their exams.

"I FEEL OVERBURDENED by the whole process of life," I said during one of our sessions a month or so later. Vincent had asked me how I was holding up as a professor at Berkeley, situated in a very demanding mental context. At the same time, I was still exploring my childhood wounding—which was very emotional. And connecting with Gloria in a heart-opened way brought me in contact with my vulnerability.

"How does that feel to you?"

"I feel like Atlas, condemned by the Olympian gods to hold the world on my shoulders for eternity," I said, letting out a sigh. "I'm like that statue of him standing in front of Rockefeller Center in New York."

Vincent reframed the metaphor. "Suppose carrying the world on your shoulders is a strength rather than a burden?"

In that moment, something extraordinary happened to me. I sensed my blood surging through my veins, my muscles flexing, my chest expanding. I became the Titan Atlas, appointed by my father as king and builder of the city of Atlantis. I looked at Gloria, reached out, and took her hand.

Our eyes locked. We both began to cry. A sequence of images flashed through my mind of all the times we had deeply connected since we met—sitting on her bed and holding her hand during the difficult talk with her mother, the sunken bath in Bali, our wedding ceremony. As I traveled through these memories, the steel gate protecting my heart swung wide open.

"Welcome back," I said softly to Gloria. "Welcome home."

She would later tell me her experience: "In that same moment, I became your queen, Pleione, mother of the Pleiades and the Hesperides."

Through the twists and turns of our life together and the deep process we were currently experiencing, we had found each other again—as soul mates—after eons and eons. I could now receive her love and offer mine. Gloria's love could now land in my heart and mine in hers. Finally, I could feel whatever pain she was feeling, or at least feel that she was feeling pain. My Atlas archetype provided a powerful metaphor: just as Atlantis had been destroyed by a massive earthquake and been submerged in the ocean, Gloria and I had been submerged in the emotional flood of the childhood wounds we had carried into our relationship—the perfect relationship destined to bring them up so we could heal them. These wounds had driven us apart, and we had lost each other in the waters of sexual exploration that we believed would bring us closer together, but never did. The many tactics we had tried now lay behind us, like the rubble of Atlantis.

This experience marked the realization that the dynamic of attack-and-defend had begun collapsing around us like an abandoned building brought down by a wrecking ball caught in a slow-motion movie. Our defenses began to break down and our hearts could now remain open, replacing the caustic old pattern with patience, kindness, and open-hearted compassion. When our hearts closed, we knew how to be together, admitting the closure to each other, which made it possible to reconnect anew as we gave our hearts time to reopen.

As our mistaken perceptions and projections dissolved, Gloria morphed into my queen. It was a major turning point. My modus operandi was beginning to include the emotional as well as the rational. The Professor's defenses were taking a back seat as he had less and less to protect, and I was emerging as a partner who could begin to openly meet his beloved heart to heart.

There I was—a professor of nuclear engineering deeply steeped in reason and logic—in two profound, inexplicable realms at once: the emotional today experiencing the spiritual yesterday. And it wouldn't be the last time.

Chapter 21

Death

Sometimes you have to step outside of the person you've been, and remember the person you were meant to be, the person you wanted to be, the person you are.
—H.G. Wells

Vincent walked between us as we approached the door of his home. We had just finished another two-day session with him, a few months after our de-meds. Stopping at the door, he placed one arm over my shoulders and the other over Gloria's.

"I'm starting a class for interns in January, and I'd like you both to join it," Vincent said. "I've been guiding your process for a year and a half now, and you two are ready to start training to be facilitators."

The intern class would focus on facilitator training—learning the basis of his deconstruction process and practicing its application—and would take place at his home one weekend a month for a year. We would be required to attend his fall and spring week-long seminars in Europe, where we would take the opportunity to visit with Paul and Françoise and share our progress and our experience working with Vincent.

After six months, we'd take a written "midterm exam" and, upon passing, be designated certified interns, ready to facilitate others under his supervision. Eventually, we would become certified facilitators and then, presumably, we'd be able to go out on our own.

I was a little startled at what felt like a sudden invitation. All I could muster in response was, "Thank you. I'll feel into it."

Noticing the surprise on my face, Vincent added, "This will be the best way to go deeper in your process, Bill. The interns will challenge you and, after that, you can continue your process by facilitating other people. And when all the interns are certified, we'll have a supervision circle, where we'll work on problem-solving."

This was a lot of information for me to take in. I hadn't thought that far ahead.

I don't recall what Gloria said, although she and Vincent had been talking about her joining the class for some time. As a young woman, she'd been on track to go to medical school with the aim of becoming a psychiatrist. However, after an early divorce, her life took a different turn. When she finally was ready to go to graduate school, while she felt best suited to become a therapist, she veered in a different direction, becoming an attorney and then a mediator and coach. Being an intern and facilitator in Vincent's work would be a good fit for her — much better than being an attorney. But for me, the prospect of facilitating another person through an emotional process was daunting. I was still a professor of engineering at Berkeley: intellectually gifted but an emotional newbie, I believed.

Still, I was honored by the invitation to be a facilitator. Despite some trepidation, I began thinking of an internship as a way to expand my own journey of self-exploration. Besides, with retirement looming within the next two or three years, being a facilitator would provide me with an interesting new part-time career and some additional income. To top it off, rather than spending one weekend a month alone in Berkeley while Gloria was training with Vincent in Grass Valley, we could learn to be facilitators together and I could deepen my process. Joining the class seemed to offer a great opportunity to be part of this seemingly new and innovative approach to personal transformation, spiritual growth, and healing. So I once again said yes.

"THE INTERN CLASS WILL CONSIST of eight other individuals who want to become facilitators, some of whom have been working with me for a long time, but none as intensely as the two of you," Vincent told us the next time we met. "And the training will deepen your own processes, whether or not you decide to facilitate anyone."

For Gloria and me, being encouraged to be interns meant that, clearly, we'd healed enough emotional trauma to be able to help others uncover and heal their emotional wounds without bringing too much of our own baggage to the facilitation.

"In this way," Vincent said, "we minimize countertransference, the danger of facilitators projecting their own feelings and issues onto the clients they're working with."

Gloria and I certainly had enough experience of that kind of projection with each other. We nodded knowingly. And he had held out the option of not becoming facilitators, which felt reassuring.

Over the next year, we trained in the intern class one weekend each month: a day devoted to group processing and a day devoted to his teaching. We also attended Vincent's seminars in Europe, which focused on the emotional and spiritual underpinnings of The Project, his interpretation of non-duality, and a devotional path to universal love and God. I was happy to continue healing the emotional and spiritual wounding of my childhood. And I appreciated the strong level of trust we could all share with each other as interns. I was ready to follow wherever Vincent led.

Vincent's gifts were most apparent when he was leading groups and seminars. He tended to be psychic, with an uncanny ability to work energetically with people to elicit unconscious material that often led to a dramatic opening or realization. These openings often washed over the entire group; in seminars, that could be well over a hundred people. Sometimes he associated the unconscious material with what Gloria and I considered metaphors of past lives, transporting people into transpersonal healing spaces, as he had done with us several times, including the opening that had transported us to Atlantis. These past lives usually corresponded to an individual's emotional congestion. All of this deepened my understanding and experience of transpersonal spaces in such a way that they began to seem as normal to me as my ordinary waking states and, at the same time, never ceased to surprise me. And because he could also meet me in the scientific realm with a breath of knowledge and interest I'd experienced with Paul, my relationship with him became ever more compelling.

"I'VE BEEN THINKING ABOUT THE CLASS coming up next week," Vincent wrote in an email to me about halfway through the internship. "Write a letter to Death. Tell Death how you felt when Death took your mother away from you. And follow it by writing what you imagine would be Death's response."

As I wrote, my hand was unsteady, my armpits were damp, and sweat rolled down my brow. The assignment felt extremely uncomfortable; I had avoided thinking about death since that year of mourning when I was thirteen. Now I was supposed to face this head on, and then read what I wrote aloud to the group. I'd become accustomed to accessing my emotions through Vincent's writing exercises, but this felt beyond what I'd been asked to do before now.

At the next class, we interns were sitting on chairs in a circle, Vincent on the floor in the center. Unable to concentrate on what anyone else had been saying, my heart was palpitating and a glossy sheen of sweat covered my body. Finally, when it was my turn, I began to read.

Dear Death,

You are the enemy! You make me feel small and helpless, like a pig going to slaughter, like the Christians being thrown to the lions, like the Jews being sent to the gas chambers. You make me feel helpless, small, powerless, humorless, weak, crushed like an ant; you make me feel sad, alone, naked, and starving.

You look like the Grim Reaper — faceless and with no name, concealed behind a hood and a cape — leaving a trail of pus and vomit, blood and guts, and piss and shit. You sneak up with no warning, hiding in the dark until it is time to strike. Yet you have many disguises: suave, with dark hair, well-built in a Brooks Brothers suit; or sexy with long blond hair in an off-the-shoulder full-length gown — to fool me, to tempt me, to cajole me, to trick me. And then, the pitchfork, the switch blade, right through the carotid artery.

You have taken them all — when you took my mother, you took a part of me. I felt helpless, alone, and frightened, and I have been fighting you ever since — denying your existence, pushing you away, hiding my eyes from you. A life and death struggle, avoidance at all costs!

Bill

The members of the class started shifting in their seats as I finished reading the letter. They were obviously unsettled — either by my candor or by the exercise itself. I couldn't tell which. And they were silent. I don't believe anyone in our class had yet confronted the subject of death as part of his or her process. I went on to read Death's response.

Dear Bill,

Nothing personal, you understand! I do my job; without death there would be no birth, no babies, no joy. No joy without sorrow. You choose when it is time to go. You choose the airplane that crashes, not I! You choose your food and diet, whether to exercise or not, your car, which freeway to drive — you choose your parents, your genes, and your family! Not I! The choices are yours, and when your time comes, I come — swiftly and quietly — no fuss, no bother — one last breath and you are gone from this plane.

It was your mother's choice to die at such a young age, not mine! Direct your anger and rage at her, not at me!

I'll be seeing you.

Death

The room remained silent. No more fidgeting.

"Any reflections for Bill?" Vincent asked, as he always did after someone's process.

After a few more minutes of silence, Vincent suggested we all take a break. I sat quietly in my chair as Gloria came up and put her arm around my shoulder — an act of loving kindness, as she appreciated the depth of my work.

In reading aloud Death's message, I could feel the guilt that I'd carried all those years begin to dissolve. I could begin to embody the truth in that message. I could begin to forgive myself as the memory of Ramesh's teaching arose within me.

I was not the cause of her death. I wasn't in control of anything.

ONE MONTH LATER, the class met again.

"Did you dialogue with Billy last night?" Vincent asked me when it was my time to process. Internal dialogues were another way of accessing regressed states of childhood wounding.

"Yes," I said. "Billy is still angry at God."

Vincent asked me to stand up and move across the room and sit in a chair away from the other participants. Then he pointed to a place where the ceiling met the far wall.

"There's God," he whispered. "What does Billy want to say to him?"

Breathing deeply, I went within and found myself as Billy — the boy who'd sat through a year of reciting daily the mourner's *Kaddish*, the motherless boy who felt out of sync with the world. Suddenly, a wailing erupted from me. With a blood-curdling scream, I cried, "You-took-my-mother-away-from-me! I-hate-you!"

Buckets of tears rolled down my cheeks. More than fifty-five years of repressed rage at God came pouring out.

Vincent then asked the women in the class to sit in a straight line on one side of the room. I sat in a chair facing them.

"There is your mother. What do you want to say to her?" Vincent whispered.

I gathered myself—and Billy screamed. "You-abandoned-me! You-gave-me-away!"

My body collapsed into the chair. And then all was serene—internally and externally.

After a while, Vincent knelt at my side and pointed to the place on the ceiling where I had focused Billy's rage.

"That was the false God," he said. "The God of your childhood who you'd blamed for all that went wrong."

Billy had cast God and his henchman, Death, as evil, Vincent explained. And, as a prisoner of my own projections, he had created The Professor, the persona that stood between me and my emotional and spiritual life. Billy finally freeing his rage had allowed Bill's heart to open even wider. And I could now feel The Professor and me switching places.

AFTER THREE YEARS WITH VINCENT, Gloria and I became certified facilitators and began leading groups and guiding people in the deconstruction process. The more I worked with Vincent, the more I learned to be in touch with my emotions and to express them effectively. I was still a year from retirement at the University, but I was finding a new sense of vigor as I integrated my personal, professional, and spiritual life. And I would include several lectures in our ethics class on my understanding of the interplay between cognition and emotion in making ethical decisions.

"The Project answers more questions than any other process addressing the human experience," Vincent would often say.

I was truly having that experience; however, when I heard him make this claim, I remembered Paul's admonition that he could appear to be a bit arrogant.

Chapter 22

Transition

Right Action is better than knowledge; but in order to do what is right, we must know what is right.
—Charlemagne

MY PALMS WERE CLAMMY. Wiping the sweat from my brow, I noticed that the dampness under my arms had stained my shirt. Standing behind a lectern on the stage in Bechtel Auditorium, I was about to address the entering freshman engineering class at Berkeley. It was August 2007, the beginning of my last semester before retiring from the University of California.

Even though I'd been a teacher for more than forty years, the nervousness I felt walking into a classroom the first day of a new semester had never diminished. However, as a result of my emotional work with Vincent, I'd come to understand the roots of this deep-seated anxiety. Needing to be perfect in my father's eyes and for the old men at the synagogue, I had been subconsciously asking myself the same questions all these years: Will I do it right? Will I give a great lecture that students will remember? Will they like me? Will they love me?

Here I stood, fifty-six years after my mother's death, approaching the end of my academic career, finally knowing where the anxiety came from. I might always have that anxiety, but it no longer held me hostage. Now I was free to laugh about it.

"Reason and logic have been the underpinnings of both moral action and scientific progress," I began. "Descartes' pronouncement 'I think, therefore I am' and Newton's scientific legacy—that a mere mortal could deduce the universal laws of nature—paved the way for the Industrial Revolution and our modern society."

I paused and looked around the auditorium at the three hundred or so freshmen eager to embark on their engineering education and, ultimately, their career in a world that was quickly changing. My inner world was changing along with it, and soon I too would be heading into a new career. This would be my last chance to offer a group of engineers something of the expanded view of life that Gloria and I had been able to present during our six years teaching the ethics course to juniors and seniors at Berkeley. So much had happened in our lives since we began teaching together. At the very least, we had dropped layers of the personas that mediated our view of each other, leading to a more whole, transparent, and responsive relationship within which we could now connect more easily in the physical, mental, emotional, and spiritual domains.

Along with a deepening understanding of my emotional life, I'd begun to feel a healthy sense of pride in my professional accomplishments. I was proud to have been a faculty member at the foremost public college of engineering in the world. During the coming year, I would be finishing up my academic career — teaching my risk analysis course and advising a couple of PhD students and post-doctoral fellows — but, essentially, this part of my life was over. I was looking forward to the next part as a facilitator in The Project, sharing the processes that had so changed my life and brought such fulfillment in my relationship with Gloria.

I went on with my talk, telling the students they were going to face some critical ethical choices regarding the jobs they would seek and the projects they would work on. I talked about the role of engineering in the world and the idea that, as engineers, they should strive to understand the impact of technological innovation on the human condition. After reviewing the major scientific and technical achievements of the past three centuries, I spoke about the human quest to understand the complexity of our world and to make meaning of our place in it.

"In addition to creating magnificent structures and sophisticated machines, all in the name of advancing humankind, these creations also shaped our place in the world."

I could feel the passion arise in me. It had taken me many years to understand and appreciate how technology shaped our lives and how our lives shaped technology. Now my goal was to motivate these young engineers to embrace a broad range of inquiry, from science and philosophy to technology and ethics—all crucial to understanding the moral dimensions of their future discoveries.

"With the tremendous speed of new scientific discoveries and technological advancements," I concluded, "we are on the cusp of a post-industrial revolution that will give us even greater opportunities to understand what we, as humans, are made of *and* who we actually are!"

I looked around the auditorium. The attention of the students was palpable. Miraculously, all eyes seemed to be focused on me—not on a smart phone or laptop.

"Are there any questions?"

A student raised his hand and asked, "Would you explain what this new post-industrial revolution might look like and how it affects you personally?" His question got to the heart of my ongoing quest: how to combine scientific knowledge and technological progress with a deeper understanding of the human heart.

"To answer the first part of your question," I began, "the Industrial Revolution and Enlightenment philosophy spawned by Newton and Descartes was based on a set of universal rules and principles emerging from a linear or reductionist paradigm."

I paused to see if the students were following me.

"Our emerging discoveries—information technology, biotechnology, and nanotechnology—are based on a new paradigm of understanding, creating a critical shift in the paradigm for both observing and understanding our physical world—and our place in it."

I paused again to gather my thoughts. How would I answer the second part of the student's question? What did this shift have to do with me personally?

Was this part of what I'd been seeking to integrate all along?

My doctoral dissertation had focused on the dynamical behavior of nonlinear systems in which even small differences in input can yield widely divergent outputs—a metaphor for the trajectory of my own life. I wanted to say some small thing that might change the trajectory of these students' lives—not just professionally, but personally as well. I cleared my throat and smiled.

"On a personal level, the path of my own career—my teaching and my research—wasn't quite as linear as I thought it would be when I was in your shoes. My personal life was highly nonlinear, having diverged from one path to another in response to disturbances, both large and small, positive and negative."

I stopped, glanced at the clock, noticed that the hour was almost over, and concluded my remarks.

"I am just now beginning to understand the consequences of all that."

VINCENT AND TINA, SHORT FOR VALENTINA, left for Europe the same month I gave that freshman ethics lecture. They had met at a seminar in Europe early in our work. Within a year, he had invited Tina and her daughter to live with him in Grass Valley as she trained as a facilitator in our intern class. We celebrated their marriage a year later.

Because Vincent had a substantial following in Europe, he decided to live there for a year teaching a new intern class, facilitating individuals and groups with Tina, and getting a first-hand taste of her cultural and familial heritage. During that year, Gloria, at his invitation, became The Project's leader in North America. It had been three and a half years since we had started working with him. After Vincent left, she would invite him back in six months to offer what she believed would be a large seminar in the Bay Area, perhaps his first U.S. event comparable in size to those he held in Europe. Her intuition proved correct.

Gloria frequently spoke on radio programs—the forerunners of podcasts—geared toward what had been considered new-age topics regarding spirituality and innovative psychological and philosophic thought that provided a counterpoint to the rationalism of the Enlightenment. She regularly did the same at bookstores throughout the Bay Area. Both of these activities drew new clients from the burgeoning community of seekers in California looking for innovative healing opportunities. Many had been followers of teachers of eastern—and sometime western—versions of mystical or metaphysical traditions. Some were people interested in consciousness change who had studied with spiritual teachers that had bypassed psychological or emotional healing, or what is commonly called shadow work.

Because she called her talks "The Art of Sacred Union" or "The Path to Sacred Relationship," she couched her work in her experience and our relationship—including our issues, explaining how the process led to the deeper emotional healing we needed. Her years of teaching at Berkeley afforded her a solid presence as a presenter, but it was probably her enthusiasm for the work and the hunger of her audience for emotional healing and a healthy relationship within a spiritual context that drew large numbers of people in an astonishingly short time. She soon had a full facilitation practice. Vincent's protocol required participants to commit to two sessions a month plus a weekend group. Based on her draw, I soon filled my weekends with groups as well.

Gloria had also begun teaching an intern class a month before Vincent departed for Europe, leaving her videos of his teaching modules. She also facilitated the supervision circle. Before long, there were enough certified interns for even more groups to form.

After teaching together at the University, where I'd essentially been Gloria's supervisor, this new experience was illuminating. Of course, we had done our individual work with Vincent in each other's presence, and I'd been in group with her for years. But in this new milieu, she showed up teaching and facilitating in a way that revealed a side of her I'd never seen or appreciated before. Having that respect for her professionally opened up an additional approach to relating that provided symmetry in our relationship. I felt that I could now rely on her to help me as I began working with people. I valued her ideas and viewpoints in a way that, in short order, illuminated what had been the patriarchal aspect of my personality, which was now in hindsight more than it had ever been in real time.

Gloria felt much more at ease teaching in this ad hoc format than she had felt delivering a formal lecture, as this method of instruction aligned naturally with bringing about consciousness change. I was learning to give up the fifty-minute lecture and to work with people the way Gloria had hoped we'd teach at the University. In fact, those years building The Project while Vincent was away took quite of bit of residual steam out of The Professor as I became a student of my beloved wife. In turn, she could trust and lean into the authentic Bill, who was no longer trapped in a self-image-preserving tug of war with her.

The people we attracted were eager to start the process almost immediately; many of them became involved in The Project for the next five or even six years. We were helping Vincent fulfill his dream of becoming a spiritual teacher with a devoted following. A psychic — the very one who had proclaimed that there were two of me sitting in front of her — had once told him there would be a couple who would "bring his work into the world."

We had become that couple.

AS I BECAME MORE CONFIDENT in facilitating people in the work, witnessing its effectiveness was further opening my heart. On one occasion, I could clearly see and feel the pain of a couple enacting the same attack-and-defend dynamic that had entrapped Gloria and me for so long. At the conclusion of the session, I came to her teary-eyed.

"That guy was doing the same damn thing I did, right in front of my face. It was painful to take in. I'm so sorry I put you through all that," I said, feeling deep remorse.

Seeing and feeling the same behavior and emotional patterns in those I was facilitating was allowing me to understand and dissolve my own patterns. And the more I dissolved my own patterns, the more effective I became in supporting others in dissolving theirs. The Professor, who had no empathy for the emotionally distraught student begging for an extension on her term paper, was now able to set aside his habituation of mental distance and to allow me to respond to emotional pain with understanding and empathy. This was certainly changing my attitude toward the students I was teaching and mentoring, and it was also deepening my work with The Project.

DURING THAT LAST SEMESTER of teaching, I found myself wondering how, in fact, I would characterize the trajectory of my life. And how would I explain it to a group of engineering students in a language they would understand?

I mulled these questions over and over. The way The Professor ended up putting it made logical sense: my life could be characterized by a series of perturbations, I reasoned, each followed by a trajectory seeking asymptotic stability; that is, moving closer and closer to equilibrium, but never quite getting there.

As Jackie Margoles had suggested, I was no different from all living systems: encased in a semi-permeable membrane; exchanging mass, energy, and information with my environment; and always in search of homeostasis. As a human being, the information exchange might be in the form of cognition, emotion, or sensation arising in response to internal or external triggers, and my responses to those would change the trajectory of my life. As a result, I would learn, grow, and change.

Had I chosen those responses based on reason and logic, or had my heart chosen to respond for reasons unknown to me at the time? Reflecting on this question, I realized that the twists and turns of my personal and professional journey had presented me with choices and decisions that were made from the heart as often as they were made from the head. I had made decisions regarding which courses to enroll in, where to live, which car to buy — any number of ordinary decisions regarding my life, utilizing the data available to me at the time. In effect, I was using a cost-benefit approach to decision-making.

But I was now aware that I had made other choices based on virtually no data at all — choices that were emotional or intuitive: moving to California when I was nineteen; proposing marriage — twice, no less; working with Vincent. These were big choices that had led to the major turning points in my life.

Many years ago, Papaji confronted me with this inquiry: "Who is asking the question?" Perhaps now I had the response: "My heart."

Now I was deciding to retire from the University of California. I had, in fact, finally satisfied my thirst for technological discovery and innovation. In its place, I was acquiring a taste for self-exploration and personal discovery. While most men of my generation feared retirement and the loss of productivity that accompanied it, I welcomed it. I had shifted my attention from engineering systems to human systems — with an emphasis on my own system.

I had never before lived my life beyond a cultural framework that shaped my values, assumptions, and beliefs. At an unconscious level, I think I had always feared feeling lost without a group that shared my values. As a child, it was my parents and grandparents who created the Jewish-American working-class framework within which I grew into adulthood. As an adult, it was the University of California that shaped me professionally. And now The Project would shape me for the rest of my life — or so I thought.

Chapter 23

Remarriage

*But Oz never did give nothing to the Tin Man that, that he didn't
already have…*
— Dewey Bunnell, AMERICA

"So far, Gloria and Bill are the only couple who have worked through all their co-dependencies and are having a healthy marital relationship."

We were sitting front and center in a large room at a retreat center on Lago Maggiore, a two-hour drive from where Vincent and Tina were living in Varese, Italy. Vincent was introducing us to the facilitators and interns associated with The Project at a biennial convention. Tina was sitting by his side on a stage facing us and the audience.

"They have mastered the art of intimate relationship," Vincent went on. "Now they can turn their attention towards their existential and spiritual issues."

Gloria squirmed in her chair, visibly uncomfortable. Shivers ran up and down my spine. I had lived in Europe thirty-five years ago — married to my first wife, with three small children—when I was a young professor spending a sabbatical year working on nuclear reactor safety at a research laboratory. Then, I had virtually no idea of an inner emotional life. Now, here I was, after many more trips to Europe, a radically different person, being held up as a model of how to conduct a successful relationship. On the one hand, I was flattered and relieved, but more important, I wondered how I would ever live up to such an endorsement.

Later that evening, Vincent asked Gloria and me if we would participate in a re-marriage ceremony to acknowledge the power of our relationship. It would be a teaching moment, he told us, providing an experience for us to reset our relationship and to acknowledge that we had resolved any caustic dynamic. Although we did not consider ourselves a perfect couple, we liked the idea of using the remarriage ceremony to recommit to our vows with fresh knowledge born out of hard work and with our eyes wide open.

On the appointed evening, Vincent rearranged the seminar room chairs to give it the feeling of a chapel. He placed a chalice of wine and three candles atop an altar on the front stage. He and I stood behind the altar and waited as Gloria walked down the aisle toward us. I offered her my arm as she stepped up onto the stage. I was young again and Gloria—looking radiant—was my bride. We took our places on either side of Vincent as he began.

"Gloria and Bill were willing to take the risk of giving up their marriage in order to find the truth within their bond," he said with reverence.

The work Gloria and I had accomplished together certainly felt risky. From the moment we admitted to each other that we wouldn't choose to marry again, knowing what we knew at the time, we both questioned whether we could make it through. But when Vincent had asked if we wanted to continue digging deeper into the nature of our marriage, we had answered with a resounding "yes!"

We now clearly understood our marriage vows in a way we hadn't at our first marriage ceremony. And here was our spiritual teacher giving us a blessing, anointing us as an ideal couple. Although, from our point of view, we were just beginning to work on our relationship as we'd intended years before. This time we were prepared to deal with emerging issues in ways that brought us closer rather than driving us apart. We were able to have fun together and grow our mutual feeling of gratitude by serving our clients as an outpouring of our love while reassuring ourselves of our new capacities. We were excited about what we had found with one another, and we translated our enthusiasm into our work.

"There have been other married or committed couples who have gone through the deconstruction process and found the unhealthy emotional truths of their relationship. However, they either left The Project, staying together in an unhealthy relationship, or separated and continued their emotional work alone."

Vincent paused and looked around the room.

"Gloria and Bill were brave enough to confront their unhealthy truths and, when they dove deeper into their process, they found each other at the far end. It was the relationship that revealed and guided their work, with all its ugliness and discomfort."

He then lit two of the candles representing the two of us. Holding both candles, he lit the third, representing our union. This simple gesture brought a portion of the audience to tears, many of them, I believe, longing for the kind of relationship he had ascribed to us. We concluded the ceremony by taking a sip of wine from the chalice.

I turned to Gloria and took her in my arms. We believed we were truly fulfilling our wedding vows to use our relationship as a spiritual path. Now we were stepping into a new chapter. Vincent looked on, smiling. He had made his point.

I WAS BUSY COMPLETING my final year as a professor at Berkeley when Vincent invited us to co-lead a week-long seminar of about a hundred people in Europe. By then, Gloria had decided she could no longer co-teach our ethics class, as a burgeoning facilitation practice pretty much filled her workdays and weekends. Still, we eagerly accepted the invitation and headed to Europe. It would be the first of two seminars—one in the fall and the other in the spring—that we would attend while

Vincent and Tina were living abroad. He called this one a King-Queen seminar, as it featured a set of teachings and processes aimed at preparing single participants for a relationship or strengthening the bonds of existing ones. Each morning I would assist him in the men's breakout group while Gloria and Sophia, the project leader in Europe, would facilitate the women's breakout group. It would also be the first seminar we attended with Paul and Françoise present.

Vincent introduced us the evening before the seminar began and asked us to say a few words to the European audience about who we were and what was happening with The Project in the States. Gloria described her activities: the new intern class she and Vincent had organized—that she was now teaching—and the plans Gloria and I were making to offer a King-Queen seminar in Berkeley. I described my facilitation activities, especially the men's group I had created and led since Vincent's departure.

"My body is here on the stage, but my heart and spirit are sitting in the audience with all of you," I said at the end of my remarks.

"You were oozing emotion up there," Paul said to me as I came off the stage to greet him and Françoise. Gloria and I had not seen them in person for more than a year. I savored his comment—another confirmation that the deconstruction process had worked for me.

"You and Françoise are living in a bubble together," Vincent said to Paul one morning during our men's breakout group. "Most people live in their own bubble, and their work is to break out of that bubble. Yours is different."

What could be wrong with their bubble? I wondered. It seemed admirable to me. Gloria and I had worked hard to form such a bubble, protecting our relationship, and caring for each other's feelings within it. Vincent saw it differently. However, as usual, I gave him the benefit of doubt. I was curious about how Paul and Françoise would work with Vincent's admonition.

"What do you recommend?" Paul asked Vincent.

"A de-med from each other, and then a surrogacy," Vincent responded.

That all seemed reasonable to me, as Gloria and I had followed the same path and it had proved clarifying. Then Vincent surprised Paul, the men in the room, and even me.

"You'll never become a king while you live in the house that had been Françoise's parents' home," Vincent said. "If you are ever going to heal your co-dependency, the only solution is to sell the house and live somewhere else."

I was shocked. I knew this directive wouldn't sit well with Paul—or, especially, with Françoise. Paul had invested a great deal in remodeling the home that Françoise had inherited from her father to make it their own. It was a uniquely beautiful and extraordinary property that sat adjacent to the Saint-Victoire Mountain range in Southern France, a setting unusual in that part of the world. The countryside surrounding their home resembled a Cezanne painting. Giving it up made no sense to me. Surely, I thought, there must be other ways to address the dilemma Vincent had described.

During the breakout session, I could feel Paul's resistance to this recommendation, and I recalled his statement to Gloria and me that Vincent could be arrogant and eccentric. Still, Vincent's teaching did make sense to me—that a man becomes a king by building his own kingdom, not by inheriting one, and then invites his queen to join him. I could see the point Vincent was making since, metaphorically, that was essentially what Gloria and I had done. I had built an academic "kingdom" that provided us with a generous lifestyle and had invited Gloria to live there with me. However, as Paul had been—and continued to be—successful in his career, he was hardly relying on Françoise's inheritance. Whether Vincent was just provoking Paul or really meant what he said remained to be seen.

When we said goodbye to Paul and Françoise at the end of the seminar, they were already preparing for the de-med. Paul also said he was looking forward to having a surrogacy.

"We'll see you at the spring seminar," we all said, almost in unison.

That never happened. Paul and Françoise decided to drop out of The Project rather than sell their home and, at the same time, Gloria and I sharpened our focus on facilitation. As Vincent's mandate to cut what he considered unhealthy ties with people outside The Project swung weight with us, we eventually severed our ties with Paul and Françoise. This was hard for us, and it would be almost seven years before we reestablished our relationship with them.

ONE EVENING DURING the fall seminar, I was working with an older German woman named Leyna, who had asked me for a private session.

"I was a little girl during World War II when American pilots bombed our family farm and destroyed our home," she told me.

I could feel her fury mounting as she spoke. Here I was, an American man of a comparable age, sitting in front of her. My father, or my uncle, who had been in the U.S. Army Air Force, as it was known during that war, could have been one of the bomber pilots, for all she or I knew.

A knot was forming in my stomach but, as I trusted the process, I asked Leyna a series of questions based on Vincent's protocol. I stayed present with her as she raged at me in German for what seemed like twenty minutes. Although I didn't understand much of what she was screaming, I clearly understood and felt her emotions. And I was able to take in what she was saying, digest it, and let it go, as I was trained to do.

Following her emotional outburst, she fell into my arms, exhausted, eyes watering. My eyes welled up too and as I hugged her, we cried together.

"You can feel me," she said. "I have a deep sense of relief, as if a fifty-kilo weight has been lifted from my heart."

As Leyna left the room, I had the realization that I was no longer devoid of feeling emotions. And that this communal moment of feeling another person's emotions was the element in which I actually became fully alive. It was a healing moment for her and one that felt deeply profound and healing for me too.

During my career as a professor, when students had come to me wanting to share emotional trauma born out of a situation in their life, I kept my distance, not just physically and professionally, but also emotionally, as my heart was closed to feeling compassion. I didn't or couldn't demonstrate empathy. Now I had nothing to fear. Since I had felt my own pain, I could feel another's. This capacity changed my life as a facilitator and as a husband, father, and teacher. Being a professor was no longer an impediment to being a human being.

I now knew I was a feeling man as well as a thinking man, and the combination of the two felt natural. My work as facilitator and teacher was becoming integral; feeling warmth and empathy in no way compromised the professionalism in my life. In fact, The Professor that had run my life for so many years was still there; however, he continually receded into the background, allowing me a deeper, fuller experience of life.

DURING THAT KING-QUEEN seminar in Europe, Vincent did several things that truly began to disturb me. While I could hear the rationale for his behavior, the emotional undertones didn't feel right. My cognitive dissonance arising from this mismatch came to the forefront with his treatment of Alma, a lovely Swedish woman who had been a Lutheran minister before becoming a facilitator. Alma was attending the seminar along with her fiancé, Lucas, and many of her clients. A spiritual marriage with Vincent presiding had been pre-arranged for the two of them, and the crowd had gathered for the ceremony during the evening break. Rather than marrying them as planned, however, he refused to perform the ritual—humiliating her in the presence of her clients.

Vincent had previously been told that Lucas had no intention of joining The Project. Waiting until that evening, he informed us all that no one could be a facilitator unless their mate did several years of individual facilitation.

Previously, he had taught that couples who were considering a marriage, first and foremost, should share a common set of values. Gloria and I certainly shared the same values as articulated in our wedding vows, so that part didn't seem off to us. Still, we had considered this as a teaching rather than a hard and fast rule, and we could imagine situations where it wouldn't necessarily matter.

That evening, however, Vincent humiliated Alma in front of the hundred attendees by describing her choice of a potential husband as indicative of her unfitness to serve as a facilitator. Gloria and I were surprised, as Alma and Lucas did share common values, including a rich spiritual life that included self-exploration. But those values didn't match Vincent's concepts.

"I would be out of integrity with The Project," Vincent said later, "and that's why I couldn't marry them."

Vincent's mistreatment of Alma was troublesome to Gloria and me. We were simply not prepared for this kind of behavior. It was the first time we witnessed him humiliating someone in public, but not the last.

WE HAD FIRST MET SOPHIA at the fall seminar in 2005, a little over a year from the time we started working with Vincent. She was essentially the leader of The Project in Europe. Most of the attendees were either working their process with Sophia or with facilitators and interns she trained and supervised. We'd met again at each subsequent seminar, at the biennial conventions, and when Sophia came to Grass Valley to work with Vincent during our intern class. It was there that she met and fell in love with Sam.

Sam, one of my very first clients, went to Europe about the same time as Vincent and Tina to live with Sophia and nurture their new relationship. Sophia continued being the leader in Europe, teaching a new intern class and facilitating individuals. Gloria and Sophia communicated quite often via email and phone, as Gloria was following in Sophia's footsteps in the U.S. I also stayed in touch with Sam.

At the seminar in Europe where Vincent humiliated Alma, he also began to publicly be critical of Sophia. At the same time, he elevated Tina as a facilitator despite the participants' negative reaction to her. In private, however, he was visibly frustrated with Tina, criticizing her for being Italian and not as "bright and articulate" as Sophia.

Gloria and I were concerned, but we took it in stride. However, upon returning home, we began hearing reports from our European colleagues that described what seemed like a continuing shift in Vincent's personality. On one occasion, for example, Sam was helping Vincent and Tina move some furniture when Vincent started screaming at Tina about something she did. Sam was horrified, as he'd never witnessed Vincent's temper. He also considered it inappropriate, as he was Vincent's client. Sam had become worried, as this wasn't the only such incident he had witnessed.

"I can't imagine Vincent acting the way Sam described," I said to Gloria, hazily recalling the warning Paul had given us about Vincent's arrogance. Although I was accustomed to Vincent saying outlandish things, I hadn't ever witnessed the kind of abuse Sam was reporting. I didn't know what to believe.

Gloria, too, seemed mystified. "We did notice some rough behavior at the last seminar, but nothing like Sam is describing."

We were to travel to Europe to visit Vincent and Tina, along with our European counterparts and friends, after my retirement that December.

"It's a good thing we're heading to Europe. We can see for ourselves." As we'd be their house guests for a week, we'd be able to witness Vincent's behavior first-hand.

AS I WAS RETIRING, I HAD CONVINCED myself that I needed my new role as a facilitator to ease my transition. Now I wondered whether I might be afraid to make waves—no matter what I discovered—to keep my position in The Project intact. Gloria and I brought our questions with us to Europe: Was the growing popularity of the work and the promise of power going to Vincent's head? Was being in an intimate relationship with Tina bringing out a side of him we'd never seen before—maybe his co-dependence?

When we arrived, we quickly learned that Vincent had demoted Sophia and taken away her groups and the intern class she was teaching. Vincent had told her that, if she ever wanted to heal her arrogance, she needed to find a humble job. He prescribed this loss of dignity to break a strong defensive aspect that lived behind this arrogance. That was the theory. Sophia had started working at a butcher shop, often waiting on people who were associated with The Project.

"Do you think he is projecting his own arrogant façade onto Sophia?" I asked Gloria one night after having been in Europe for several days.

"That's possible," Gloria replied. "Maybe she had some countertransference. But he's supervising her. The accusations he's couching as arrogance were behaviors made at his behest. I don't understand why he isn't helping her work it out rather than demoting her."

When we visited Sophia at the shop, we found that she had accepted her fate with grace. This was a woman who had led the entire facilitation program in Europe and had attracted several hundred people to The Project. She had been teaching the interns, supervising the small band of facilitators, and growing The Project in Europe. Before that, she'd been a successful entrepreneur and a student of several prominent non-dual spiritual teachers.

Gloria found Vincent's treatment of Sophia deeply disturbing. At dinner one evening with Sam and Sophia, we learned what had happened since Vincent and Tina arrived. Tina had taken over the leadership position. While Vincent taught interns the protocol, she facilitated the interns, along with anyone else who had previously worked with Sophia.

Later that night, Gloria asked me, "Do you think Vincent took the leadership and the clients away from Sophia as a ploy to elevate Tina? They're always worried about money and, just the other day, he confessed that Europe is a 'cash cow' for him."

"I don't think it's just that," I said. "He wants status for her."

"Sophia is devastated but also sincere in wanting to work her shadow," Gloria pondered. "Perhaps Vincent sees something we haven't seen or felt, and this was a move that will ultimately benefit her."

"He hasn't been harsh with us," I said. "Thus far, he has been appreciative for all the people we've attracted to The Project."

"Still, Vincent did give me a bizarre admonition during a supervision meeting I had with him this afternoon."

"Tell me."

"I asked him if there is anything special I needed to keep in mind with someone who has an eating disorder," Gloria began. "I was referring to Phillip, the new client I recently started working with who you haven't met yet. Vincent told me to fire him. He doesn't want 'fat people' associated with The Project because it doesn't look good."

I just shook my head, unsure how to respond.

Ultimately, Gloria decided to facilitate Phillip's process despite Vincent's proclamation, thinking he would see the beauty of his soul shining through his corpulent exterior when he finally met him. And, in fact, he did see it, albeit a year later.

"DO YOU THINK VINCENT was being a little hard on Tina during dinner last night?" Gloria asked me the night before we left. "He seemed to be criticizing everything she said."

"I just think he's under a lot of stress," I responded. "Teaching and facilitating in a foreign culture is work, as we know."

"Tina seemed fine with what he was saying," Gloria said. "I think she understood and felt supported by us when we observed that he was in content, and she was in context. But it was difficult for me to make sense of his bizarre behavior."

During that same dinner conversation, with Vincent facing me and Tina facing Gloria, I shared a transcendent moment with Vincent—another experience my rational mind could not explain—similar to what I had with Gloria when I felt we were in Atlantis. In this case, I had the distinct feeling that Vincent and I were having two conversations at once: one in the present and the other almost two thousand years ago.

This time, Vincent and I might have been in Judea at the Last Supper, a teacher and his disciple, two seekers forging an eternal bond. What was clear was our common purpose: to bring Vincent's teaching to a larger audience—to the world. I could smell the desert air and feel a hot breeze on my face. I felt connected to the brother I never had. And I realized how lonely I had been, first growing up as an only child and then later, with a father who was emotionally absent. I began to realize how hungry I had been for a spiritual teacher who could help guide me back to the mystical aspects of religion, which I left behind after my mother's death. In addition, I appreciated the experience of an intimate male presence like I'd known with Paul. Vincent had seen to it that I severed my relationship with Paul, and he soon moved into his place.

When we came back to the reality of the present moment, I was left with the feeling of cognitive dissonance I'd felt since the beginning of the visit. How could a man generate so much love? And how could he convey me into a dramatic transpersonal moment that seemed to heal any insecurity I might have had? I believed he saw and reflected to me the immensity of my being, as well as a reality outside the normal bounds of day-to-day consciousness. Yet his capabilities seemed correspondingly linked to the intensity of the abuse we were beginning to glimpse with others.

We returned home filled with images of our remarriage ceremony and the transpersonal experience I'd had with Vincent at that last dinner, leaving behind memories of Vincent's seemingly erratic and abusive behavior, which just faded away. The goodness we experienced submerged any seeds of doubt that had been planted.

Chapter 24

Max—The Warning

*Like us, they have personalities, moods, and emotions; they laugh
and they play. Some show grief and empathy and are self-aware and
very likely conscious of their actions and intents.*
—Virginia Morell, ANIMAL WISE

I COULD HEAR THE EXCITEMENT in Gloria's voice.
"The house next door to Vincent and Tina is for sale.
I love it. I talked to the owners, and it hasn't even
been listed yet. They'll sell it to us without using a
real estate agent."

Gloria was calling from Grass Valley, where she was
visiting with Vincent and Tina. They had recently
returned from Europe, intending to make the U.S. the
base for The Project. This small town, known for its
artistic and spiritual community, already had a dozen or
so of his followers, most of whom had been traveling to
the Bay Area for monthly groups with us during his
absence.

"What's it like?"

"An open floor plan with a large high-ceiling living
room," she raced on, "a country kitchen and formal dining
room, floor-to-ceiling windows overlooking huge lawns, a

natural swimming pool and waterfall, with the Sierra Foothills in the background. The house will be great to hold our groups and there's a lovely room for individual facilitation."

"Sounds like we'd be living in the country," I said.

"We would—but only ten minutes from town. I'll text you some pictures, so you'll get an idea. The owners and I have even discussed the price."

The home and grounds were stunning. It was our dream house, our Shangri-La, the place we would live out the remainder of our lives. The added bonus seemed to be that Vincent and Tina were living on an adjacent property just up the hill. We could see the possibility of forming an intentional community of like-minded people—the kind of community Gloria and I had spoken about in our wedding vows.

Our home in Berkeley sold quickly. Moving into our new house was surprisingly simple and easy. The whole thing was *bashert*—"meant to be" in Yiddish—our destiny. Many of our clients, especially those intending to join the next intern class that Gloria and I would teach together, were moving to Grass Valley too. Others would commute to Grass Valley for individual sessions and groups that we would offer in our new home.

We were now co-leaders of The Project, along with Vincent and Tina, and we were creating a property to support the work. He invited us to be members of his newly formed Board of Directors as he incorporated The

Project as a not-for-profit corporation, and I would soon become Chairman of the Board.

Gloria thought that living close to Vincent would give her immediate access to him, making it easy to get the supervision she thought would elevate her own work as a facilitator. And so did I. We believed we could use anything that came up for us in our facilitation, in the same way we did within our coupledom, as spiritual work. Now that we had worked out so much between us, we agreed that the possibility of learning about ourselves in our work with clients was the next frontier and having Vincent close at hand to ask questions and receive feedback seemed an amazing opportunity.

On a personal level, and perhaps even more important to me, was the huge change involved in leaving the university system, which had provided an anchor for most of my adult life. Being part of the community represented by The Project gave me a sense of purpose and place to ease my transition.

"You're just like family," Vincent proclaimed when we moved in. I felt welcome, with a new sense of security, as I left academia. Living next door to him would be the perfect way for my new career as a facilitator to unfold.

ONE NIGHT, SHORTLY AFTER we had moved into our new home, we heard screaming and yelling coming from up the hill. A few minutes later, Tina showed up on our doorstep. She was on the brink of hysteria.

"I don't know what he wants from me," Tina cried out as she fell into Gloria's arms.

Gloria sat down with her on our couch, and I sat across from her.

"I'm terrified of him," Tina sobbed. "He almost threw me down the stairs. I'm afraid for my life."

Gloria and I stared at each other in disbelief. During our trip to Europe, we had heard talk of Vincent's abuse from others in The Project, and we'd witnessed his temper flare a few times. However, we had managed to find excuses and to dismiss the behavior. Now it was literally on our doorstep and undeniable.

"What does he want from me? More passion? More sex? To be more relational! For me to enlighten! What is wrong with me?"

They were supposed to be *the* model couple. Beyond anything we'd heard or seen, we were stunned by her outburst.

"How can I do any of those things when I'm terrified of him?"

Our little dog Max jumped into her lap, and we all sat together, trying to comfort and reassure her. Dismissing this experience again as stress—this time, due to their recent return from Europe—was no longer ringing true. Maybe they were just like many other couples that get into fights—I had witnessed similar behavior with my aunts and uncles. However, he was supposed to be our teacher. We would never have spoken so harshly to each other the way they did, even in the worst of our fights when we were really letting it rip.

I don't remember whether we walked her back home or whether Vincent came and got her. But I do remember the stark contrast between his behavior before he went to Europe and his behavior after he returned. I began to question whether anything had changed, except maybe our proximity.

MAX HAD ATTENDED ALL OUR DAY-LONG sessions when we were Vincent's clients and had attended all the intern classes. When the class ended and Vincent certified us, one of the facilitators joked, "Max should be certified too." In fact, he did serve as an emotional support dog. Often when clients had deep emotional outbursts, Max would jump into their lap and lick their tears. On several occasions, Vincent even used Max in his energy healing work by letting him rest on a client's chest. When he was asked to do an energy clearing of a home someone was going to rent, he used Max to "mark the spot" where any negative entities might be hiding. Max dutifully obliged.

That's what made it even more puzzling when, two months after we moved into our new home, Vincent launched into a completely unexpected concern.

"I've heard through the grapevine that your focus on Max is illuminating your codependent behavior again," he said, looking at Gloria.

Vincent and Tina had come down the hill to visit with us, and we were sitting on our deck looking out over the lake and the distant hills. I'd just poured him a glass of his favorite wine, a pink merlot, and was happily settling into being the host in our new home.

"Max is being used as a medication to cover your existential pain and the emptiness between you two," he went on.

"I don't feel there is emptiness between us," I said, looking at Vincent incredulously. "In fact, there is a growing flow of love between us that we've never experienced before."

"Max is medicating the pain and fear you feel from leaving the university, Bill," he continued. "I heard you say that men shrivel up and die once they retire. Maybe you'd feel your fear of death if the dog wasn't there to make you happy."

Looking directly at Gloria, he said, "And you'd feel the emptiness that exists between you two without the struggle your relationship was built on—and the fear of your death too."

Vincent showed no emotion either in his face or his body as he said this, which was uncharacteristic of him. I didn't recognize him this way, and I was speechless.

"You can't see how emotionally unhealthy your clients' relationships are because of your own relationship with Max." He seemed to be on a roll. "This means you can't facilitate them, let alone teach an intern round or anyone else, as long as you have him. The only way you two can move to the next level of your own relationship is to give Max away or—better for him, just put him to sleep."

I looked over at Gloria. The alarm on her face was quickly shifting into despair.

"It would be much easier for Max to reincarnate with a new family in his next lifetime," Vincent continued, "than for him to adjust to a new family now."

We were even more surprised when Tina nodded, indicating her agreement with him.

"I don't see how you can represent and lead The Project as long as you medicate with Max," Tina said in her thick accent. Her face was stone cold too.

Were they trying to provoke us? To push us aside in order to elevate Tina the way they did with Sophia in Europe?

"We are Max's stewards," I said, feeling pain in my heart. "He's part of our family, just like you are with your daughter."

"Don't be ridiculous!" Tina exclaimed, mimicking the way Vincent would brush off any reasoned reply. "He's a dog, not a person."

I felt like hitting her over the head with an iron skillet.

Vincent quickly changed the subject, asking about the status of several of our clients. We gave him a quick rundown, finished our wine, and said goodbye.

"I CAN'T BELIEVE VINCENT told us to get rid of Max," I said to Gloria after they left. "I thought he loved Max. And he had said getting a puppy was good for our relationship four years ago."

"I remember," Gloria said.

And now here we were, grief-stricken and panicking at this sudden reversal.

We had moved to Grass Valley with the intent of being project leaders, to facilitate, and to teach the next intern class. In fact, our financial planning included another ten years of income as facilitators. We had not intended to retire completely. But without facilitation and the intern class, we would be doing just that. Still, we couldn't let Max go.

"What are we missing here?" Gloria asked me, tears in her eyes. "What are we not seeing about our relationship that Vincent does?"

We were accustomed to trusting Vincent's intuition. After all, working with him had cleared out all the immeasurable emotional gunk in each of us, which had allowed our love to blossom. He had been kind and sympathetic to us during our de-meds and had stayed with me every step of the way towards emotional and spiritual renewal.

We sat in silence. For Gloria, losing Max would be like losing a child. For me, it would be like losing a dear friend.

"I'm in agonizing pain at the thought of giving Max up. But is the constant joy I feel with him covering some unhealthy pattern I'm not tracking?" Gloria was desperately trying to make sense of what was happening.

"Maybe some people are jealous of the love we have for Max," I suggested.

Gloria took that in, and after a long pause, she wondered aloud, "Given the issues he and Tina are having in their relationship, do you think he is projecting his ideas about relationship onto us?"

"What do you mean?"

"Is it possible that he justifies his discontent with Tina by insisting that, if a couple isn't constantly having turmoil, they must be medicating on something?"

"That is an interesting theory. Just as bad is the possibility that they are looking for a way to justify taking away from us all that we've built while they were gone," I said. "On the other hand, maybe there's some truth to what Vincent told us. The issues in my first marriage were plastered over by our focus on the kids."

Silence again. My heart was pounding in my chest.

"Maybe Vincent and Tina are just challenging us to self-question our behavioral patterns, and that's all it is," Gloria mused. "There must be something we're supposed to learn."

Vincent had used this strategy of challenging emotional limits with the de-med process for many clients. He had done so with us as we took our separation to a painful emotional limit.

We were in a daze for several weeks, letting ourselves imagine the loss of Max or The Project. At the same time, more than ever, we recognized that something was going on with Vincent and Tina that didn't feel healthy.

It seemed clear that Vincent meant it: we would have to retire from The Project or give up Max. Now what? We felt trapped, as we were deeply involved—on several levels. We both looked at Max. He was fast asleep on his favorite overstuffed living room chair.

We sat down to discuss the situation. I shook my head. "This is for real. If we stop being facilitators and lose the income, this house will be too big and too expensive for us," I reasoned. "Unfortunately, it wouldn't make sense to sell it now that the economic downturn has wiped out a good part of our equity. We'd lose a big chunk of our life savings. Still, giving up Max would be a betrayal of our hearts."

"Oh my God, Bill. This is the kind of thing that happens to people in cults. Is this really happening to you and me?"

Vincent had often said, "The Project is based in love, not fear." Still, in this moment, we were wrapped in fear.

"I trust you, Bill, and your good heart and conscience," Gloria said. "This is a clear opportunity for me to 'lean into you' to handle this for us. Will you?"

Vincent had been teaching and asking women to "lean into" their man. Whether or not that practice was ultimately a justification for his patriarchal ways, we decided to try it. There seemed to be some truth to it, but we felt it had to be mutual.

"I'll put my faith in your judgment and abide by your decision," she said.

Mentally confused and emotionally pained, I nodded yes.

WE SENT MAX TO A DOG CAMP for three months—a place he was familiar with, since that's where he usually stayed when we were traveling. Because the camp owners had been Max's trainers and had several small dogs of their own, we knew he not only was in good hands but that he would probably have a blast. We were essentially trying out giving him away. We even made a tentative arrangement that they would keep him.

In fact, the pain of life without Max during those three months did take us to our emotional limit once again. His absence conjured up feelings of emptiness in us, but we couldn't tell if it was a sense of being childless or the loss of trust in Vincent, along with the pain of being forced into an impossible situation. Whatever the origin of our discomfort, the situation had us relying on each other in a new way.

Meanwhile, we had absolutely lost our trust in Tina and were never again able to feel her compassion. Rather, she felt cold and disconnected, which seemed to corroborate Vincent's judgment of her, which he shared with us in private. In addition, this series of events was leading to a shift. How we went about facilitating couples was diverging from Vincent's protocol.

For ourselves, we were clear that loving Max took nothing away from us. Quite the opposite: it produced more love and endless joy.

Still, I needed to solve the problem of Max. In stark contrast to my previous dynamic of jumping right to a solution—which had always been a sore spot between

Gloria and me—I allowed myself first to feel my pain, and then Gloria's pain, down to the bones.

Then the solution came to me. Or perhaps I should say, The Professor whispered to it me. He was always there in the background now, ready to handle Vincent when I felt confronted by him, in the same way I had learned to handle my father. And Gloria was beginning to draw on her experience of dealing with an irrational and emotionally immature mother. We were, in effect, recreating the relationships we had had with our parents, who had narcissistic tendencies. I believe Vincent was now revealing himself as our narcissistic boss, rather than trusted mentor. We were simultaneously seeing the pattern and the irony of the situation, in that we were beginning to mistrust a man who had taught us how to break those very patterns.

So one night at dinner during a weekend retreat we had organized, I suggested to Vincent and Tina that we get a second dog—a female.

"In that way," I said, "we would focus less on Max, and …"

"That's it!" Vincent exclaimed loudly before I could finish my sentence. "You two can focus on each other, and so can the dogs."

Tina nodded in agreement and promptly changed the subject.

In hindsight, I believe Vincent needed a way out of a situation he had created, and The Professor provided one.

He really couldn't afford to lose us—we were the main draw that filled The Project's coffers.

Gloria and I found a five-year-old female Maltese that was up for adoption by a breeder, now that she had finished her breeding years. We brought her home, eager to try this solution. Max ignored her. So did Vincent and Tina—they never came down to meet her. Our attempts to potty train her failed, as did teaching her to walk on a leash. Clearly, she'd spent her entire life in a kennel. Ultimately, we returned her to the breeder. The whole matter ended and was never brought up again—by anyone. Max resumed his emotional support efforts in groups and sessions and was always welcome at Vincent's seminars and workshops. He'd often place himself at Vincent's feet and, oddly enough, Vincent would be disappointed when Max missed one of his events or ignored him.

In the end, I couldn't figure out whether Vincent had been just testing our limits around what we'd do with respect to his commands or orders, or whether he really believed Max was in the way of Gloria and me having a healthy relationship. Still, one thing was for sure: we were clear that we could no longer have an authentic relationship with Vincent and Tina. When asked why he prescribed something in any way that might have challenged his wisdom or authority, he wouldn't answer. Instead, he would feign his enlightenment: "I'm always in the present moment; I don't remember why I said that." As for Tina—her responses were incomprehensible.

"SHOW EMPATHY FOR THE INNER CHILD," Vincent often would say in our training during the intern class, "but not for the strategic self."

The strategic self, as he would call it, was a persona developed by an individual to protect them from feeling emotions. In my case, it had been The Professor. Gloria's version was a persona sometimes called The Lawyer who could out-argue anyone. There was also a side of her that Vincent called The Caretaker: her compassionate, caring side. While her clients loved The Caretaker, Vincent tried to convince Gloria that this part of her represented an unhealed aspect of herself that emanated from fear rather than love. He often told her she needed to be "tougher" with her clients.

While in Europe, Vincent had concluded that the way to break unhealthy emotional or behavioral patterns for certain people—if the pattern or behavior was emanating from their strategic self—was to not feel any empathy for them at all.

"You give tough love when you really care for a client," Vincent would often say, as a way of explaining what began to look like increasingly abusive actions.

I had accepted this mantra at first, assuming Vincent and Tina were acting with skillful strategy. It never occurred to me that they didn't feel empathy, even though the whole paradigm was built on this capacity.

But I was increasingly recognizing that they were projecting their own unhealthy patterns in full view of everyone—along with a set of elegant justifications.

Although Vincent's writing and speaking about The Project still seemed internally consistent to me, I began to see and feel how his actions were not. Tough love was beginning to look like emotional abuse. I was expected to be tough with my own clients but, instead, I found myself attempting to protect them from his harsh outbursts. Occasionally, it worked. And while I was expected to seek his advice on implementing the deconstruction process, I was beginning to realize that something was terribly wrong.

Chapter 25

Undermined

Power tends to corrupt, and absolute power corrupts absolutely.
Great men are almost always bad men.
—John Emerich Edward Dahlberg-Acton,
1st Baron Acton

"HOW IS NORA DOING?" Vincent asked me at one of our monthly supervision circles.

We'd been living in Grass Valley for five months now, but we maintained our practice of sixty or so people in the Bay Area. Nora had been one of our clients there, and we saw her once a month when we went to Berkeley to offer individual and group facilitation. While many of our clients in the Bay Area were moving to Grass Valley, Nora was reluctant to do so.

"Nora made great progress working with Gloria," I answered. "She was able to access her emotional body and worked the issues she had with her mother. But we felt she might benefit from working with me."

I paused for a moment, and then added, "It's something you recommended," assuming he might not remember.

Our small group of facilitators, six of us in Grass Valley, sat around a large rectangular table in a restaurant on a Sunday evening following a weekend seminar. Vincent was seated, as usual, at the middle of the table, like a king holding court. At least it was starting to seem that way to me.

Each of us gave Vincent a status report on those clients who were facing a challenge in their process, and we asked questions about how we might proceed. As his behavior had begun to change, we had become protective of our clients, avoiding saying too much. However, there seemed to be informants in our groups who would give him a heads up before we reported any difficulties at the supervision circles. What and how much to tell him and still seek his advice had become a balancing act. Sometimes his reflections were helpful, whereas at other times they were counter to our own intuition—or counter to our sense of decency.

I still clung to the belief that he knew more than I did as a facilitator, especially when I didn't understand his directive regarding a person's process. Nor did I understand why he got so upset when any of us made what he considered to be a mistake. It seemed to me that mistakes were part of the learning process. Over my many years as an educator, I'd taken my students' errors in stride, as affording them an opportunity to learn something new. But when a facilitator did something Vincent thought was wrong, even if it was perfectly reasonable, he'd go into despair over their judgement. It didn't take long to realize that it was in everyone's best interest to soothe him. We'd have to reassure him that it was our fault for not understanding him or the protocol, rather than faulting what he had previously instructed us to do. We gave up on expecting him to take responsibility despite it being a fundamental premise of the work.

Vincent gave me a stern look. "Nora should quit her acupuncture practice in Oakland, move to Grass Valley, and join the next intern class this coming January."

I was surprised. A notice had been sent out announcing the new intern class, and Nora hadn't applied. I knew from our work together that she wasn't drawn to Vincent. She had had a negative reaction to him at the last two seminars because he reminded her of her father. I felt that Nora was making progress and thought it would be premature to attempt to use that reaction to work out the issues with her father.

Still, the next time I met with Nora in Berkeley, I decided to test her reactivity and I brought up the idea of the intern class.

"I believe you'd make a great facilitator, given your training and background working with people."

She looked surprised.

"A number of people in my group are moving to Grass Valley to join the next intern class," she responded.

A look of sadness crossed her face. "Some of them are good friends of mine. I'll miss them."

"Gloria and I will facilitate each of the interns individually or as a group, so you can continue your process with us," I said, aiming to reassure her. "Vincent will only teach the facilitation protocol and offer a seminar every three months. You won't have to interact with him if you don't care to, although it might be a good thing for you."

At first, I was trying to convince Nora to make the move, still giving Vincent the benefit of the doubt. But I also knew it was important to support Nora in finding her own self-authority—a core issue stemming back to her father. Nora took all of this in and said she would think about it. I went away feeling unsuccessful, having caught myself in my own father projection with Vincent. I had hoped to report back to him that I had changed Nora's mind, even if doing so was against my better judgment.

"TELL NORA WE CAN'T SERVE her anymore if she doesn't want to move here," Vincent said when I told him what had happened.

I felt very uneasy about relaying this directive to Nora; I believed she could still benefit from the work wherever she lived. And I didn't like threatening her or anyone else as a manipulation. It felt cult-like.

To my relief, I didn't have to tell Nora about my conversation with Vincent. At our next session, she said she'd talked to her friends and decided to move to Grass Valley after all. She would join the next intern class. Within a month, Nora gave up her apartment in Oakland and was preparing to leave her acupuncture practice as well. She found a place to live in Grass Valley and attended one of Vincent's weekend events. Several days later, she came to see me.

"This isn't working for me. I'm moving back to Oakland." Nora was emphatic. "I just don't like it here — Grass Valley is too small for me. I don't want to give up my acupuncture practice. And attending Vincent's lectures won't work for me either. I just don't trust him."

I found myself caught in the awareness that I too was starting to lose trust in Vincent. Questions swirled in my head. When did I begin to lose faith in him? We owed so much to him for the work we had done together. He was brilliant, but his behavior had become erratic. What happened to our being independent contractors? He had skillfully turned that arrangement into a ruse. If we disagreed, he would threaten to take away our certificates — not in retaliation, he would claim, but because we were demonstrating that we weren't qualified if we had a different point of view or couldn't deliver his brand of tough love.

I came back from my thoughts and doubts to offer empathy to Nora. "I can feel your sadness. My heart aches for you. Is there anything else?"

Nora shrugged. "Vincent tells me it's my 'A' destiny to become a facilitator. Otherwise, I'll be following my 'B' or even 'C' destiny and not living up to my soul capacity. Give me a break, Bill!"

This sounded to me like another veiled threat on Vincent's part. While it didn't matter whether I believed in his prediction or not, Nora clearly didn't. Vincent claimed access to the Akashic Records, which are purported to contain the complete life history of every human being—past, present, and future. Gloria and I did have a strong experience of a past life together in Atlantis that had a huge impact on my own development. All of this was part of Vincent's teaching. But Nora was my client, and I wanted to trust her own realizations without Vincent undermining me at every turn. I asked her to go on.

"Even though Vincent knows I am unhappy here, he sent me an e-mail saying I have a contract to meet my soul mate at a coffee shop here in Grass Valley." She was speaking quite rapidly now. "He told me that, before incarnating this lifetime, my soul mate and I had made a contract to meet at Fable Coffee."

"Wow!" I was surprised, as that kind of statement felt very invasive to me. Nora didn't resonate with the notion of soul contracts, and a statement like that would only drive her away.

"How does that land for you?" I asked.

"I don't care," Nora said angrily. "It's nonsense, so I'm going back to Oakland. I just want to continue to work with you and Gloria when you come to Berkeley."

I was silent for a few moments as my thoughts raced: This is so confusing. If I tell Nora that it's okay to go back to Oakland, I'll surely incur Vincent's wrath—he'll accuse me of being weak. He expects me to counter Nora and insist she stay. But Nora and I are making progress, and she is beginning to trust me. That is something new for her, given her relationship with her father. If I insist that Nora stay, she'll probably leave anyway. If I cut her loose, I'll be terminating her process at a crucial junction on her emotional path.

I took a deep breath.

"I respect your decision to return to Oakland," I said. "And I'm happy to work with you, as I am sure Gloria is, during our monthly trips to the Bay Area."

I was relieved. I felt that respecting Nora's decision was best for her—although certainly not for me in the face of Vincent's pressure.

Within a day, Nora was packed up and on her way back to the Bay Area. She quit The Project during our next session in Berkeley, a month later.

At the next supervision circle, I briefed Vincent on all that had transpired—some of which he had already heard through the grapevine.

"None of you can see what I see," he said sadly, drawing the group's attention to his loneliness and his grief over how he had overestimated our capability. "No one can meet me."

Then he began to berate me in front of the other facilitators in the most demoralizing and traumatic way, emphasizing my weakness in not being tough enough on Nora.

"You don't know how to give tough love," Vincent said, shaking his head. "You're too soft a man."

After several moments of silence, Vincent continued, an air of superiority in his voice. "Well, you two can work with Nora if you want. But she can never, ever come to anything I offer. I don't want her there projecting the rage she has toward her father on to me!"

That statement was obviously referring to Nora's tendency to confront him in public, which Vincent did not like. Hoping for a semblance of redemption in my teacher's eyes, I pressed the situation further.

"But aren't you the perfect foil for her to work through her father issues?"

My hope in asking this question was to let Vincent know I understood how the protocol worked by triggering an emotional response in a client. I thought this might be a good teaching moment and a way of taking his attention off me. By this time, I had learned that this was one of the ways to handle Vincent.

Vincent waved his arm, shrugging off my question. He'd hear none of it.

"It's a shame," he mused. "There's a young man going to Fable Coffee every day this week for coffee, knowing he's supposed to be there, but not why. He's waiting for the love of his life, and she won't show up because she's afraid of being in a healthy relationship!"

Feeling like a character in *The Twilight Zone*, I recognized that I was caught between a father projection, causing me embarrassment over a mistake, and anger at Vincent's lack of compassion. He was undermining me at every turn. Based on my experience as a professor who had successfully mentored students and empowered faculty for more than half my lifetime, I knew in my bones that his approach was wrong and would end badly.

"MAYBE I'M NOT CUT out to do this work," I said to Gloria that evening. "I never had self-doubt about my work as an engineering professor, but maybe Vincent is right that I know nothing about being an emotional body facilitator. I might as well quit."

"I'm sorry this is so painful, darling," Gloria said compassionately. "Your father was critical of your behavior, but he knew nothing about mathematics, physics, or engineering, so he couldn't criticize you in that domain. Vincent's criticism hurts even more because you respect his intellect. You had The Professor protecting your vulnerability. Now he's in the shadows and you are without his protection—you are laid bare. This is exactly what makes you a great facilitator."

"Thank you, Gloria," I said.

She moved closer, as I had seen her do many times with clients when they were in a painful process.

"That small boy who was hammered by his father when he was so vulnerable is still hurting every time

Vincent criticizes you—retraumatizing the boy," she said. I felt her love engulfing both of us. "Billy needs you to be with him when Vincent comes after you. I can feel you are there for him now."

A familiar quietness came over me. Gloria and I had developed our own "love-bubble," which we later heard described by Stan Tatkin in his book *Wired for Love*. Ours had developed naturally as an outgrowth of our individuation and now provided a zone of safety, care, and devotion toward each other's well-being. After our years of emotional growth and the relationship stress between us, we naturally found ourselves on the other side of it, and the bubble surrounding us had become our anchor and our haven—a zone of mutual nurturance and love. It felt healing to inhabit this bubble together. My heart felt at ease. I could calm Billy.

"This love-bubble is exactly the kind of sweetness I'd always believed was possible between us," Gloria said.

"It's a dynamic Vincent would have called codependence," I quipped.

"It's too bad he didn't avail himself of our years of research together and what we've discovered about relationships," she added ruefully. "His ideas sounded good, and some were, but his actual relationship isn't impressive at all."

Following the episode with Nora, Gloria and I became even more concerned about Vincent's disturbing pattern, which was becoming difficult for us to explain to ourselves. While he promised the work would build self-authority, the opposite seemed to be true. If anyone disagreed with him, he quickly diagnosed the opposition as emanating from the so-called strategic self or persona that needed to be dismantled. Of course, he never diagnosed his abuse in the same way, except for a few well-placed admissions, strategically interjected to prove his sincerity.

Still, there were many times that he was right about dismantling someone's strategic self. And by now, I was committed to the work and couldn't see the vicious cycle I was in. I was trapped in a loop that made me doubt my own truth. Added to this, Gloria and I felt a sense of responsibility to protect our clients, compounded by our appreciation of all that we'd learned from Vincent over the years and the loyalty that emanated from it.

AMID THESE INCIDENTS, GLORIA and I were increasingly being hooked by contradictory messages that played into our own confusion and touched on our still unhealed childhood wounds from parents with narcissistic tendencies. Vincent might be his charming, friendly self to us, and then an hour or so later send an email to Gloria or me that would typically begin with "How could you?" followed by a reminder of some way we had let him down. Rather than explain what had occurred or what we had experienced, I would answer with some version of "I'm sorry that I caused you so much pain in having to write this email to me." I had learned to protect myself from my father's criticism as a child by apologizing to him first, before telling him what had happened. I had become so habituated to this tactic that I repeated it in the face of Vincent's criticism.

With time, Gloria and I came to learn that, from childhood, we could be considered empaths. Vincent's behavior was typical of how a narcissist hooks people like us—by getting us to feel his pain rather than our own. As Vincent was sinking the hook in deeper—he was a master at it—I had chosen to stay connected with him. But, despite my misgivings, it was also clear to me that I had some additional personal work to do: my father projection was slowly building inside me, with Vincent as the perfect trigger.

My association with Vincent and The Project fulfilled other needs as well. Since leaving the University and moving to Grass Valley, my world had gotten small, as I didn't have time to make friends outside the facilitator circle—a small circle that included Vincent and Tina. During the summer, they would come down for a swim. On those occasions, I continued to enjoy discussing everything from politics to religion and from physics to metaphysics with Vincent. I was hungry for these talks. While I still had Gloria, I no longer had my colleagues— or Paul, for that matter—with whom to have these rich conversations.

For a while, we continued to benefit from the seminars and retreats as well. The talks he gave always seemed to provide new information about the human condition, and he certainly played into my ego.

He'd often refer to me when he used a scientific or technical analogy to make a point at a workshop or seminar: "Isn't that right, Professor Bill?" or "Am I right about that, Doctor Bill?" Sometimes he'd hold his arm out in a gesture for me to explain the scientific principle—and I usually did—and end his solicitation by saying, "You got it right." I still needed his "Atta boy," since they'd been absent in my childhood.

Meanwhile, Gloria and I continued to notice his seemingly increasing erratic behavior, rationalizing it to ourselves for the sake of keeping our life intact.

SIMON, AN ORGANIZATIONAL DEVELOPMENT consultant and one of Gloria's clients, had been taking prescription medication to deal with long-term depression and anxiety. Although she hadn't been working with him very long, they had come up with a reasonable schedule for Simon to wean himself off the drugs. Naïvely, Gloria revealed her excitement about Simon's progress to Vincent during the coffee break at a seminar.

"He is very sincere, and he's adhering to his plan," she enthusiastically told Vincent during the morning coffee break.

Apparently unimpressed by Gloria's assessment, Vincent simply looked at her without comment. As we gathered back in the seminar room, he stepped directly in front of Simon.

"You are nothing but a drug addict," he announced for all hundred and fifty attendees to hear. "We can't serve you anymore as long as you are taking any medication."

Simon's face turned beet red. He sank into his chair as if punched in the gut. Vincent must have had some idea that he needed to shock Simon's defenses but, instead, Simon was traumatized and devastated. After several seconds, he stood up and walked out. Gloria quickly left the room to speak with him.

"He felt misled," Gloria told me, recounting their conversation. "He thought this was a love-based process."

"How did you respond?"

"I told him Vincent must have sensed that tough love was needed to wake him up."

Gloria described how Simon had expressed appreciation for her and said that he could feel her love and respect for him. Her support had made him feel safe enough to start giving up his medication.

"But I never saw this coming," Simon had told her. "What Vincent did was abuse, not tough love. Tell me, Gloria, do you agree with Vincent?"

My curiosity was aroused. "What did you say?"

"Bill, it was such an awkward moment. I agreed with Simon, yet I represent Vincent's work. How could I disagree with his judgement regarding a client?"

"So ... do you disagree with Vincent's assessment?"

"Yes, I do disagree." Gloria sighed deeply. "Simon said he could have continued working with me, but not in the context of Vincent's influence. He quit. Now I feel terrible that I even told Vincent anything about his process."

I put my arm around her as she wiped her tears.

MORE THAN EVER, GLORIA and I wanted to teach and facilitate the next intern class. As Vincent's behavior became increasingly inconsistent, we were losing trust in him. We felt uniquely qualified, since we had recruited and facilitated most of the class over the past years, and we knew these people and their process well. And while we were still working with our own triggers and projections toward Vincent, we were steps ahead of the interns. Vincent had updated the protocol and developed new approaches for training. This all felt exciting and promising.

About a month before the intern class was to begin, Vincent and Tina came to our home to discuss the revised protocol with us. We were engaged in what felt like a very stimulating discussion when Vincent suddenly stopped and, seemingly out of the blue, turned to Gloria.

"Tina and I are going to take over the entire intern class," he said. "You can keep working with whoever you want in the Bay Area, but we'll be working with everyone here."

The floor dropped out for Gloria and me.

"What?" Gloria exclaimed, shock fully visible on her face.

"We've heard about some of the things you are doing with your clients that are hurting them," he said.

I was momentarily transported back to Europe when Sophia had lost the intern class for a similarly asserted reason: harming her clients. Now—as then—the actual reason was to justify Tina and Vincent taking over. I was angry.

"Those clients were triggered because of the very things you told her to do!"

Vincent calmly began listing the accusations made by her clients. After a moment, Gloria cut him off.

"Those were interventions you insisted I make. They're not things I would have done otherwise."

He stared at Gloria with a blank look on his face. "I don't remember. I'm in the present moment." He paused then, turning to Tina as if he knew she had something to say.

"It's Vincent's paradigm," Tina asserted. "He should lead the training."

When he started in again with an example, Gloria stood up. She had heard enough. We left for home.

IT HURT TO WATCH OUR OLD CLIENTS driving up the hill to Vincent and Tina's home for their classes and groups. I felt like an outcast. We also speculated about how to make up the difference in our income.

"We still have our clients in the Bay Area," Gloria said. "We could build on that again."

We did continue co-facilitating our Bay Area group and Gloria and I even gave talks again. However, our heart wasn't in it as it had been in the past. Yet another petty altercation arose with Vincent. Finally, I was fed up. I quit.

As usual, Vincent tried smoothing things over the next time I encountered him walking by our house. I wondered whether, now that I was out from under his authority and independent of him, I might still be able to share some other kind of relationship with him. That remained to be seen.

Gloria continued as a facilitator for a little while longer. Once I quit, the wounded boy, Billy, began to relax even more. After I took a position as a part-time administrative law judge with a federal agency to make up some of the lost income, I began to feel more like myself again. Still, I hadn't spoken my full truth, following a pattern I learned early in life—to focus elsewhere. That "elsewhere" would reveal itself shortly.

Chapter 26

Standard of Care

The unleashed power of the atom has changed everything except our modes of thinking, and thus we drift toward unparalleled catastrophes.
We shall require a substantially new manner of thinking if mankind is to survive.
— Attributed to Albert Einstein

"THE FIRST STEP IS A LUMPECTOMY where we remove the tumor," the surgeon explained. "Then I'll refer you to a hematological oncologist for chemotherapy. After chemo, you'll be referred to a radiation oncologist for treatment."

Our heads were spinning. It was February 2012.

"But, what if I don't do chemotherapy and radiation?" Gloria asked. There was an edge in her voice.

"Well, these procedures are considered the standard of care for breast cancer." The surgeon looked at each of us to see if we were still with her. "The treatment I outlined is supported by clinical trials," she assured us, "and your health insurance will pay for it. No questions asked."

Gloria ended up having three out-patient surgeries: the lumpectomy; a lymph node dissection, as cancer cells were detected in her left armpit; and a port emplacement for possible chemotherapy. After ninety minutes of agonizing uncertainty, I would receive a page and go to a little private consultation room to await the surgeon, who would debrief me on the results of each surgery. I'd sit on a small loveseat before a coffee table with out-of-date magazines, facing an empty chair.

I'd study the nondescript wallpaper. *Was it purple-gray? Or was it gray-purple?* A print of an Impressionist landscape painting adorned the far wall. *Was it a Renoir or was it a Monet? Just look at the signature,* I told myself. Then I'd play out every horrible scenario in my mind: We found more than we thought was there. I'm terribly sorry, but your wife died on the operating table.

The door opened, and the surgeon appeared with the news about the tumor and her directive on what would follow. "Gloria did really well. She's in recovery and they'll bring her out shortly," she announced. "You'll be able to take her home this afternoon."

My heart would leap each time the hospital staff rolled Gloria's gurney down the hall to the dressing room. She'd smile at me, and my fear would begin to fade. Her eyes would close as she drifted off to sleep, and I'd fall in love with her all over again. It didn't matter how she looked or what state she was in. I was thrilled to bring her home for her recovery. I'd have her all to myself.

I would have liked to believe we were done after the three surgeries, but the cancer cells found in the sentinel and auxiliary lymph nodes called for post-operative treatments. Would it be a course of chemotherapy and then radiation, as the standard of care dictated? Or would she choose just one of the treatments? Or—none of the above?

"WHY PUT YOURSELF THROUGH the pain and misery of these treatments?" Vincent had stopped at our home a week after the cancer diagnosis. "You've lived a good life. So you die in five years. Stop making such a big deal about this lifetime. Before you know it, you'll be in your next one."

In retrospect, that marked the precise moment Gloria was done with Vincent and with being a facilitator of his deconstruction process. There was no way she would ever be able to reconcile the way he discounted the decisions confronting her. Vincent prided himself on teaching from a context where emotion is primary, yet he never seemed to feel the fear we were both experiencing. But even more disturbing than bypassing Gloria's emotions, he was downright cruel.

"You have to get bigger than the cancer," Vincent went on. "Bigger than the medical paradigm."

While there was some value in Vincent's admonition for Gloria, there was no prescription for how to carry out his advice. The stress he was causing Gloria made her emotional state worse, not better. There was no empathy, no comfort, no feeling. We'd have to figure it out on our own.

Gloria was still reeling from his words when she received an email from him later that night that made the situation worse.

"It's your own fault, taking all those hormones post-menopause, trying to recapture your youth," he wrote. "Take responsibility for getting cancer."

Now I too had finally had enough. Gloria was emotionally fragile, and I needed to protect her from Vincent's onslaught.

"Stop treating my wife this way," I wrote back to him. "Your insensitivity is making her emotional and physical state worse."

He responded with the kind of taunt that emotional bullies resort to. "I've lost all respect for you as a man," he wrote. "You have become codependent. You're projecting your mother onto Gloria, still trying to save her life."

Furious, I wrote back, "I don't want your respect, nor do I need your respect. Your respect means nothing to me."

I turned to Gloria, who was sitting next to me at the computer. "The end of our association with Vincent is very close. But unfortunately, we're neighbors."

Several days later, I was pulling weeds from our front lawn when he walked past our house. He smiled and acted as if nothing had happened.

"I know, I know," he said. "You're just protecting your wife. It's all okay. I would do the same thing."

Although he had attempted to smooth over our damaged friendship, I was becoming very wary of him.

IT SEEMED THAT I HAD BEEN working on my mother issues my entire adult life and, just when I felt I had some resolution, the breast cancer diagnosis had brought them up again. Gloria's diagnosis was, of course, the latest and most powerful instance of breast cancer among the women in my life. My mother had died from breast cancer, my cousin Leslie had succumbed to it, and several of our family and friends had survived it. And I had, in a profound way, charted my emotional and spiritual life around it.

But what became the most terrifying to me during those three surgeries was the waiting when I could do nothing but sit with my mind running through all the worst possible scenarios. Outpatient surgery was scheduled first thing in the morning, a God-awful time. I'd see Gloria off—surrender her—then I'd walk through the medical complex to the cafeteria. With a mug of coffee and a doughnut, I'd try to stay sharp and awake. My iPad became my link to the outside world. I tried to answer emails and text family and friends. But my mind would take over.

Up to this point, our long-term planning assumed that I would die first. After all, I am eight years older than Gloria. Now I was experiencing a deep-felt sense of aloneness as never before, at least not as a mature adult. My fears ran wild through my mind: "What if she dies before me? Who will I be without this partner? What will I do with my life alone?"

There was also the more immediate question: "How will I cope with the cancer diagnosis and the standard of care treatment plan?" Although the diagnosis was Gloria's, the post-op treatment plan would become our problem to solve.

I understood that I would have to be present with Gloria on a minute-to-minute, hour-to-hour, and day-to-day basis, and not exist in some future or past time. Simultaneously, I recognized how the past had conditioned my experience of the present. And I knew that the future was highly uncertain.

"YOU HAVE TO MAKE SOME immediate decisions about the chemotherapy," the oncologist told us the first time we met her. It was a week or two after the last of the three surgeries—the port emplacement.

"What's the rush?" Gloria asked. "I'd like to get some second opinions."

"You'll have to decide within six weeks," the oncologist said. "It's the standard of care."

The oncologist began explaining the two courses of chemotherapy Gloria could choose from and described the pharmaceuticals that might be used.

"There are short-term side effects like hair loss, nausea, compromised immune system, and exhaustion," she had explained, "and there are long-term side effects like increased risk of bone cancer or leukemia, and even heart disease. These effects are especially pronounced for the preferred protocol."

We were shown the infusion room where the chemotherapy would be administered. There were a dozen or so leather-covered reclining chairs arranged in a semi-circle facing a central nurses' station. Each chair reminded me of a Barcalounger, albeit with an IV standing at attention next to it, as if to protect the chair.

About half the chairs were occupied by individuals at various stages of their treatment. Some had already lost their hair, some were listening to music through ear buds, others were sleeping or being attended to by a caregiver. The sight of the patients, the sounds of the pharmaceutical names for the chemo—Taxotere, Adriamycin, and Cyclophosphamide, and the atmosphere of doom and misplaced hope infused us with such dread that we left the building like two drunken sailors on shore leave, weaving and wobbling through the parking lot. We both felt ready to vomit.

The prospect of the love of my life undergoing that torture was almost too much to bear. And yet this was what the standard of care dictated. None of it felt right.

Damn standard of care.

GLORIA AND I DECIDED TO GO BOTH inside and outside the traditional medical community for second and third opinions from the best specialists we could find. We sought help in the San Francisco Bay and Los Angeles areas.

"The lymph node pathology tells me you have 'micromets,'" one well-known pathologist in San Francisco told us. "That's a name for very small tumors. While micromets would still dictate chemotherapy, the pathology also indicates that the tumors have cells that divide slowly."

He went on to say that, because the tumors were highly estrogen dependent, the use of a drug to eliminate estrogen production meant that chemotherapy wouldn't add much to preventing a recurrence.

"In fact," the pathologist said, "because they are slowly dividing cells, I doubt chemotherapy will do anything."

"But chemotherapy is the standard of care," Gloria said.

"Sometimes the standard of care has to catch up with new scientific information as it becomes available," he explained. "We know a hell of a lot more now. That's my opinion."

We were shocked and confused. We had been pretty much convinced that chemotherapy was necessary.

"So, there's no need for chemotherapy," I said, wanting to make sure I understood.

"That's my opinion," he reiterated.

When we proposed these ideas to another highly recommended oncologist in San Francisco, however, he was alarmed. "Do you want to die?"

Gloria was speechless. So was I.

"I would insist that my mother undergo chemo," he went on.

"What about your own wife?" I asked him sharply.

"Yes, the same."

"And if it were you?"

He refused to answer me, throwing up his arms in disgust.

Gloria was determined to make a decision out of love rather than fear. It's one thing to consider the prospect of death. It's another to be told you have no choice in the matter by a mere mortal; Death had told me otherwise in his letter to me. Still, we really didn't know who to believe. The decision was gut-wrenching.

BACK IN OUR BAY AREA HOTEL ROOM after that difficult encounter with the oncologist, Gloria received an email from Vincent. She blanched as she read it to me.

"How could you leave Tom without a session?" Vincent wrote. "There is no one else who can work with him."

"I told Tom that I was not going to facilitate anymore, but I didn't know yet who would work with him," Gloria wrote back.

Because Gloria felt a deep sense of responsibility to her clients, she put up with a lot of Vincent's cruelty for their sake. But this was too much.

"You've left him in the lurch," he wrote back. "It's unforgiveable."

Gloria turned to me, leaving Vincent's email unanswered. "Actually, Bill, it's Vincent who's unforgiveable. I've transferred all my remaining clients to Tina or to some other senior facilitator. Tom understood that. He may not have liked it, but he understood."

"That's it. I'm done with The Project altogether," I said.

"Bill, I can finally agree with you."

"I WANT YOUR HONEST OPINION about what I should do." We had returned home from travels seeking second and third opinions. "What do you really think? How do you really feel?"

"I don't want to be a patriarchal know-it-all and tell you what to do," I responded. "But neither do I want to be a wishy-washy panderer, telling you that any choice you make would be okay with me. I'll need time to digest everything we've seen and heard."

I was beginning to feel a deep sense of remorse that I had trusted Vincent in the emotional arena regarding my clients. His recent behavior toward Gloria demonstrated to me that I probably had better instincts than he did. In the past, I had allowed myself to defer to him even when I sensed he was wrong. I now began to realize the depth to which I could trust myself in matters of the heart and spirit rather than relying on a spiritual teacher. This was a transition I'd have to manage on my own. Vincent's behavior was making it easy for me. The trust Gloria placed in me also enhanced my ability to trust myself.

In searching for answers to Gloria's questions, I had to be honest, direct, compassionate, and completely present with her. In other words, I would have to tell Gloria what I truly felt and thought about chemotherapy *and* that the choice was, indeed, truly hers. I'd be there either way. As engineers who had attended my safety and risk classes would learn, "*and* logic" is always more robust than "*or* logic" in determining the safety of a system. I had proven this mathematically.

The Professor's intellect was now in service of his heart.

Suddenly, too, Papaji's and Ramesh's teachings on non-duality were making sense and proving useful, as they could be applied effectively to keep both options open. In this "*and*" worldview—my scientific understanding of chemotherapy's effects and Gloria's choice—we were up against the medical, insurance, and pharmaceutical complex and its standard of care.

The decision-making process Gloria was using demonstrated the very nature of our new understanding. On one side, there was the medical establishment's information with its many conflicting ideas about cancer treatments. On the other side were a host of alternative treatments we learned about, such as nutraceuticals and mistletoe. All this new knowledge was useful to Gloria. Augmenting this information were reports from the women she'd met who were already recovering from breast cancer and who shared information regarding their choice of treatment and how their diagnosis was different or similar. Gloria took in all the data, as did I.

"How are you going to make a decision, Gloria?" I asked her one evening.

"The answer will have to find me," she answered. "I'm waiting for my decision to arrive."

This was what Jackie Margoles had taught: as one gathers more and more specific information, a "difference that makes a difference" will emerge, revealing an answer. This was an exquisite approach, and Gloria wasn't reaching for an answer. I was in awe of how she navigated the uncertainty and chaos, and I certainly would abide by her ultimate decision.

To support her approach, however, I began to read all the literature I could comprehend and some that I couldn't. I tried to interpret what the tumor and lymph node pathology reports were saying about the molecular-genetic nature of the tumor cells to learn how they would respond to chemotherapy. I learned about new tests that employ this information to generate individually tailored approaches to treatment. I read about blood tests that measured circulating tumor cells in the bloodstream—another way of deciding whether chemotherapy was needed at all. I could find no scientific—or even anecdotal—evidence to support the claim that a decision regarding chemotherapy must be made within six weeks of a lumpectomy, as we had been told.

What astonished me was that many of the medical specialists we encountered were unaware that such tests existed. Several thought they did not apply in Gloria's case and told us they'd have never ordered them in the first place. I actually had to interpret statistical data for one very highly regarded oncologist at the UC San Francisco Medical Center.

As I enlisted The Professor to determine whether the risks of the short-term and long-term side effects outweighed the potential benefits of chemotherapy, I realized that this was the kind of question I'd been addressing professionally for most of my career. Here was that elusive Aha moment: all the academic work I had researched and taught regarding risk-benefit analysis was now available to help me support my beloved's decision-making. The Professor did a standard risk assessment calculation and determined that there was a less than five-percent reduction in the already small chance of recurrence for her type of breast cancer.

Aside from this small risk, chemotherapy just didn't feel right to me for Gloria's diagnosis. And there was some relief in knowing that I had finally learned how to stay in touch with my emotions instead of relying on heady calculations—or on a spiritual teacher, for that matter. Still, the questions recurred: Was I afraid to deal with the side effects of the chemotherapy? Was I afraid to see my beloved under such pain and discomfort—both emotional and physical—even if chemotherapy proved beneficial?

I also wondered how I would begin to respect my initial emotional response to each situation, and then use reason and logic either to support that emotional response or to discount it. This was the same approach

Gloria and I had endeavored to teach our students in the ethics course. We ultimately got there by trusting our emotional path, and I employed reason and logic to overrule self-doubt.

Meanwhile, Gloria had set the date to begin chemotherapy. Even though she had not yet decided what to do, the port she'd had inserted into her chest was ready to deliver the poison directly into an artery close to her heart.

I went through my calculations and continued to research the benefits and risks of chemotherapy, providing Gloria with my research findings, including my own opinion. The day before her first treatment was scheduled, she had tea with a woman she'd met who had recently completed chemotherapy. This person had a different type of breast cancer and reported a very different tale.

The last and fourth opinion Gloria had received was from a very well-respected oncologist at one of the best cancer centers in the country. He also was steeped in the latest research out of Europe, Israel, and the alternative research community in this country. He told Gloria that chemotherapy would not help her. To Gloria's amazement, the woman who met with her that afternoon had sought a similar second opinion from this same oncologist, who happened to be friends with her husband, also a physician. He had told the woman she must have chemotherapy, given the molecular biochemistry of her particular tumor. Finally, an oncologist who didn't practice one size fits all.

At this dramatic turn, the evening before she was scheduled to begin, the answer found her. Gloria chose not to do chemo. Her decision was based on solid ground and a fair dose of intuition. Several weeks later, the new genetic testing results would prove her right.

THAT SPRING, VINCENT HAD ARRANGED the biennial convention in Sedona, Arizona, for all the facilitators and interns in Europe and the U.S. — about forty people in all. We had attended the four previous conventions, first as interns, then as facilitators, and finally as leaders. We had always enjoyed hearing Vincent present his new ideas regarding facilitation and catching up with our European peers.

"I'm not going," I said to Gloria. "We're not facilitating any longer and I don't care if we'll miss being with friends."

"I agree," Gloria said. "After all, we've been through with Vincent, I can't imagine going either."

When word got out that we were not planning to attend the convention, we started receiving emails and phone calls from facilitators and interns, many of whom had been our former clients or had become our friends through The Project.

"Vincent is going to hand me my intern certificate," one wrote, "and it wouldn't be the same without you guys."

"You've been my facilitator since the beginning of my process," another wrote, "and you are still leaders of The Project, in my view."

Vincent called, offering to cover the cost of attending.

Based on these emails, our own need for a vacation, and our desire to have closure with the facilitators and interns, we decided to go. This would be our way to say goodbye and create resolution for ourselves. In addition, we loved Sedona and the people who would be there. Considering Vincent's offer, we reasoned that we wouldn't find ourselves in an altercation with him and that this experience would provide a way to complete this phase of our life.

We were sitting at breakfast the first morning with the "family" — Vincent, Tina, and two senior facilitators — as if nothing had changed. Suddenly, Vincent turned to Gloria.

"I'm sorry for the way I've treated you," he said with tears in his eyes as he reached across the table and attempted to take her hand. "It wasn't your fault, after all."

During the conversation, it became clear that he was referring to his criticism of her work that had prompted him to take away her clients and her responsibilities as a teacher and leader. It seemed he was truly sincere. As usual, he had forgotten the harsh interchanges regarding Gloria's cancer diagnosis and treatment and his whole history of emotional abuse during the last several years. Once again, his selfish interest in The Project trumped care and congruency.

Vincent explained that all the facilitation behaviors he had criticized in Gloria were his fault. He took responsibility for what he considered his deficiency in teaching and mentoring her and for asking her to deliver the wrong interventions.

Needless to say, we were shocked. And even more so when he announced his apology to Gloria at the opening session of the convention for all to hear. While we fully appreciated Vincent's public statement, something about it felt off, as though he had turned the teaching into a display of his magnanimity, proving wrong any of the current rumors throughout the community that he never took responsibility for his mistakes. Therefore, although we thoroughly enjoyed the company of our friends and peers, our intention didn't change regarding participation in future seminars and retreats.

While in Sedona, Gloria received the genetic molecular test results she was waiting for. The tests showed that conventional chemotherapy would not be effective for her tumor cells. While we had both come to the same conclusion several weeks before, that she shouldn't undergo chemotherapy, the test data supported our feelings—she now had certainty in ruling chemotherapy out.

"WHAT SHOULD I DO ABOUT RADIATION treatments?" Gloria asked me when we returned from Sedona. "You're the expert."

"I'm not quite an expert in this field," I said, "but I'll take the same approach I did with chemotherapy."

While I could have assumed that the radiation facility staff knew what they were doing, and that the equipment that generated the radiation was modern and reliably maintained, I needed to meet the staff and see the equipment myself. I came away with a good feeling that Gloria would get proper treatment at the facility. I conveyed all that I felt and knew to Gloria, and then it was up to her to decide. And decide she did.

Each weekday, over five weeks, I would take Gloria to the facility for radiation treatments. Max would accompany us there and would sit with me in the waiting room, anxiously waiting the half hour for her return. As expected, Gloria came home more and more fatigued as the weeks progressed. Max would jump up on the bed and lie down next to her while they both slept away the afternoon. Gloria elected not to have a radiation booster at the end of five weeks as dictated by the standard of care. This was Gloria's decision. And it felt right.

AFTER VINCENT'S APOLOGY IN SEDONA, as self-serving as it seemed, Gloria and I no longer felt compelled to completely sever our relationship with him, as we previously thought we would. We were no longer facilitators; neither he nor anyone else involved in The Project expected our active participation. From his perspective, we'd gone about as far as we could in our process—or anyone could, for that matter. We were like the grandparents, invited to all the family events to provide some sense of continuity and grounding.

Vincent and Tina remained neighbors for another year, then moved five miles closer to town. It was a huge relief for us. Now we were alone in the enclave where we'd hoped to create a community. We could take a deep breath and begin to find ourselves again, removed from Vincent's ever-present energy.

Chapter 27

Intermezzo

Dogs' lives are too short. Their only fault, really.
— Agnes Sligh Turnbull

"MY ONCOLOGIST IS RUNNING LATE," Gloria had said. "Could you make a salad, steam some vegetables, and set the oven to 350 degrees? And while you're at it, set a pot of boiling water for the pasta. I'll handle the rest when I get home."

"Not a problem," I replied as I hung up the phone.

Gloria was determined to know that I would be self-sufficient if she didn't survive the cancer or passed before me. I was determined to make sure that her concerns were allayed.

It was almost twenty-five years after our first encounter over cooking when Gloria called me at home that afternoon. I saved the document I was working on and glanced at Max, sleeping on his mat in my office. Max was an integral part of our family. He lived inside the love-bubble we had painstakingly created, which was filled with kindness and care. Max helped Gloria through the cancer travail, easing her anxiety and always bringing a smile to her face.

As I got up from my desk to walk down the hallway to the kitchen, he stirred, stood up, did that little head-to-tail body shake that dogs sometimes do, and then followed me.

In the kitchen, Max sat at attention, his head moving back and forth between his bowl and me. He watched every move I made, hoping for a scrap of food to fall his way.

"I'll feed you when we eat," I said to Max.

That evening, as I was setting the table before Gloria's arrival, I lifted a wine glass out of the cabinet and several other glasses fell to the floor and shattered. Years earlier, such an event would signify a calamity, throwing me back to the shame and confusion I'd felt as a child when a similar accident happened.

I recalled being six or seven years old, with my mother and aunt on a shopping trip to a department store. At some point, when they were involved in the kitchen department, I wandered off to explore. There was a display of crystal glasses stacked in a pyramid towering above me. I must have been fascinated with the way the light shining on the glasses formed some sort of fractal pattern, producing a rainbow. Perhaps wanting to see how the light might move, or how stable the pyramid was, I touched one of the glasses in front of me on the bottom row. The whole display came crashing down, leaving me surrounded by broken glass and terrified.

Maybe I'd concluded then and there that I was no good around things in the kitchen.

But this evening I was no longer that traumatized little boy and Gloria and I were on the other side of attack-and-defend. There was no need for shame now.

"I broke some of our good wine glasses," I told her as soon as she walked in the door.

"I'm so sorry," Gloria said. "I hope that didn't upset you."

Gloria understood how intimidated I get in the kitchen, and the concern she had for me was written on her face.

"It's really not a problem, darling."

As I swept up the broken glass, I could feel my love for her — and for the frightened Golden Boy.

"IT LOOKS LIKE MAX HAS AN INSECT bite on his right side," the groomer said to me about four months after Gloria's radiation treatments ended. "Have your veterinarian check it out if the lump doesn't go away in a week or so."

After two weeks, the lump was still there. We took Max to the vet. He agreed it probably was an insect bite.

"Use this ointment," he said. "Bring him back in two weeks if it doesn't go away."

It didn't go away. Two weeks later, the vet took a blood sample and examined it under his microscope.

"The blood cells don't look normal," he said. "Let's do a biopsy tomorrow. I'll send the tissue to a pathology lab in Sacramento."

Gloria, Max, and I sat in the waiting room the next day until the vet's assistant came out and said everything was ready. I stood to walk Max toward the operating room where the biopsy would take place. He refused to move. I gave a little tug on his leash. Max was usually responsive and knew what a tug meant. But today he just sat down and refused to move. So I picked up this seemingly healthy eight-pound dog and took him into the room.

"Come back in three hours," the assistant said.

We were running some errands when Gloria's cell phone rang.

"You better come quickly," the assistant said. "We need to make some decisions regarding Max."

When we arrived, Max was on a ventilator, unable to breathe on his own. The vet told us that, when they administered the anesthetic for the biopsy, Max had gone into convulsions. Lesions under his tongue were indicative of a lethal brain tumor.

We called our cousins who still had Max's brother Sammy. Max had been an integral part of their lives too.

Gloria and I sat in the surgical room with Max still hooked up to the ventilator, wrapped up in a blanket across our laps. We were heartbroken.

"You've been a real pal, Max," I whispered as tears streamed down my face. "Thanks for gracing my life."

"He took the last remnants of the cancer from me," Gloria said, convinced it was true. "The last full measure of devotion."

We both nodded yes. The vet gave him the fatal shot and removed the ventilator tube.

And we wept, and we wept, and we wept.

AFTER MAX'S DEATH, WE WERE BOTH still reeling from Gloria's cancer diagnosis and treatment. She was feeling the side effects from the radiation and from an estrogen inhibitor she had been taking for almost a year. As this regimen had thrown her into a second menopause, she was struggling with low energy and physical discomfort. While she was also struck with the grief of losing our precious Max, we both felt reassured as her fear of a recurrence mysteriously disappeared after he left us.

While stepping back as facilitators had been our choice, we were feeling that loss as well. After Vincent's public apology to us in Sedona, we were less apt to distance ourselves completely from him and the rest of the community. And when Gloria's diagnosis had looked grim, she was very concerned that I would be alone and isolated if she passed, so we chose to stay connected to the community, although at a distance. Vincent had offered us gratis attendance for his weekend seminars, and we'd drop in every so often out of curiosity. But we became restless with the content in a relatively short period of time. I couldn't help feeling that we no longer belonged there. At the same time, we really didn't feel a part of the Grass Valley community, either. So accustomed were we to the jargon and mindset of The Project, we experienced a state of animated suspension, not quite sure where we belonged.

On the rare occasions we went to a seminar, I'd look around the room at our friends and former clients and sense their process. It seemed they were changing and maturing without noticing or facing the kind of abuse we'd experienced. When Vincent called someone out in a way that felt abusive to me, they seemed to work with it better than we'd been able to do.

Despite working through the trauma from the cancer diagnosis and treatment—and Max's death, this was a special time for Gloria and me. We had developed a deeper sense of intimacy with each other than we'd ever known. Our intimacy was actually enhanced by our mutual isolation. After the cancer treatment, being together became paramount. Every day was a blessing. We reconnected with old friends on our infrequent trips to the Bay Area, as well as with some friends who had moved to Grass Valley, tentatively finding our way as if we'd been in a distant land trying to find points of common understanding.

We also became more involved with our family. For my birthday, my sons, now straddling the age of fifty, invited me to join them in the Bay Area to attend three Oakland A's–Yankee baseball games, since I'm a lifelong New York fan. The games turned out to be a side activity, as we spent most of the time getting to know one another once again. It was the first time the three of us were alone together since their high-school days—until now, there had always been wives and grandchildren present when we were together.

"Ask me any question you have about my life or your life growing up," I started a conversation that first day, "while I still have enough mental capacity for recollection and to give you an answer."

By the time I started asking my father questions about things I wanted to know regarding his early life, our family origins, and—especially—my mother, his mind was cloudy, and his memory had faded. For the next three days, my sons and I entered a series of heartfelt intimate conversations about my life and their lives that not only brought us closer together but also opened a channel for them to come to me with whatever professional or personal difficulties they were and would be confronting. My sons know I'll give them an honest answer.

"I'm not a father who will meddle in my sons' lives; they are adults, and they can take care of themselves and their families," I've said to my daughters-in-law and even to my friends. "I've become a good listener, but when asked for advice, I will be straight with them."

My daughter—that's a different matter. I tried to be just as honest and forthright with her, but it didn't work out. We are estranged, and perhaps that's a story for another time.

During the winter holidays, Gloria and I travelled to Southern California to celebrate with my son's family—in the summer, they'd visit us for swimming, fishing in the local lakes, and hiking the numerous trails. But we mostly spent our time together, alone. I relished having Gloria to myself. She was grateful to be with me. This was the first time in our many years together that we spent so much time alone, always seeming to have needed community around us in the past.

As we recalibrated our lives, remaining mostly isolated from The Project and savoring the sweetness of our newfound intimacy with each other and with family, we also realized that an underlying trauma remained unaddressed. Initially, when we stopped working with clients, we felt the pain of the loss. But now this was different. What we didn't realize was that remaining even tangentially connected to The Project kept us subject to a different kind of trauma, and that we were unable to fully integrate that experience and move on. The nature of that trauma would become clear several years later.

I began writing. Timidly, I wrote essays about my life. Remaining active at the University from afar, I also wrote and lectured about the relationship between emotion and ethics. We barely noticed that we had remained board members for The Project. The board met twice a year to discuss the budget and plans for upcoming seminars and retreats. Perhaps, subconsciously, remaining on the board kept me feeling a part of something and, while doing so, I no longer had to go through the adjustment of finally being "out of school."

"I HAD A VERY VIVID DREAM LAST NIGHT," Gloria said one morning. "I was an oil painter living in France toward the end of the nineteenth century."

I listened intently as she recounted the dream.

"I saw the painting the artist was working on—vibrant, with abstract multicolored flowers. I could feel what the painter was feeling—a state of ecstasy and oneness with God. She was having a spiritual breakthrough as she splashed paint on her canvas."

Within days, Gloria bought the paints she would need to recreate the image from her dream. She had painted as a young woman but was discouraged from pursuing the life of an artist by her parents. Ultimately, her emotional work had given her permission to rekindle that early yearning to be an artist. She now began to pursue it again in earnest.

Not long after Gloria had that dream, she saw a film about a French artist called Seraphine of Senlis. The artist in her dream bore a marked similarity to Seraphine. As she watched the film, Gloria wept and began shaking as if something were moving in her in a mysterious way—a feeling she remembered from the moment we sensed we were in Atlantis.

Several months after her dream and the discovery of Seraphine, we traveled to France following a professional meeting I had attended in Northern Italy. We drove to Senlis and parked in the village square. Gloria, never having been in that town, nor knowing where the artist had lived and painted, walked directly to her home as if in a trance-like state. The front door was locked, but a metal plate indicated that we were at the right place.

Fortunately, the little museum nearby that displayed Seraphine's art was open. As we went inside, Gloria began crying—there facing the entry was the painting from her dream. After studying a display of Seraphine's paintings, we went to the French Gothic cathedral where Seraphine had prayed every day. We had read about her strong devotional relationship with the priest. Sunday morning mass was being conducted when we arrived; the liturgical music and choir voices pulled us in.

When I entered, I wept. Who would have thought The Professor—a Jewish one at that, with his scientific and mental capabilities—would once again be transported back in time and, perhaps, to another lifetime? Had I been that very priest who was a source of comfort to the artist? Was Gloria that artist in a past life? Is this the tie that originally brought us together? Or was it just our minds playing a trick? It was second nature for me now to ask these questions.

Gloria was good at painting and approached it with enthusiasm and passion. Her renewed love of art thrilled me. I had been enamored by it as a boy and her excitement aroused a remembrance of my delight roaming the halls of the Metropolitan Museum of Art. Along with my engineering courses, I'd also studied art history in college. My passion for the arts that had lain dormant arose in me as well. We took great pleasure wandering through museums in each place we visited, as I recognized the famous paintings we'd encounter.

BETWEEN GLORIA'S AND MY EXPERIENCE of teaching ethics to engineering students and of facilitating a spectrum of individuals and groups, we had developed a new understanding of the role emotion played in ethics and morality. When the Dean asked me how we could transfer our experience to other instructors who would then teach ethics after I retired, Gloria and I developed and taught a two-week summer short course focusing on pedagogy and content. We offered this course for three summers—once before Gloria's cancer diagnosis, once during her radiation treatment, and once the summer afterwards. Gloria and I taught the first one; my postdoc and I taught the second and third iterations.

By this time, Gloria and I had refined our approach to teaching, concentrating on "moral emoting," a term we invented as an antecedent to moral reasoning. Rather than treating emotion as irrational, as was a common practice, we believed it brought salience to ethical issues. We also believed that engineering professors who taught ethics should be aware of their own value systems regarding education and technology and be able to articulate them. Gone was the tension between us, as we seamlessly wove together our knowledge and experience—as if we were playing the Bach double violin concerto—harmonically interdependent yet independent in rhythm and melodic contour. I was deeply sorry I couldn't play that music with her the last two times I taught the ethics course.

Two colleagues, my postdoc, and I applied for and received a three-year National Science Foundation grant to develop an innovative approach for teaching engineering ethics. We framed it as a process by which instructors would receive, reflect, and reframe their student's values, assumptions, and beliefs regarding an ethical dilemma. This approach was informed by my years as a facilitator—and what my postdoc renamed meeting students "where they're at," a skill for which I'd become adept as a facilitator.

In April 2015, towards the end of the NSF project, I was invited to deliver a paper at an international conference in New York City called Ethics in Biology, Engineering, and Medicine. In addition, I was invited to write a paper for publication in a peer-reviewed international journal describing my work on engineering ethics. Our work on ethics education was gaining attention among scholars and practitioners across a spectrum of disciplines beyond engineering. I had incorporated the ideas we'd developed previously and was exploring a new idea as well.

WHILE GLORIA AND I HAD DISTANCED ourselves from The Project, the appreciation I felt for the breadth of Vincent's knowledge in the emotional arena didn't wane, even though his failure to treat us with compassion and empathy during the cancer ordeal showed me he hadn't embodied this knowledge. Still, I continued to respect his intellectual authority and thought this esteem could be enough to maintain our relationship. As an academic, my comfort in trusting his apparent level of expertise had allowed me to maintain the status quo with him in a collegial way that felt oddly reminiscent of my relationships with senior faculty members who had mentored me as a young professor.

However, when encountering the Vincent I now knew, something would come over me that felt guarded and cautious. I could feel Billy astutely continuing to seek approval and, at the same time, I could feel his fear. Was I still looking for that "Atta boy" I hadn't received from my father? Was I still needing something from him to buoy me as I explored bringing concepts related to emotion into my work? Was I afraid to go it alone without an institution or mentor behind me? Whatever combination was operating, it had a discernible hold over me.

"I've been working on a concept I call 'Self-interest versus the social contract' as a way of framing certain ethical conflicts," I told Vincent a week before Gloria and I left for the conference in New York. "I first got the idea after that trip Gloria, Paul, Françoise, and I took to Damanhur in Italy."

I described to Vincent that Damanhur was a federation of communities based on ethical and spiritual values created as a laboratory for experimenting with sustainable ways of living in harmony with nature. Falco, the founder, who was also a charismatic spiritual teacher, had explained to us that Damanhur's value system sees the individual as both I and We, which means honoring an individual's lifelong process of self-exploration while also recognizing the individual's responsibility to the community through service. From this idea, I began to understand that many ethical issues arise out of an I-We dilemma—the difficulty of balancing self-interest versus the social contract.

"It all comes down to motivation," he responded. "Does the motivation underlying self-interest come from a healed emotional state or an unhealed emotional state?"

"That feels like a key in determining moral behavior in this complex world we live in," I answered. "Maybe I'll end the presentation with that question as a way of stimulating discussion."

As time went on, I would explore my motivation to stay close to Vincent. Clearly, staying close had a bright side and a shadow side—and everything in between. On the brighter side, I was influenced by my years as an academic, constantly citing sources and consulting with authorities. So, although I had been distancing myself from him, my sense of academic integrity called for giving him attribution in my writing and presentations. However, on the shadow side, I was suspicious of an "unhealed" aspect I attributed to Billy's need for approval. I hadn't yet integrated his healing enough to recognize that part of my motivation to stay connected to Vincent remained unhealthy, even as I began to write papers and lecture on the notion that motivation is a key to moral emoting—and to being able to distinguish healthy versus unhealthy moral emoting. In effect, while the attribution required giving him credit, I justified my continued conversations with him based on unhealthy motivation: I was getting Billy the "Atta boy" he had lacked from his father.

Before the cancer diagnosis, I had thought of citing Vincent's books in my research to help him gain access to a larger audience. He'd shared several ideas with us about how to work with the University faculty that were very useful. And I still deferred to his expertise around emotion, all the while not quite realizing how much I knew about emotion because of my very own access to it. I remained in communication with him, still feeling hurt and cautious, but trying to rise above these feelings. My relationship with him felt distant—stiff and a little bit contrived. It reeked from the very thing he warned us against—being with people with whom you couldn't be real.

After all the years of experiencing Vincent's mercurial moods, I had good reason to feel guarded. According to his own standards, the only alternative would have been to tell him exactly how I felt—which I'd already done, to no avail—or to step away. Instead, I consulted with him as I might have consulted with any colleague—even one with whom I had very little relationship. If real intimacy necessitates being truthful, Vincent had long ago made that kind of intimacy impossible.

This was my social contract with Vincent: albeit infrequently, we both enjoyed discussing new ideas, discoveries, and concepts with each other—the galactic alignment of the Earth, sun, and center of the Milky Way in December 2012 and the discovery of the Higgs Boson, to name a couple. And we each had our own self-interest in maintaining that social contract. Whether or not the self-interest was healthy for either of us would soon be revealed.

"I'VE BEEN DREAMING ABOUT MAX," Vincent told us over the phone.

Gloria and I had heard from Vincent only infrequently during her year of convalescence. Yet now, out of the blue, about three months after Max's passing, he was contacting us about a dream he had had several nights in a row.

"Normally, I wouldn't tell you this," he continued, "but I feel Max has reincarnated into the same breed of dog, somewhere in eastern Pennsylvania."

While we couldn't even think of getting another dog and were still very much grieving the loss of Max, we were curious. I wasn't prepared for another dog, especially a Maltese, but Gloria was missing the comfort of Max's warm body curled up against hers. So she did a little Internet research and found a breeder in eastern Pennsylvania who had one single male Maltese puppy born at just the right time to coincide with Vincent's dream. We felt called to follow up. Gloria contacted the breeder.

"We're keeping the puppy for show," the breeder said.

We laughed with each other that, if in fact this was Max—we had no idea or sense of what might be true about animal incarnation—he would have a totally different life as a fancy show dog outside New York City. We could picture him with his long, white, silky hair down to the ground with the hair on his head tied up with a black bow. Quite a different picture from Max with his hair cut short, full of the mud, dirt, and sand from the trails we hiked on most days.

Three months later, we took a trip to Italy to visit old friends who had a home there. Gloria would have a chance to paint the Tuscan landscape and visit the major museums in Italy that she'd never been to as an artist. And I, as a student of art history, absolutely delighted in visiting these museums by her side. On our way home from Europe, we received a telephone call from the breeder.

"The Maltese puppy is yours. He's a bit too big for the breed standard."

We arranged to meet the breeder at a baggage carousel in the Newark airport. The puppy licked our faces and looked at us as if to say, "What took you so long to get here?"

We took him home. He has been with us ever since. Bogie, named after the famous actor Humphrey Bogart, is a beautiful dog.

"You couldda been a contenda," I like to say to him, paraphrasing Marlon Brando's famous line in the movie, *On the Waterfront*. But Bogie is nothing like Max. The only thing that remains the same is the love Gloria and I feel for him. And his love for us. We now felt complete once again.

Chapter 28

Dissolution

If you meet the Buddha on the road, kill him.
— Zen koan

"HI SAM, what's up?"

I was standing on the corner of 8th Avenue and Bleecker Street in the Greenwich Village section of Manhattan when I heard my cell phone ring. Seeing his name, I answered the call.

"It's just terrible here on the ground, Bill."

Above the cacophony of noisy traffic and building construction, I heard a sense of urgency in Sam's voice. Gloria and I had been in New York City for more than a week. I'd given the ethics presentation that morning at an international conference and was walking from the subway to our friend's townhouse. Gloria was painting cityscapes with her New York artist buddies and one of her favorite teachers. I knew that Sam and the senior facilitators were in the midst of a busy schedule preparing for an upcoming presentation and workshop in the Bay Area.

"What's happening, Sam?"

"Tina's left Vincent, and he has asked the senior facilitators for help. Several of us went to see him last night," Sam said without taking a breath. "He looked just like Howard Hughes when they finally found him dead."

Sam paused for a moment as I tried to take in his words.

"That's the best way I can describe it."

Howard Hughes, the famous American business tycoon, inventor, aviator, and recluse was practically unrecognizable when he died—long hair and beard, overgrown fingernails and toenails. Yet when I'd seen Vincent a week or so before leaving for New York to discuss some ideas concerning my presentation, he was his affable self, neatly groomed and wearing his signature outfit.

This was shocking news. "Oh my God, has he gone nuts? What's he like?"

"When I stopped by to see him today, he was on his couch surrounded by stuffed animals representing his emotional parts," Sam said quickly, "and it seemed like he hadn't showered or shaved in several days. No one seems to be in charge of The Project. There's no leadership."

"Gloria and I will be home in a week and—"

Sam cut me off. "You don't understand, Bill. Vincent is supposed to teach a class Friday, and we have a seminar this weekend. What should we do?"

Because Gloria and I were still board members, Sam believed we could do something. We had run The Project while Vincent lived in Europe. Maybe he thought we might have the space and wisdom to help now.

"It's been years since we've been involved in the day-to-day work of The Project," I said.

"Everyone is in a state of shock," Sam persisted. "We have no idea what to do."

I thought for a minute about what I would have done at the University. I had handled organizational crises before and knew how to be diplomatic about the situation until I could discern for myself what had happened to avoid misrepresenting the details.

"Have a staff member send an e-mail to everyone stating that the class on Friday and the weekend seminar are cancelled for now and that they'll be offered at a later time," I said. "Have her add that Vincent will be taking a sabbatical leave for the next six months to work on some personal stuff."

I was shaken by Sam's call. Gloria and I had begun building a life tangential to The Project. We had separated ourselves to heal from the emotional abuse we had personally experienced. The idea of being pulled back into the drama of the organization threatened to bring the trauma back.

That evening, Gloria received a text from one of the board members asking us to come home as soon as possible for an emergency meeting. We spent the rest of the day discussing this urgent request, ultimately choosing to cut our trip short. The cry for help was deep. As we talked, we realized how much love we had for these people who had been our colleagues, friends, and former clients. Even though we hadn't been in touch recently, we felt called to respond and to be part of the community. Although we had reservations for dinner at a trendy New York restaurant to celebrate our wedding anniversary the next night, with the frequent calls and texts coming in, we realized we wouldn't enjoy it. Instead, we celebrated the event by flying home.

"How ironic," I commented to Gloria. "After being marginalized and put out to pasture by Vincent, we end up the responsible parties."

"Maybe this is why we stayed on the board for so long," Gloria mused.

THE NEXT NIGHT, EVERYONE ON THE BOARD, including Tina—that is, everyone except Vincent, met in our living room. Some of the senior facilitators attended as well. We began to hear, openly and honestly, for the first time, about how each of them had suffered emotional abuse and how each of them had also tried to keep it a secret. As the meeting unfolded, we also began hearing the shocking story of Vincent's unraveling.

During the preceding three months, unbeknownst to us, Vincent had sent emails to all the active facilitators and all the interns, blaming them for his need to abuse them. He proclaimed that they were not stepping up to the high mark he had set for them, either in their process or in how they were representing The Project to the outside world. Only a couple of the two-dozen people who received the message had responded within twenty-four hours, so he'd sent another abusive email describing his despair at their inaction. He wrote that he could live with the world not accepting his life work, but he could not live with the prospect of the world never receiving his life work because of the emotional immaturity of the facilitators and interns.

As we listened, a deep sadness permeated our living room. So many groups and individual sessions had taken place here — sessions that had ended in the genuine joy of self-discovery and emotional healing. Now, everyone was revealing the emotional abuse they had incurred from Vincent, sharing feelings they had kept secret from their partners and friends out of fear of criticism, humiliation, and even ostracism. Tina spoke about how Vincent's emotional abuse had led her to leave him.

Sitting next to Gloria throughout, I felt her anger and heartache.

"Damn him!" she cried out.

The people in this room, with their stories of abuse, were those same people we had worked with over the years. While Gloria and I had our own experience of Vincent's abuse during our last days as facilitators, we had also held that privately. At the infrequent board meetings or at other events we attended, our friends and former colleagues had praised him, The Project, and the work itself. Now, after listening to everyone, we realized that we were not unique in keeping our thoughts and feelings about Vincent's abuse to ourselves. Ironically, silence was embedded in a culture that touted truth-telling.

We had long been aware of Vincent's abusive behavior toward Tina and yet, as a couple, they had seemed to work it out. And on the surface, it seemed as if things were changing with the new leadership team. Vincent had said repeatedly that he just wanted to teach and leave individual and group facilitation to the facilitators.

Gloria and I had great faith in the new and upcoming facilitators and believed that, when they took over leadership, the direction of The Project would be uplifted. We had stayed, in part, to support them. Unfortunately, most weren't admitting to each other the underlying private abuse that everyone seemed to be experiencing. Gloria had worked with and trained them as far back as the Berkeley days, when she had first become a facilitator. They were now friends of ours; some had been colleagues.

"I'm so sorry he hurt you all that way," Gloria said. Her remorse was palpable. "I was so busy distancing myself that I didn't see that all of you were suffering, as I did. Had I known, I would've tried to stop it. From a distance, it seemed all of you were thriving and that our experience was unique."

"We thought the abuse was unique to each of us too," someone said.

After hearing from all the members of the board, as well as from several senior facilitators, the board took the only step we deemed possible: we fired Vincent and voted to dissolve The Project. The vote was unanimous. Although Tina abstained from the vote, she concurred with the board's action. Since The Project was a legal entity, we also voted to hire a law firm to file the necessary court papers to dissolve the non-profit.

At the end of the meeting, Gloria and I were personally tasked with delivering a written letter terminating Vincent's employment. We did not feel that sending the letter by email, as was his custom, would be right, given the magnitude of what we were doing.

"ARE YOU READY FOR any reaction from him?"

We were standing at Vincent's front door, the letter firing him in hand, ready to deliver it to him. Gloria nodded yes. I took a deep breath and knocked.

Vincent opened the door. He looked quite neat and proper, dressed in his usual black tights and long-sleeved polo shirt. But he looked sad and withdrawn. I handed him the letter terminating his employment. He held it, opened it, read it, and mulled it over for a moment.

"It was not unexpected," he said.

"At least you realize it," Gloria said.

"And thank you for doing this yourselves, in person."

I momentarily remembered how many emails we had received blasting one or the other of us with unfounded accusations about our facilitation that he had solicited from others. I felt the anger arising in me.

"Even though you delivered hard reflections by email, I wouldn't do that," I said forcefully, recalling his stated belief that, by sending criticism via email, he would give the recipient time to digest its content. "I've always thought sending emails was actually the coward's way out."

He seemed to ignore my anger and invited us to sit down. I wondered how many times we had sat opposite him on this couch, first as his clients and later as his colleagues and friends. More than a hundred, I guessed. This time was very different. The power gradient had shifted.

As we sat down, he began to give us his intellectual assessment of what had gone wrong. Gloria stopped him.

"This is not a teaching moment, Vincent!"

Gloria's face was red with anger. This was the first time I had witnessed her turning her anger towards him rather than turning it inward. I felt relief.

"Of course not," he said. But his look was puzzled, as if she had interrupted him while he was creating a new way to describe and heal the human condition. Seemingly devoid of emotion, he nodded, although I doubted that it was a nod of agreement. I couldn't tell whether he had absorbed anything we said.

"Do you realize that some of your emails to the senior facilitators and interns were so abusive and humiliating that they were afraid and embarrassed to show them to anyone? Do you even realize how damaging that was for them?"

This seemed to have an effect. Vincent smiled, as if savoring a moment of cruelty, and then, as if caught out, he quickly assumed a look of regretful surprise.

We described some instances of the abuse shared at the meeting, along with a few instances we had experienced.

"Others have shared this with me," he said dismissively, as if to convince himself that his behavior was somehow not as awful as it really had been. After all, these weren't isolated incidents: he had abused everyone equally.

"Do you think you guys could have a glass of wine or coffee with me in a few years, maybe?" he asked meekly. "Maybe even invite me out to dinner?"

That was the last straw for both of us. He just didn't seem to feel his impact on all these people involved in his organization.

"I can't imagine that would ever happen," Gloria responded. "Not if I ever want to really heal the damage you've done."

I reflected on the dichotomy of having received so much in the way of self-discovery and healing in the first years of our work with him and then, in the later years, so much abuse. At that time, I did not know how to reconcile these opposites.

As we walked toward the door to leave, he stopped us to offer one more explanation. "You know, I'm not like other spiritual teachers and gurus. I can take the criticism."

I turned to face him. The anger I had tried to suppress now came roaring out.

"Other spiritual teachers might not know what they're doing," I said. "But you do. And guess what? You are like the rest of them. You're just a mean son of a bitch!"

We haven't seen him since.

Chapter 29

Aftermath

*The louder he talked of his honor, the faster we
counted our spoons.*
—Ralph Waldo Emerson,
THE CONDUCT OF LIFE: A PHILOSOPHICAL READING

THE PROJECT WAS OVER. The board retained an attorney to legally dissolve the non-profit before disbanding. All remaining funds were donated to charity. Gloria and I remained friends with some of the board members and senior facilitators, while others moved away, eager to go on to other things. With heavy hearts, we severed our relationships with the few people who remained close to Vincent at the end. All scheduled trainings and seminars were cancelled, and The Project's websites taken down.

Within six months, Tina and Vincent got back together again and, shortly thereafter, moved to Arizona. After several attempts at starting a new project there, we heard from a former facilitator that they had moved to Europe, where he still had a following. That was the last I heard about him.

In the aftermath of the dissolution, however, I found myself on an emotional roller coaster. During the ensuing year, Gloria and I scoured the literature, trying to understand Vincent's behavior, as well as the nature of organizations such as The Project. We found an abundance of information describing the characteristics of cults and cult leaders that seemed to match our experience. Over the years we were involved in The Project, the two of us had conversations—between ourselves and with other facilitators—about whether we had been part of a cult. Vincent had even brought up the subject of cults in seminars and workshops, attempting to counter the chatter that was cropping up online and to convince all of us we were not in one. Alarmed parents, family, and friends who had been cut off at Vincent's suggestion, or even disgruntled former followers, wrote that The Project was a cult and that he was a cult leader. At this point, we no longer needed to deny the truth—we realized it was essential for our process to accept it.

"I UNDERSTAND WHY WE got so involved with Vincent when we first met him," I said to Gloria one day shortly after the dissolution. "But I can't stop asking myself why we stayed associated with The Project so long."

"Those first few years were very powerful," Gloria said. "We transformed ourselves and our relationship, and the results we experienced gave us a sense of trust— at least, we trusted the process we were in."

"Do you think we simply didn't separate the process from the man?"

"I think that's true. At least at first," Gloria responded. "But we felt so grateful for the process. Not only did we want to keep it going but also to share what we'd learned."

"It was an exhilarating time," I added.

"He had answers to my existential questions that resonated with me," Gloria mused. "But still, I wonder — was he attempting to hook us, or to help us, or both?"

"I was hooked by his brilliance and in awe of his teaching ability," I said. "He could simplify even the most difficult and complex subjects about the human condition into terms that were easy for me to digest. As a teacher, I put a lot of faith in that. But I was also afraid that, if we left, I would lose the emotional access I seemed to have gained working with him."

Gloria's most vulnerable patterns hooked her as well. She was less worried about staying emotionally open and more concerned about the existential fears that had always motivated her spiritual journey — reconciling a deep sense of anxiety about life and death issues. Vincent's certainty had given her a sense of peace. His spiritual paradigm, that included both the non-dual as well as a love for God, brilliantly resonated with her. However, she experienced highs and lows like mine after the dissolution and began to ask the same kinds of questions.

We were sitting in our garden one day, having another long conversation about why we overlooked what began as personality "quirks" that would eventually reveal emotional abuse.

"Let's face it, he's a smart guy," I reminisced. "Probably a genius."

"Well, he's certainly charismatic," Gloria mused. "He was able to speak on just about any subject with intelligence and fervor."

"And hold an audience for an hour and a half! That's not easy."

"Right. And he was charming—a delightful raconteur. He loved to entertain, and he provided a built-in social life for us," Gloria chuckled. "Even though we felt isolated."

I paused, recalling all the stimulating conversations we'd had over the years. He was a big personality—intelligent and innovative—who fancied himself a larger-than-life leader. It was no wonder we were captivated by him—his message resonated with us.

"The bottom line is that I became dependent on his clarity. I believed that, without him in my life, I couldn't maintain the openness I had come to embody. I was afraid I'd lose the connection with you. I feel ashamed when I think about my insecurity."

"Thank you for admitting that to me, honey," Gloria responded. "It's a big step to come to terms with those feelings. The fact that you can admit that insecurity—and the pain and shame that goes with it—proves that you haven't lost anything."

GLORIA HAD LOOKED UP the definition of narcissism. She read it to me aloud: "Narcissistic personality disorder is a mental condition in which people have an inflated sense of their own importance, a deep need for excessive attention and admiration, troubled relationships, and a lack of empathy for others."

I nodded. "I don't know if he's a narcissist or not. But those characteristics you read sound similar to his behavior."

As I continued to read books and articles, it became clear to me—although difficult to admit—that the man I had trusted to be my spiritual teacher seemed to demonstrate many characteristics of a narcissist. Vincent had often called himself "the ultimate adjudicator of reality." This, I learned, is a claim commonly made by such leaders. He was a charismatic leader of an organization we were concluding to be a cult. And I had fallen for his message.

I had been able to rationalize Vincent's behavior, as he was interpreting the world through the lens of The Project—an interpretation that seemed to match my experience, to feel internally consistent, and to assuage my existential fear. The work I'd done healing the emotional wounding of my youth and resolving the issues cleaving my marriage provided proof to me of The Project's value. What escaped my awareness was that my issues with my father had set me up to be vulnerable to Vincent himself—perhaps beyond what would have served me in healing those issues by illuminating my father projection. Vincent's seemingly narcissistic tendencies had recreated my father's milder version. I had reacted to him the same way I did to my father—stuffing my feelings. And as I did with my father, I made myself small and meek, surrendering to him—although Vincent would say I surrendered to my process—for the sake of emotional and spiritual growth.

However, as my facilitator, teacher, and supervisor, either he didn't recognize this pattern in me or didn't care—once my usefulness no longer served him—because he never helped me unravel it. Rather, he seemed to play on my pattern or to shame me for it—perhaps for his own advantage or for unhealthy reasons typical of a cult leader. Over time, surrender became ubiquitous in my life until my sense of choice was lost to me, much as it had been with my family, and certainly in relation to God during that year of mourning.

In reading the literature, I began to feel that Vincent was motivated by his belief that he was superior. Daniel Shaw, a psychotherapist who works with ex-cult members, explains that the "extreme narcissist's life purpose becomes to sustain his delusion of omnipotence; he must prove his superiority, over and over again."

Delusionary cult leaders, as Shaw calls them, believe they are entitled or infallible. And they need constant reinforcement of that belief. In other words, while the explicit mission of The Project was self-improvement in the emotional domain and enlightenment in the spiritual domain—both noble endeavors—at the same time, I believe, the implicit mission of The Project was to feed Vincent's insatiable need for dominance and power over his acolytes.

"This show is all about you," Vincent liked to say at the opening of a seminar or workshop. "But I'm the star in it."

Although he said this in jest, and the participants would laugh, there was much truth in it. Moreover, Vincent appeared to be intolerant of criticism, continually commending himself and devaluing those around him publicly. He taught that anything you saw or felt that was horrible about his abusive behavior was coming from your shadow, not his. If something he said or did didn't feel right, it was just a projection of your own inner turbulence, flaw, or unhappiness. Although this is consistent with many psychological models, he used this "truth" to absolve himself of any responsibility for his impact. From his point of view, I reasoned, he was always right, and you were always wrong.

I felt depressed when I realized I had been following a cult leader. My sense of self felt shattered. I had ignored the warning signs and made excuses, all the while convincing myself that what I was witnessing was not so. In fact, it wasn't until The Project was dissolved that I realized I had abdicated my freedom, even as an adult. I'd marched forward within the University, clinging to the identity of The Professor for dear life, using his authority to protect me from the vulnerability I was afraid of. Later, when I had allowed myself to be vulnerable with Vincent, the very thing I had feared happened: I was controlled by an outside authority, just as Judaism had controlled me in my youth.

How could I have known at the time how profound that simple act of firing The Project's leader—a surrogate parent—would be? Now Billy could finally relax, knowing that I was there to nurture and protect him. And I felt the freedom of being able to make a mistake and then openly admit it. The power I ultimately took back with my own vote to dissolve The Project was a critical step in my evolution built on many years of deep work, much of which, ironically, I had pursued with Vincent.

Several years of therapy followed The Project's collapse. When I was finally able to admit to myself and to everyone else that I had been in a cult, I sensed a heavy blanket lifting from my body. With this realization, I had a newfound feeling of freedom as my sense of self coalesced.

"LOOK, SHAW LAYS IT OUT," I said to Gloria one day. "He says that a cult is comprised of concentric circles—we were in the outer circle for a year and a half when Vincent was our facilitator. It was during those days we worked out our trauma and a lot of our relationship strife. We didn't realize what would happen as we got closer to him."

"But the evidence was so clear when we became part of his inner circle."

She had a point. When he invited us to join the intern class, we became members of his inner circle—a dozen people devoted to Vincent's explicit mission, which we assumed to be helping people. At the time, we were not aware of the implicit mission, which we now recognized as Vincent's self-aggrandizement. As more people joined us, The Project became a series of concentric circles around him, dedicated to both missions. When we became leaders, especially after he left to live in Europe for a year and we were the ones closest to him, the abuse intensified—partly due, I believe, to his competitive nature and partly that the intimacy seemed to go hand in hand with abuse. Unfortunately, by then, we were deeply invested in The Project.

Now we were learning from Shaw that, with most cults, people in the outer circles are unaware of the emotional abuse until they move closer and closer inward. This was what happened for Vincent's followers who attended his workshops and seminars. By then, many felt that it was too late for them to leave.

As interns, facilitators, and leaders, Gloria and I got to know a group of people in each concentric circle on a very intimate, emotional basis. These were "seekers"— people with varying personal histories committed to healing and growth. The emotional bond among the people in each circle became strong. Because of the trust built between and among us, we were intimately connected with the people we worked with. The humility and honesty were palpable as people described, in the most elaborate way, the childhood wounding they had experienced. I was in awe as they authentically worked their process, creating moments of profound connection and healing. I loved these people and our interactions, which made my life richer and more meaningful. I didn't want to lose these relationships. Being part of a community dedicated to what I thought was cutting-edge transformational healing warmed my heart. I loved the intimacy. Traveling with people into transcendent realms transported us in space and time—there were times when I could almost hear the angels singing. In some ways, it became addictive. Gloria and I wanted more of it, and many of our regular associations outside The Project didn't offer anything like that.

"When we became members of his inner circle—after transforming ourselves and our relationship—I was convinced of the value of the work," I said to Gloria. "And I wanted to teach this stuff."

"All good reasons for staying," Gloria said.

"Looking back, I can see that I was conflicted. I was insecure when I compared myself to him but excited that I could be an emotional body facilitator and have a whole new career that would carry me through retirement."

Gloria nodded. "Before meeting Vincent and imagining yourself a facilitator, I think you dreaded the idea of retiring."

She was right again. I had observed my father and both of my grandfathers wither away after they had retired—a very scary proposition for me. Once I had experienced the work giving me exactly what I needed, the hook was in. I believe Vincent understood my yearning—and Gloria's too, for that matter—to feel valuable, to use my skills, to have a meaningful life.

"Once I became a facilitator, I needed him at a whole new level and he knew it," I said. "He seemed to know he could begin to treat me any way he wanted, and I would overlook his abusive behavior."

"Little did I know I was reinforcing Vincent's implicit need when I worked so hard to bring people into The Project," Gloria sadly acknowledged. "I wanted to share our experience. Still, I had my shadow part in trying to get his approval, like I tried with my mother."

"I understand. We were terribly entangled, much the way that Shaw describes, Gloria," I said, feeling compassion. "I put my all into The Project—it became my life. In some way, I became attached to becoming a facilitator the same way I created an identity of being a professor—or even a husband or father."

As Gloria looked at me, I could tell she was feeling my heart. It was in much the same way I felt it early in our relationship when we were falling in love. We both started to cry.

"I can feel your goodness, Bill Kastenberg, and I love you. We got a lot out of being in the cult." She caught her breath, then continued. "Cult. I can barely say that word. But I don't know if we'd be in this place had we not gone through it all. In that sense—and I hate to say it because I am still so angry and hurt—it was perfect. And we went through it together, my love."

"It's freeing, though, isn't it?" I responded. "I was afraid we'd lose the magic of our relationship. I didn't trust myself. I didn't trust that I would be able to tap into my heart and express what I feel for you as I can now."

GLORIA AND I CONTINUED TO deconstruct our entanglement with The Project over the days and weeks after its dissolution.

"I believe I was afraid of being humiliated in absentia if we left," I said one day, shaking my head. "If I didn't keep participating in The Project, I would have been a pariah."

I paused momentarily, recalling those times at a seminar or workshop when Vincent had berated someone who left The Project. "It's just Vincent doing his thing," I'd say to myself, not realizing the subliminal message. *If you leave, that's what will happen to you.*

"I could feel the fear at the time, but I just chose to ignore it."

"Does that remind you of anything?" Gloria asked.

"Of course. It reminds me of the year I went to the synagogue and was castigated by the rabbis for crying.

But I knew that if I refused to say the *Kaddish*, I'd have been an outcast."

As my emotions overtook me, I felt Billy and the fear of humiliation he had carried all these years. I wept. Gloria was there with me, enveloping me in her tenderness, care, and love.

Ultimately, my healing after the collapse of The Project required both self-forgiveness and self-acceptance. At first, I judged myself harshly for having maintained the connection to Vincent—even at a distance—during the years he abused Gloria so badly after her cancer diagnosis and after we'd resigned as facilitators. I understood that I was motivated in part by our fear of being humiliated and by the doubt I still carried about my ability to navigate my emotional and spiritual landscape without him. What I came to realize, however, was that I could not have accessed this old fear if I had left him before the experience was complete. By feeling my fear in its fullness, I was able to reclaim another piece of myself. Now, finally, with The Project's demise, and accessing these deeper fears, I found that the power to have a deeply spiritual and emotionally rich life emanated from my own authority. It was only with this insight that I could both answer the questions that were gnawing at me and stop asking them.

I shared these realizations during another conversation with Gloria, as we continued making sense of why we stayed so long and allowed the abuse to continue.

"At the most meta level, you stayed until your work with him was finished," Gloria mused. "In that way, staying was absolutely perfect. But that doesn't answer the question, at a more practical level, of why an intelligent man like you, and many others like you, got hooked."

Gloria and I sat in silence for a few moments as she completed her thoughts.

"Yes, what I never thought about before is the simple fact that, as long as you remained in the cult, hoping for more healing, you were always trying to 'not be you,'" she said, surprised when she realized the dichotomy this idea illuminated.

"I don't think it has to do with intelligence," I responded. "It's all about the emotional bond between teacher and disciple—that is stronger than rationality."

Gloria nodded in agreement.

"Leaving the cult let me be me, not only because the psychological knot with my father was untied but also because I no longer needed to heal and change who I am. I could finally be me, perfect as I am in my imperfection," I concluded, as tears of relief streamed down my cheek. I could now be anyone I wanted to be. I could actually be myself.

I HAVE LEARNED THAT there is, within all people, a fundamental need to belong to a family, a tribe, a religion, a political party, and—for me—to an academic community. We are hard-wired to not only desire these connections but also to require them for survival. Once we have an emotional connection, we are often unwilling and unable to let it go. I was clearly emotionally connected to Vincent and had difficulty letting go.

Cognitive dissonance can be defined as the holding of contradictory beliefs. This is the very dissonance that children experience when their reality is denied by their parents, and they turn the doubt inward and blame themselves. Yet the need for connection remains so strong that, for example, battered wives will plead with judges not to sentence their husbands to jail.

The dissonance I experienced with Vincent, echoing the atavistic feelings living in my psyche, made this pattern familiar. The early loss of emotional connection—my mother's illness and my father's distance, coupled with Vincent's intermittent abuse and threat of withholding connection with the involved community—resulted in cognitive dissonance that was crazy-making. In the case of The Project, the need for connection explains why individual board members could not leave until they were newly connected against a common foe. And so we united. Not only did we unite to leave The Project, but to destroy it as well.

WHEN I INITIALLY SAID, "Sign me up," I was desperate to heal the emotional and spiritual wounds I had suffered from my mother's death and the events that followed. As I look back at my relationship with Vincent and the path I travelled with him, I'm left with a deep sense of appreciation and gratitude, coupled with anger and disappointment. My healing was real and deep and keeps growing. At the same time, the trauma I suffered from the abuse was equally profound. Yet, even with that trauma and my recovery from it, I took another step toward healing, leaving me in a whole new place in the world with myself and with others. Did I have to experience an abusive relationship with Vincent—one that mimicked the relationship with my father—in order to heal? I don't know. I'll never know. Obviously, the way this experience arose in my life had to have been perfect because of where I am now. But I certainly can't ethically recommend to anyone that they join a cult led by a narcissistic leader to heal. This is another dichotomy for me—so much healing combined with so much betrayal and abuse. I have pondered how to reconcile the two while writing this memoir, always being reminded of important teachings I've learned throughout my life. I have heard and felt each of my teachers speaking to me as I have tried to answer this conundrum.

"The answer is metaphysical," Vic had said to me in a different context that felt germane. "It's domain specific," is another answer that rang true in my heart. I believe it's okay to go meta to reconcile this dichotomy in the context of perfection, as long as the wounding in the personal domain is addressed and healed. I don't know—and can't even speculate—whether my journey could have happened any other way. But here I am today with my beloved.

Chapter 30

Sunshine and Rain

A painting is finished when the artist says it is finished.
—Rembrandt

SEVERAL YEARS HAD PASSED since the dissolution. The Mauritshuis in The Hague had reopened its art collection after a major renovation. Gloria and I had spent a week in Delft, where I gave a series of invited lectures at the Technical University on my approach to teaching engineering ethics. Before returning home, we decided to visit the museum to see some of Vermeer's most important and well-known paintings. Upon arrival, Gloria and I began a walk through the galleries—a set of rooms on the second floor—built around two central grand staircases. The pattern reminded me of the real estate properties laid out along the outside edges of a Monopoly board.

In visiting the museum, we were anticipating seeing Vermeer's best-known work, *The Girl with the Pearl Earring*, for the very first time. As we turned into the Vermeer gallery, we were both struck by the simplicity of this beautiful painting—a timeless rendering of a young girl looking at the viewer over her left shoulder, her body slightly turned away, her face bright in full light, her hair covered by an oriental turban, and a pearl dangling from her left ear. Noticing her slightly parted lips, I felt she was about to speak to us—or perhaps she had turned toward us because we had startled her. The painting left us breathless.

We were equally struck by Vermeer's *View of Delft* as he saw it more than three hundred and fifty years ago. His simple likeness of the cityscape, rendered from across the harbor, looked very much as it does today, albeit without large freighters and modern buildings. At its center, the painting depicted a gate to the city flanked by several small sailboats in the foreground and church steeples pointing to the cloudy sky in the background. Those same steeples define the center of Delft today.

Gloria had honed her painting skills over the past few years and enjoyed painting on the streets of this charming city, capturing the very views Vermeer had memorialized. Viewing Vermeer's masterpieces, we delighted in his technique, his color choices, and his use of perspective, and I regaled with her recollections from the art history courses I had taken as an engineering undergraduate.

Of course, we viewed *The Goldfinch*, a stunning painting of a bird by Carel Fabritius, thought to be Vermeer's teacher. I had no idea it was in this museum. The small painting had adorned the cover of a Pulitzer Prize-winning novel of the same name. Serendipity—it was the very book I'd been reading on the flight over.

As we moved effortlessly from painting to painting and gallery to gallery, I felt fully present with Gloria. As we turned another corner, I was immediately drawn to a Rembrandt self-portrait—one of the last portraits he completed during the year before he died. I was taken by the introspective look on his face and the softness of his eyes, the windows into his soul. Here was Rembrandt in a remarkable, self-probing, and utterly honest examination of the artist as both outward and inward observer, as a participant not only in his own life but also in his own moral growth. His eyes seemed to be staring into the face of his own death—a stance I'd avoided since I'd been a boy standing at my mother's grave. Averting my eyes from death in those days of my youth kept me half alive as an adult—unable to open fully to life, incapable of fully loving.

Yet here I stood, still timid, though I was now unafraid to glance in that direction and embrace the curiosity I sensed in Rembrandt's honesty. I saw Gloria at the other end of the room, gracefully engrossed in another painting. As she studied the painting, her mature beauty took my breath away once again. Leaving the Rembrandt, I stepped toward her, accepting the realization that the next journey would entail our separation at some unknown point, but with the willingness to feel the beauty and the catastrophe of this life—to feel it all—the ultimate dichotomy. Like Rembrandt, no doubt, I'd looked deeply into my being—

my fears, my life, and my morals—and was now ready for the final chapters.

As we left the museum, I realized—perhaps for the first time as an adult—that I had been there with my beloved as a mature man, unfettered by the events of my childhood. I had the strange feeling that the dense fog that had surrounded me for most of my adult life had lifted and I could now feel the sunshine. While I could recall my days exploring the Metropolitan Museum of Art in New York—with my mother, ever the observer, waiting for me in the lobby—I no longer felt Billy looking for her or expecting her to be there waiting for him.

This insight felt profound to me, and I shared it with Gloria as we left the museum, arms interlocked, she on my left, close to my heart. We took a leisurely walk through The Hague, discussing the paintings we had so admired. As we walked, I noticed the sidewalk cafés beginning to fill with the late afternoon crowd, deep in conversation while sipping their espressos or apéritifs. We arrived at the train station just in time to make our way back to Delft as the sun began to set and a light rain began to fall.